THE SWINDON BOOK COMPANION

BY MARK CHILD

The Towns and Villages of the Windrush Valley
Abbey House and Gardens, Malmesbury
Downton and the Tanning Industry
English Church Architecture: A Visual Guide
Discovering Church Architecture
Discovering Churchyards
Churches and Churchyards
County Guide to Wiltshire
Swindon An Illustrated History
Hometown History: Swindon (*for children*)
Swindon Old Town Through Time
Swindon Central Through Time
All For the Empire (*with Roger Trayhurn*)
The Swindon Book
The Swindon Book Companion

Swindon local history monographs
Blunsdon House Hotel
Book Club Associates at Swindon in the History of the Book Clubs Movement
Fairs and Markets of Swindon
Fred Stevens: The Magpie of Kingshill
Frederick Rowland Young and his Free Christian Churches in Swindon
From a Packet of Pins: A History of Barnes Coaches
Ken White: Artist, Muralist and Painter of Trompe L'œil
The Man Who Printed Prehistory and Other Mazonowicz Swindonians
The Mills of Swindon
Swindon Chinese Jazz Club 1960-1963
Swindon Water Company: How Piped Water Came to Swindon
Wick Farm, Lydiard Tregoze and Some of its Occupants
Wyvern Theatre, Swindon: The Years of Council Management 1964-1994

Other publications
King Alfred's School, Wantage: A Defining Moment, 1954-1960
The Little Ships of Dunkirk
Bluebird A Dream of a Boat in Six Acts
Electric Boating

THE
SWINDON
BOOK
COMPANION

Mark Child

First published in the United Kingdom in 2015

by The Hobnob Press, 30c Deverill Road Trading Estate, Sutton Veny, Warminster BA12 7BZ
www.hobnobpress.co.uk

British Library Cataloguing in Publication Data
A catalogue record for this book is available from the British Library

ISBN 978-1-906978-30-3
Typeset in Octavian and Franklin Gothic Heavy 10.5/12.5 pt. Typesetting and origination by John Chandler

Printed by Lightning Source

The Swindon Book Companion is dedicated to my wife
LORRAINE CLAIRE CHILD,
my constant in life,
and to our children OLIVER *and* LAUREN.
Also to ADAM *and* JOANNA.

THE SWINDON BOOK COMPANION

A Full Head of Steam Swindon-born Kenneth Rupert Ausden (1924-2009) was headmaster at Even Swindon junior school when he wrote his first stage play, an amusing documentary drama with music about the changing face of Swindon and the effect of the decline of steam on the railway workshops there. *A Full Head of Steam* centres on a home-occupier who refuses to be evicted from his railway village cottage that has been scheduled by the local authority for demolition. In a series of flashbacks, he recalls the birth and development of the town between 1840 and 1972, with particular references to railway works redundancies and the decline of steam railways.

The set of *A Full Head of Steam* includes a section of the railway cottages and four railway locomotives of as many periods, which slide on and off the stage. It also makes use of slides with historic images, which, in the original production at the Wyvern Theatre, were projected onto either side of the stage. The scheduled opening night, 18 April 1972, was delayed when problems affecting the theatre carpenters' workshop meant that the set was not ready in time for the actors to rehearse with it. Ken Ausden wrote on his original title page for the play: 'A play about a dying railway town for a living Wyvern Theatre'.

The Wyvern Theatre production was directed by Roger Redfarn, resident director of the Belgrade Theatre, Coventry, and the designer was Swindon-born Adrian Vaux. The delay of two nights meant that the especially invited civic guests had to be moved back, and the public who had seats for the first two nights had to exchange them for later in the run, which continued until 29 April. The play starred film and television actors Richard Beale and Anthony Booth; John Gower, the grandson of an engine driver; and Bernard Taylor. The last-named, who played the parts of Victorian and Edwardian landowners in Swindon, was a Swindon-born actor who studied at the town's art college and then at Chelsea College of Art. The Wyvern production included three schoolboys, one part being taken by the most recent head boy at Ken Ausden's school.

Aerated Water Works, College Street This establishment, custom-built in 1878, on land next to a terrace of three houses, was in the business of making soft drinks for eight decades. Its originator was probably Samuel Smith, a chemist in Regent Street who relocated to nearby Bridge Street where he was also a stationer, and the business was initially in the name of 'Smith & Pope'. By 1880, the name of the company had become New Swindon Aerated Water Company, secretary J. Moncrieff, of whom nothing is known. Soon, its manager would be Charles Hall Barker.

C.H. Barker (b. 1860) was the son of Charles Barker and, like his father, was born at Finchampstead, Berkshire. Charles (the elder) was born in 1831 and, by the 1860s, he was licensee of the Roebuck Inn, in the marketplace at Wokingham. During that decade, he relocated to Swindon, where he took on the Great Western Hotel in Station Road. By 1881, he was retired, and living at Bella Vista Villa, Bath Road, with his wife Mary and their children, one of whom was twenty-one-year-old Charles Hall Barker, who at that time was unemployed. However, early in the 1880s, he became licensee of the Wellington Commercial Hotel in Gloucester Street (interestingly, it would later become the Wellington Temperance Hotel), and in 1885 he is documented as manager of Swindon Aerated Water Company ('New' having by then been dropped from the name.) He became licensee of the Lower George Hotel, Gloucester in 1886.

It is likely that C.H. Barker went to Gloucester to gain experience in the licensed trade, because the Barker family continued its association with Swindon Aerated Water Company. Charles Barker (the elder), now living with his wife Mary at 87 Clifton Street, Swindon, became a coal merchant, and Swindon Aerated Water Company in College Street immediately added a coal dealership to its core business. By 1895, Charles Hall Barker had returned to Swindon

and had become licensee of the Golden Lion public house at 43 Bridge Street, just a few hundred yards away from the aerated water works. In that year, the latter's business name was again changed, becoming Barker & Co. Charles Hall Barker and his wife Maud were living at Elm Villa, Wellington Street by 1901. Barker & Co. continued to trade as 'mineral water manufacturers' from the College Street site until the 1950s. (See also College Street.)

Aeroplane, first to land in Swindon On Saturday, 27 July 1912, Henri Salmet (b. Paris, 1878) became the first aviator to land in the town. Salmet was a former mechanic at the Blériot Flying School based at Hendon aerodrome, where he learnt to fly and gained his aviator's certificate in 1911. The following year, he was contracted by the *Daily Mail* to fly a 'Wake Up England' tour around the country. That newspaper had a political agenda based on what it saw as the UK's failure to respond seriously to what it regarded as the aeroplane's potential as a military threat in Europe. Henri Salmet arrived at Swindon as part of this programme, landing in a two-seater Blériot XI-2 in a field off the Coate Road at Piper's Corner that belonged to Thomas Hooper Deacon, Swindon's premier horse seller. The crowd, which numbered some 30,000 people, covered several surrounding fields. Salmet was greeted by George Brooks, mayor of Swindon, and the deputy mayor, Tom Butler. In a thick French accent, the aviator announced that he had just two minutes' worth of petrol left, but once topped up he gave an exhibition of flying. Afterwards, Swindon Territorials roped down the aeroplane, and some of the town's boy scouts escorted the aviator to his car.

Salmet was driven to the Empire Theatre, where manager Alfred Manners had arranged for him to give an address to a packed house on methods of flying and the value and use of aviation. The ticket price was in support of the Victoria Hospital Fund, to which cause Salmet also contributed a cheque. George Brooks told the audience that 'other European countries were taking up aviation and employing it as a power for resistance', adding 'it is time we did something in this country'. This was the serious side of Henri Salmet's visit. Brooks had been asked if the people of Swindon would be prepared to subscribe to the 100,000 Shillings Fund to assist the War Office. Salmet had intended to leave Swindon the next day, but was prevented from doing so by 'the boisterous state of the weather'. He eventually took to the skies at 4.50 a.m. two days later.

Anderson, Robert Charles ('Bob') (b. 1947) Known as 'The Limestone Cowboy' in his darts-playing days, Bob Anderson won the Winmau World Masters in 1986, 1987, and 1988 – the first person to do so in three consecutive years – and the World Professional Championship in 1988. He was born in Winchester, Hampshire, the son of Harry Charles Anderson and his wife Hazel Irene, née Grant. Harry Anderson was a pork butcher in Winchester who, early in the Second World War, suffered a massive injury whilst undertaking specialist training on Salisbury Plain. He saw no active service, but was a member of the local Home Guard, the so-called Dad's Army. He worked for Vickers Armstrong at Hursley Park, Winchester, and came to the company's South Marston works in 1951, finishing in the contracts department. Harry also co-founded Stratton Youth Club. Meanwhile, Bob Anderson was educated at South Marston Primary School, Upper Stratton Junior School, Headlands Grammar School, and Swindon College.

Sport played a large part in his early life. He played football for Stratton Youth Club, Swindon NALGO, Athletico, Wootton Bassett Town, Highworth Town, and Shrivenham. Concurrently, he played darts for local teams: The Baker's Arms, the Kingsdown Inn, the Rat Trap, Gorse Hill Working Men's Club, and the NALGO Club at Penhill. As a junior, in 1963 he won the England Schools' Javelin Event, and was so good at this sport that he was picked as one of the British Olympic javelin team at the 1968 Olympic Games in Mexico. However, he broke his arm and was therefore prevented from taking part. By now, he had taken up his first job, being employed from 1966 as a clerical officer with the then National Assistance Board in Maxwell Street. In 1969, he was promoted to executive officer, and was transferred to the Ministry of Agriculture, Fisheries & Food in Lincoln. The following year he married his first wife, Mary Benstead, and they had two children. Bob Anderson played football for Lincoln United and, when he was living and working at Guildford in the early 1970s, for Guildford City, Woking, and Farnborough Town. He was a very good footballer, who might have made more of a career in the sport had not a broken leg prevented him from doing so. The family returned to Swindon in 1972 when he was appointed to the Department of Health and Social Security, where he became a higher executive officer in 1981. He resigned from the DHSS in 1985 to become a professional darts player. Bob Anderson moved to Somerset in 2001, and in 2004 married his second wife, Sally Attwater.

Artillery Arms beerhouse Until the mid-1850s, what became Regent Street was little more than a trackway extending eastwards from Bridge Street across the Wilts & Berks Canal. Isolated cottages and houses were built alongside it, and then small terraces. In one of these, a couple of hundred yards west of the Rifleman's Arms, which was erected early in the 1850s, a beerhouse was established c.1855 and called the Artillery Arms. The first keeper of the place was James Edward Toe (b. Swindon, 1822), a boot and shoemaker, who lived at 16 Westcott Place. He was followed by J. Herbert, and then by Charles Watts (b. Whitechapel, London, 1828), who lived with his family in a cottage a little further along the road. Watts styled himself as 'cellarman'. Arkell's bought the beerhouse, c.1864, when the recently widowed Louisa Watts (b. Swindon, 1832) was in charge. Three years later, the company acquired the adjacent house, and later remodelled the interior of both properties, and re-fronted the whole to give a unified appearance. Louisa Watts was followed at the Artillery Arms by Thomas Latter (b. East Peckham, Kent, 1843), who lived over the beerhouse with his wife. Thomas had been a carpenter at East Peckham, and in Swindon combined that trade with the occupation of beer retailer. He remained there until 1891, when he moved to the Eagle at 7 Regent Street, and Thomas Claughan (b. Durham, 1825) took over the Artillery Arms at the age of sixty-six. Claughan had previously been in charge of The Sun at 50 Bridge Street, where his wife and daughter – both named Mary – had been the barmaids. He died in 1892, after which date Edward Thomas took over at the helm. The Artillery Arms closed in 1936, by which time W.H. Woolworth's store was next door. The beerhouse was demolished to make way for Woolworth's extension to the east.

Averies Recycling, fire at Marshgate Averies Recycling (Swindon) Limited was a private company that was registered on 22 July 2008. It operated a skip hire service, and had a number of waste and skip businesses in Swindon and the surrounding area. In 2010, it acquired Swindon Skips. In 2012, the Environment Agency brought charges against the directors (Lee Averies and David James Averies), alleging at Swindon Crown Court that between January 2010 and September 2011 the firm 'kept, treated or disposed of controlled waste in a manner likely to cause pollution or harm public health'. A further charge was that they also operated a 'regulated waste facility', during two stipulated periods in 2010 and 2011, without a regulatory permit. Some of the charges also related to another of their companies, Swindon Reclamation Limited. The case was referred to Bristol where, at the Crown Court in 2013, Lee Averies pleaded guilty to causing a nuisance to neighbouring businesses with dust generated by its waste operations, and also to operating a waste transfer station without an environmental permit. He agreed that appropriate measures were not in place, or followed, to control dust escaping at the company's Swindon Marshgate site. He was fined £2,000; for the other offences, the company was fined a total of £11,000 and ordered to pay £60,000 in costs. The judge at the trial highlighted the impact of the nuisances on Averies's neighbours, and the potential for polluting a nearby stream. Also in 2013, some 750 tonnes of material caught fire at the Swindon Skips site.

The Averies Recycling case, and the portents of the judge, were soon to be raised again. In July 2014, the Environment Agency visited the Averies site and raised concerns about security. Two weeks later, on 21 July 2014, fire broke out on the firm's premises at Marshgate, an industrial estate at east Swindon, close to residential streets and a retail shopping park.

It was clear there was going to be a problem from the moment Wiltshire Fire & Rescue Service was called to the scene at 5.51 p.m. on 21 July. The Service quickly built up a company of six fire engines, two water carriers, an operational support unit and an incident command unit. Military firefighters brought specialist equipment from RAF Brize Norton, and crews from Cricklade, Malmesbury, Marlborough, Royal Wootton Bassett and Stratton St Margaret abandoned their day of industrial action over pay. As the flames and the black smoke gathered momentum, Swindon Borough Council became involved, as did the NHS, Environment Agency, Public Health England, and the Wiltshire Police. Air quality began to be monitored. By the next day, the burning smell was all over Swindon, and people with breathing problems were told to keep their windows closed. Footpaths around the area were closed. Additional fire crews came from Corsham, Ludgershall and Ramsbury.

Ten days after the fire broke out, Swindon was told that the site was expected to burn for weeks, and the Environment Agency began to monitor the nearby River Cole. Attempts to remove dampened waste from the site, so that firefighters could deal with the fire beneath, were at first thwarted when local protesters successfully lobbied against the suggested site, a former park and ride at Groundwell. Eventually, contractors were called in to remove the waste to a landfill site at Chapel Farm, Blunsdon. The fire continued at Marshgate for fifty-seven days before, on 15 September 2014, it was officially declared to be extinguished. Averies Recycling (Swindon) went into administration on 29 December 2014.

Bartlett Brothers This firm of monumental masons are (2013) at 84 Victoria Road. Its origins lie in the birth of William Bartlett at Latton in 1795. He married Mary from Marston Maisey, who was two years his junior, and he worked as an agricultural labourer. The couple had four boys: Henry (b. 1823), John (b. 1826), William (b. 1829), and Thomas (b. 1833). The family lived at Bridge Row, Latton. When he was in his late forties, William (the father) became blind, could no longer work, and by 1851 was a pauper. He died, a widower, in 1873.

In 1855, William (the son) married Mary Ann Hinton (b. 1833) in her native Cricklade, and the couple lived there together for more than thirty years at West Mill Lane. He became a stonemason. They had three children: Richard George (b. 1856), Sarah (b. 1861), and Alfred (b. 1865). By 1881, William was described as a master stonemason. Mary Ann Bartlett died in 1887. In 1888, William married Fanny Clapton (b. Down Ampney, 1846) but hardly survived the union; he died on 19 January 1889, leaving her just £122.

Life dealt unkindly with the former Fanny Clapton during this time. Having lost William Bartlett, master stonemason, she took up with John William Gosling, former bootmaker and then the innkeeper of the Three Horseshoes in the High Street at Cricklade, whom she married in 1890. He died in 1900, and Fanny took over the Three Horseshoes.

Of the children of William and Mary Ann Bartlett, Richard George became a bricklayer, and Alfred started out as a pupil teacher at St Sampson's National School in Cricklade. When their father died in 1889, Alfred gave up the teaching profession and took over his father's business as a stonemason. In 1890, he married Leah Annie Brown (b. Newton Tony, 1867) at Mere in Wiltshire. For a while, the couple lived at West Mill Lane, Cricklade, where their first child, William Alfred, was born in 1891.

In 1884, Richard George Bartlett, the bricklayer, married Mary Wakefield (b. Fairford, 1861) and the couple set up at Walton Villa, William Street, in New Swindon. Significantly, Richard George must have encountered one of Swindon's principal builders of the time, George Wiltshire, who lived at 22 Bath Road. About 1893, Alfred, Leah, and their son William Alfred also came to live in Swindon. It was there that their remaining three children were born: Charles (b. 1893), Dorothy Margaret (b. 1896), and Nina Frances (b. 1898). George Wiltshire died in 1897 and, the following year, 22 Bath Road was sold to Alfred Bartlett. The exterior of the premises was lime-washed and became known as 'The White House', and has since remained thus. By 1911, his two sons William Alfred and Charles were working with him, from the same address, also as monumental masons. Richard George Bartlett, the bricklayer, relocated to 84 Kingshill Road, where he died in 1912, leaving Mary just under £280. Of their children, Alfred James (b. 1886) had joined the family business as a stonemason; George (b. 1891) aspired only to be a riveter's labourer in the GWR Works; and Lily (b. 1895) was in dressmaking.

Alfred died at the Wiltshire County Asylum, Devizes in 1916. He left almost £850. His two sons changed the company name to Bartlett Brothers, which it has remained. Leah Annie remained at 22 Bath Road, where she died in 1934. (See also Wiltshire, George.)

Bates, Ralph (1899-2000) Author, poet, traveller, political activist and one-time Professor of Literature at New York University, Ralph Bates was born in Swindon, where he spent the first three decades of his life. He came from a railway family; his grandfather, Alfred William Bates (b. Horley, Gloucestershire) was a GWR engine fitter; his Swindon-born father Henry Roy Bates (1875-1925) was variously a railway fitter and turner for which he had served (1889-96) a seven-year apprenticeship in the Works, and a lathe man. Ralph Bates's mother, Mabel Stephens, née Rosby (1878-1955) was also born in Swindon. When Henry died, he left nearly £500, and granted probate to Ralph William Rosby, Mabel's brother, a wood turner who lived with the couple in the early years of their marriage and who became a cabinet maker and latterly a fine art dealer. On her death, Mabel left over £3,000 to two other of her children, Roy Stephen Bates, who was a railway turner, and Leslie Alfred Bates, who was a railway coppersmith.

Before he turned to writing, Ralph Bates was also destined for a career with the GWR. He would have attended the Swindon School Board's school for boys (opened 1881) in Sanford Street, and then the Swindon & North Wilts Technical Schools (opened 1897) in Victoria Road. When he was seventeen, Ralph Bates joined the GWR as an apprentice fitter, turner and erector, and became a union man, thus firing his political spirit. During the First World War, he served as an infantryman with the 16th Queen's Royal West Surrey Regiment. Afterwards he re-joined the GWR (1918-c.1930) working in the chain testing house. By now a member of the Communist Party, Bates began travelling first to Spain (and later Mexico, and America where he settled), and writing. In 1928, at Kensington Registry Office, Bates married Winifred Eades Spink (b. London, 1898), a teacher and Communist Party member. His first book, *Sierra*, was published in 1933. It was followed by *Lean Men: An Episode in a Life*, 1934; *Franz Schubert*, 1934; *The Olive Field*, 1936; *Rainbow Fish*, 1937; *Sirocco and Other Stories*, 1939 (reprinted as *The Miraculous Horde and Other Stories*, 1939); *The Fields of Paradise*, 1940; the *Undiscoverables and Other Stories*, 1941; and *The Dolphin in the Wood*, 1950.

Between the mid-1930s and the end of the decade, Bates crossed the Atlantic on several occasions, each time describing himself as 'author'. In 1938, he deserted Winifred and his children and took up with Eve Salzman (b. 1913), whom he eventually married in New York. Ralph Bates is Swindon's forgotten author, probably because most of his writing was published after he left the town. An account of his life and work can be found in *Ralph Bates: Swindon's 'Unknown' Author* by Michael Yates (Ex-Libris Press, 2014).

Bath Road, No. 68 The organisation that brought piped water to Swindon was Swindon Water Company, whose offices were in the Corn Exchange, Old Town. In 1872, it changed its name to Swindon Waterworks Company, and the following year moved into temporary accommodation at 42 Cricklade Street, the offices of its solicitor. This gave them the time to custom-build their own offices. These were designed by William Henry Read, architect, and were built, 1875-6, next to market gardens on the north side of The Sands by George Wiltshire. The property was stylish, elegant, homogeneous and beautifully proportioned, with the overall appearance of a substantial villa. Built of brick with freestone quoins, the front elevation was of five bays and two storeys. Its central section was pedimented, and the quoins that picked it out at first-floor level and the arched central carriage entry that admitted onto the street created a beautifully balanced picture. The upper windows were square-headed, except for the one above the porch, which was shoulder-arched, and the ground-floor windows were round-headed. The windows in both levels had moulded jambs. It was one of the most attractive buildings in Old Town.

The property was numbered 68 Bath Road, and the Swindon Waterworks Company moved in on 4 July 1876. It comprised residential accommodation for the manager of the company's waterworks, the secretary's office, and a boardroom. On 4 October 1895, the Swindon Waterworks Company moved out. In their place came the Swindon Water Board, which took over the premises before establishing their own offices elsewhere in Bath Road. No. 68 continued to be an architectural gem in Bath Road until it was demolished in the 1960s. The Girls' Friendly Society acquired the site, and spent £51,000 building its first hostel for young women since the Second World War. The hostel was named Townsend House, after Mary Elizabeth Townsend who founded the Society in 1875, and was opened by Princess

Margaret on an official visit to Swindon in 1968. It could hardly have been more out of keeping with the general architecture in Bath Road, but was an example of how the local authority's planning department of the day was prepared to compromise in the face of property development. The hostel closed in 2008 and, despite efforts to turn it into flats, remains empty.

Bavin, William Dorling (1871-1948) At the end of the First World War, the Government decided to establish a National War Museum, and H.M. Office of Works was charged with collecting material for its museum and library. The Office of Works wrote to Swindon Borough Council seeking examples of its wartime printed ephemera. The Council agreed to this, and decided to compile a 'complete record in permanent form of local activities, charitable and otherwise, in connection with the War'. With this in mind, it negotiated terms, 1917-18, under which W.D. Bavin would undertake the project which was expected to occupy his spare time for 'at least two or three years, and will probably cover at least two or three volumes'. In the event, *Swindon's War Record* was published in one volume in 1922.

Very little has ever been written about the author, and both Bavin and his seminal book have been almost forgotten, as has the fact that he compiled all of the town's official printed guidebooks between the 1920s and the 1940s. Recently, Darryl Moody, Head of Swindon Local Studies Archive, has investigated W.D. Bavin and his work, and the information in this entry is from his research.

W.D. Bavin was born in Lincoln, the eldest son of William Bavin (b. Sheffield, 1841) and his wife Maria Elizabeth, née Dorling (b. Woodbridge, Suffolk, 1846) who married in 1869 in Lincoln and were both 'commercial clerks' in a local iron foundry. After some time, 1893-95, as an assistant tutor at Westminster Training College, a Methodist foundation in Horseferry Road, London, he was employed, 1895-97, as an instructor of pupil teachers at Bath Technical College. In 1897, he was appointed the first head of Swindon Pupil Teacher Centre – a day training facility which opened that year (the building later became Euclid Street School) for teachers at Swindon Board schools. The following year, he married former draper's assistant Jessie Bralsford (b. Lincoln 1872) at Lincoln. They lived in Goddard Avenue, Swindon, where they had two daughters, Evelyn Jessie (1900-1982) and Helen Muriel (1907-1990).

Bavin was appointed head of the Swindon Higher Grade Elementary School when the Euclid Street building was thus redefined in 1903 to take boys and girls. His wife Jessie died in 1915 and, three years later, he married Helen Georgina E. Metcalfe (1882-1959). He was appointed headmaster of Sanford Street Boys' School in 1919. During the Second World War, he published *America Gets Around*, a guidebook for the use of US service personnel stationed in Swindon. Among his other publications were two volumes of pocket notes for Sunday school teachers (he was President of the local Sunday School Union), and a book on practical and applied arithmetic. His interest in the education and welfare of youngsters found him variously founder and president of the Swindon Triangle Boys' Club, vice-chairman of the Swindon Juvenile Employment Sub-committee, and founder and chairman of the After-Care Committee. He was also a borough magistrate. Bavin and both of his wives were buried in Radnor Street cemetery.

Bays, Edward & Co. see Ironmongers in Wood Street

BBC Wiltshire Sound radio station In 1964, the houses and shops in the section of Prospect Place immediately off Victoria Road were demolished, and their place taken by office accommodation. *BBC Wiltshire Sound* was created in the former AMI House, an office block that had remained empty for some time on the corner of Prospect Place and Victoria Road, when it was purchased by the BBC and remodelled into studios. The station began broadcasting on 4 April 1989, and was officially opened three days later by Douglas Hurd, then the Home Secretary, who unveiled an illustrative plaque designed by stonemason John Lloyd of Great Bedwyn. On 11 November 2002, the station split into two, *BBC Radio Swindon* and *BBC Radio Wiltshire*. (See also Brunel FM; GWR Radio; Radio 105.5; Swindon FM; Wiltshire Radio.)

Beehive, Prospect Hill For the best part of thirty years from the 1840s, railway village and New Swindon residents who wished to go to Old Town had to follow a difficult route between fields through the hamlet of Eastcott. Part of this route was called Eastcott Lane, which admitted eastwards into Prospect Lane. The gradients were steep and the pathways narrow, and the journey required walkers to climb over two stiles. This continued until c.1870, when Prospect Street was built up on the line of Prospect Lane. (It would later be named Prospect Hill, and its southern continuation became Prospect Place.) Also, c.1870,

Western Street was built immediately to the west of Prospect Street; and in the angle formed where the two converged, Philip Cockbill built the Beehive in 1871. Cockbill had built, 1863-64, the Belle Vue brewery on Victoria Street, and an inn adjacent at the rear. The Beehive on Prospect was his only other venture. It would have been a good time to open a public house on Prospect Hill, and in a prime position, although, for eighteen years, only an off-licence was allowed. When it was granted its full licence in 1889, the first landlord was Henry James, who came to Swindon that year from London, where he had worked as a milkman. James, his wife and mother were originally from the Faringdon, Berkshire area. All three were installed at The Beehive, together with his three sons, one of whom, Walter, had been blind from birth. Later in the 1890s, the family relocated to London, where Henry worked as a cowman. Edmund Perrin and his family succeeded him in Swindon. The Beehive was refurbished in 1985 and was internally re-modelled in 2014 under Andy Marcer, who had been landlord since 1992, and Morrell's, its long-time brewery. (See also Reilly, Noel.)

Beer retailers in 19th-century Swindon Pigot's directory for 1830 lists just a handful of named inns and public houses in Swindon. A decade later, New Town was started beneath the old settlement, and in 1842, other directories begin to include the inns and public houses being opened in New Swindon. However, at all times throughout the 19th century the compilers of these lists were selective, rather than comprehensive. The 1830 Pigot also mentions the town's maltsters, who were William Butler in Newport Street, Henry

Tarrant at Eastcott, and the two High Street businesses of William Farmer, and Sheppard & Tuck. Beer retailers did not make it into the directories until 1842, when the first to be recorded were William Bizley of High Street, and John Jones and Isaac Wheeler, both of Newport Street.

In the early 1840s, the origins of the small beerhouses extant in the New Swindon area were founded on the needs of the earlier canal constructors and workers, and these beerhouses were largely supported by the farming community thereabouts. Then, premises were custom-built and licensed to serve the growing GWR workforce, but New Swindon's general retail infrastructure was relatively slow in development. It relied for a while on that of Old Town, on the hill to the south. This provided the opportunity for the expansion of beer retailing in Old Town, as well as presenting a wide open market in New Swindon. Traders there were quick to respond, particularly in Westcott Place, which was begun as a private development just outside the railway village in the mid-1840s. By 1848, within a few yards of each other, Elizabeth Cave, Henry Cross, Henry Hinton, Thomas Hurcomb, and Richard Pearce Smith had all set up as beer retailers in Westcott Place.

One of the effects of foot traffic between New Town and Old Swindon at this time was the establishing of beer retailing along the route through Eastcott. By 1848, George Bishop, who was also a 'cowkeeper', had begun to supply beer there, as had John Page, and William Smith, who was also a carpenter. The combination of beer retailer with some other occupation was common practice. In Old Town, for example, John Compton of Cricklade Street was also a gardener; William Simmons of Newport Street was

also a stonemason; and Charles Smith of Lower Town was also the local mail carrier. Other beer retailers in Old Swindon by 1848 included Edward Henry Delaunay and Isaac Wheeler, both of Newport Street; John Jones in Prospect Place; and, in Albert Street, Lucy Rogers and William Walker. One or two of their premises emerged as named beerhouses but, for the most part, these were individuals selling beer. Just two years later, fifteen beer retailers were listed for Old Swindon, and there were twelve in New Town.

The next half-century was to make a considerable difference. In 1850, Old Swindon had a population of about 2,500; there were some 2,000 people in New Swindon. The GWR Works accounted for an estimated workforce of about 1,200. At the end of the century, the number of employees at the Works was nudging 12,000, and the combined population (Swindon was given its charter of incorporation in 1900) was approaching the 44,996 logged at the 1901 census. The railway made for thirsty work. By 1900, there were some sixteen named beerhouses and fully licenced pubs in Old Swindon, and in New Swindon the tally was fifty-three. There were several wine and spirit merchants and, as the nineteenth century rolled into the twentieth, the independent beer retailers were listed as:

Old Swindon
John Wilkins, 6 Albert Street
Henry Game/Christopher Gale, 7 Albert Street
William Morrison, Belle Vue Road
Henry William Bennett, 14 Cricklade Street
Andrew Smith, 41 Cricklade Street
Frederick Hooper, 37 Cricklade Street
Lydia Offer, 26 Devizes Road
Frederick Bishop/Ada Jane Bishop,

28 Devizes Road
James Henry Barns, 52 & 54 Newport Street
Harry Maylott, 56 Newport Street
Emily Day, 63 Newport Street
Alfred Strange, 30 North Street
George A. Godsell/Ernest Greenwood,
9 Prospect
Edwin William Hughes, 44 Prospect
Charles H. Fenn/Edmond Perrin,
55 Prospect
Henry Baden, 8 Union Street
George Strange, 33 Victoria Street
Stephen Brown, 45 Victoria Street
Albert George Lay, 27 Wood Street

New Swindon
Robert Carrier/Arthur George Nott,
76 Albion Street
Thomas Gardiner/Richard Bishop, 31 Bridge
Street
Frederick Davies/Edward Hastings Hart,
37 Bridge Street
Arthur A. Powell/William Martin, 50 Bridge
Street
James Gray, Carfax Street
Frederick George Leighfield, 49 Cheltenham
Street
John Skinner, 57 Cricklade Road
Ernest Herbert Hayward, 241 Cricklade
Road
John Charles Taylor, 256 Cricklade Road
Charles Praeter, 1 Cromwell Street
Frederick George Pound, 109 Dean Street
David Townsend/Sarah Townsend, 9 East
Street
Gabriel Morrel, 14 Eastcott Hill
Edwin Fifield/Richard Caunter, 27 Eastcott
Hill
William Shail, Ferndale Road
Thomas Evans/Charlie Smith, 4 Fleet Street
John Miles/Thomas Tranter, 15 Fleet Street
A.L. Pryce, 22 Fleet Street

Alfred William Young, 34 Fleet Street
Thomas Rasey/Walter George Barnard,
50 Fleet Street
Eliza Cove/Ellen Eames, 16 Harding Street
Albert Rice/Ellen Woodhouse, 13 Henry
Street
John Kempston/Frank Robert Hornblow,
15 Henry Street
Charles Riddiford Thomas, 6 High Street
(Emlyn Square)
Alfred Edward Morgan, 12 High Street
(Emlyn Square)
Charles Thomas Hartwell, 16 High Street
(Emlyn Square)
William Knapp, 25 Medgbury Road
Thomas Garland, 92 Medgbury Road
Thomas Catchmie, 1 Merton Street
Joseph Maylott, 22 Oriel Street
Edith Rake/Thomas Cullerne, 23 Princes
Street
Eli Rowland, 33 Regent Place
Henry William Thomas, 7 Regent Street
Thomas Eddie/John Gigg, 25 Regent Street
William Richard Stone, 29 Regent Street
Henry Chandler, 40 Regent Street
Thomas Edward Wise, 63 Regent Street
Sarah Sweet, 66 Regent Street
Charles Stance/Maurice Bert Phipps,
88 Regent Street
Henry George Hughes/Louis Francis
Howell, 14 Rodbourne Road
George Henry Strange, Oxford Buildings,
Rodbourne Road
William James Little, 1 Rolleston Street
Georgina Williams, 6 Sheppard Street
Frank Edward Tanner/Stephen Ogbourne,
1 Station Road
William Westlake, 43 Theobald Street
Albert Edward Tunley/Samuel Sparrow,
18 Vilett Street
Sarah Ann Page/Thomas Henry Little,
3 Westcott Place

Frederick George Carpenter/Jessie Stratton, 23 Westcott Place

Henry Lewis, 43 Westcott Place

William Charles Lock/Edwin William Hughes, 66 Westcott Place

William Stephens, 144 Westcott Place

William Griffin, 28 Whiteman Street

By this time, the retailing of beer in Swindon, in one way or another, was at its height. Several main routes and areas had opened up, along which the sellers had become established, a number of whom devolved on the ingress and egress of the GWR workers. These were High Street (later to be named Emlyn Square), New Swindon, the roads east of the railway station and works, and particularly the line immediately to the south of the railway village, taking in Westcott Place and Fleet Street. These were all routes taken daily by the massive and thirsty railway workforce. Many of these people also passed through Bridge Street and Regent Street, and beer retailers opened up there before these roads became lined with general shops and, before Victoria Road was opened, providing an alternative route between the new town and Old Swindon. The other route that provided beer retailers with opportunities to trade was the original way across the Wilts & Berks Canal, up Eastcott Hill and through Prospect. By 1900, if new traders had established themselves as beer retailers facilitating the needs of mobile groups of people, no such criteria worried Old Town. The increased number of beer retailers there, largely supported the community on the hill. It is interesting to note how they developed in the Cricklade Street/Albert Street/Belle Vue Road area – Old Town's red-light district. (See also Pub landlords in 19th-century Swindon.)

Beint, Eric William (1922-2008)

In the local government reforms of 1974, Swindon lost its borough status and became submerged in the newly created, larger Borough of Thamesdown. It was the only town in the country to lose its identity in this way, which further angered its residents who were already appalled that the name per se had been changed. None were more aggrieved than Eric Beint, son of the cartoonist W.E. Beint (see below), and he mounted a high-profile and non-stop campaign to have Swindon's borough status reinstated. This involved writing to government departments, Members of Parliament, and individuals who potentially had influence in such matters.

Eric was born in Swindon, trained locally as a car mechanic, served as a fitter in the RAF during the Second World War, and then joined the GWR as a railway fitter. In 1939, whilst on holiday in Blackpool, he met Joan Marshall from Burnley, and the couple were married there in 1943. They moved from Swindon to Burnley in 1956, and it was from there that Eric Beint conducted his campaign. The importance of this in the history of Swindon may be judged by the fact that when the town was restored as a unitary authority in 1997, Eric Beint was guest of honour at the celebrations in the Civic Offices.

Beint, Kenneth John (b. 1933)

The artist and muralist was the son of W.E. Beint (see below). Born in Swindon, he went to Ferndale School and Euclid Street School, and obtained a National Diploma in Design after attending a full-time course at Swindon School of Art 1949-53. He followed this with an Art Teacher's Diploma (also writing a thesis on aspects of Swindon's history) at Birmingham University, 1953-54. Then he wrote directly to Swindon's Borough Education Officer for a job, and was rewarded with the post of art teacher at Pinehurst School, eventually relocating as head of art at Commonweal School, where he remained for fifteen years until he took early retirement in 1983. At Pinehurst School, he taught Ken White, who would go on to have an international career as an artist and muralist.

Like his father, Ken Beint had an artistic alter ego. An accomplished painter of landscapes, streetscapes, murals and still lifes, he was also a signwriter and illustrator, which he turned into a full-time business following his retirement from teaching. Between 1955 and 1975, he taught part-time at Swindon School of Art. He became much in demand in Swindon for painting whole shop windows with cartoon characters and storybook characters. One of his largest commissions was a mural 100 feet long and 8 feet high, depicting a French street in the 1930s, painted for a wine event sponsored by the *Sunday Times* and the Bordeaux region of France, at Olympia, London. When Swindon's Brunel shopping mall was being built, the Borough Council appointed Ken Beint to paint numerous pictures of Swindon landmarks on the fronts of empty shops before they were filled for the first time. These included a King Class locomotive going through the station; the town hall, the Baptist tabernacle, and a landscape of Coate Water. He followed these in the Brunel Centre with a 75-foot-long panorama of Wiltshire, a compendium of landscape, individual buildings of note, and depictions of horse racing. Always an enthusiastic cricketer and supporter of the sport, he designed the logo for Swindon Cricket Club.

Beint, William Edward (1895-1977) Will Beint, cartoonist and caricaturist, was born in Swindon, the second of seven children of Eli Hicketts Beint from Bradenstoke, a frame builder at the GWR Works, and his wife Fanny, née Newman, from Wootton Bassett. Eli was also, at one time, draughts champion of Wiltshire. Will left school and became an office boy at the Co-operative Society bakery store, served in the First World War, and afterwards joined the GWR as an office clerk in the general stores. Over the years, he became an inspector of stores for the whole GWR system, and continued in the company's employment until he retired. In 1921, he married Winifred Ada Jane Spanswick, and the couple had six children.

Normally a quiet man, Will Beint had a triple life. Throughout the 1920s and '30s he trod the boards as a comedy turn, either dressed as a country yokel, performing as a magician, or entertaining as a lightning magic picture artist. This was the clue to his other occupation, the incisively observed and beautifully drawn caricatures and cartoons with which he illustrated publications by the Borough Press, drew sporting cartoons for Swindon's *Football Pink*, and illustrated the national Sunday *Empire News*, all signed in a very distinctive way. He also published a book of his sports cartoons, drew his own greetings cards, and left numerous drawings of work colleagues. His illustrations have become very collectable.

Bell Close, circus at see Tarrant's *Recollections*

Belle Vue public house This is currently known as Long's Bar, fronting Victoria Road. When it was built by Philip

Cockbill, 1863-64, this part was his brewery, and the public house was adjacent to the rear, admitting onto Belle Vue Road.

Philip Cockbill was born at Kelmscot, Oxfordshire, in 1828, and was the son of a carpenter and wheelwright, himself taking on the occupation of carpenter. In 1849, he married Elizabeth Williams (b. Highworth, 1823), and the couple briefly took on the White Hart public house in Newport Street, Swindon, before handing over to Eliza Cocks, early in the 1850s. Whilst at the Belle Vue, Cockbill styled himself 'carpenter and publican'. Philip and Elizabeth relocated to 59 Belle Vue Road, where their six children were born between 1853 and 1864, whilst Philip worked as a carpenter.

At the time, Victoria Road (then called Victoria Street) extended no further north from the junction with Bath Road than about 100 yards, beyond which stretched allotments, gardens and orchards. A track ran eastwards from the end of this short roadway towards Christ Church, and abutting it to the north was a portion of land owned by Revd Henry George Baily, the vicar of Old Town. In 1863, Cockbill negotiated to buy this land and immediately set about building his brewery and public house. It made sense to place the public house at the Belle Vue Road end, all the better to attract clientele from the terraces being put up in that area. In the year he opened, 1864, he was advertising himself as a 'licensed brewer' selling 'genuine home-brewed beer at the Belle Vue Inn, Belle Vue Road. Elizabeth Cockbill died in 1869; Philip gave up carpentry and thereafter styled himself only as a brewer. He died in 1873, and the business was taken over by his fourth child, William Cockbill, who put it on the market in 1877. The following year,

it was acquired by Arkell's the brewers, who immediately shut down the brewing side of the business. William Cockbill continued to run the pub, in all for a decade, and Arkell's later remodelled the buildings so that the entrance to the public house was at the Victoria Road end.

Betts, Alexander Alfred (1858-1928) Between 1889 and 1898, Betts was in Swindon operating as a portrait and landscape photographer at 59 Prospect. Born at Brighton, Sussex, he was the son of artist turned photographer Alfred Betts (b. Bristol, 1831) and his wife Zilpah, née Carr (b. Holloway, London, 1835). The couple met when both were living at Merthyr Tydfil, Glamorgan, married in 1856, and went to live in Brighton. In 1859, the family moved back to Merthyr, where Alexander's six siblings were born. Between 1879 and 1882, Alexander Alfred Betts was one of the managers of The Soho Bazaar School of Photography, the successor of The London School of Photography, with premises in the capital in Oxford Street and Soho Square. Afterwards, he made much of this connection in his advertisements. In 1887, having spent some years as a photographer in Derby, Betts married Mary Isabell Davies (b. Richmond, Yorkshire, 1862) the daughter of a papermaker in Blackburn. Almost at once, the couple relocated to Swindon, where their son Victor Alfred John Betts was born in 1892. Betts informed his potential customers that: 'Enlargements of every description (whether taken by Mr Betts or elsewhere) can be made from any picture, in all styles of finish, while the thorough preservation of the likeness is kept throughout. Special attention paid to the re-production [*sic*] of faded or other portraits'. He continued to operate at 59 Prospect until 1898, when the family removed to Fleetwood, Lancashire, where they were to remain. The Swindon premises were taken over by two short-lived photographic businesses, John William Huff, from 1898-1900, and H. Dobbinson, in 1901. Mary Isabell survived her husband by just two years.

Big Screen, Wharf Green In 2007, regeneration began in Wharf Green, an area alongside Canal Walk that had hitherto contained a miscellany of walkways, large planters for bushes and shrubs and, for a while, a statue of local acrobats of the early twentieth century, the Great Blondinis. This project was the first of seven areas in the centre of the town that had been scheduled for remodelling and refurbishment under a £1 billion programme co-ordinated by The New Swindon Company on behalf of Swindon Borough Council and the South West Regional Development Agency. The Wharf Green project included the first permanent BBC Big Screen to be installed in the south-west of England. It measured thirty-five square feet and was affixed to the north side of the Brunel Centre's west car park, overlooking the area that had been re-shaped into an open plaza that facilitated viewers.

The idea was that the screen should provide entertainment, including live streaming of some BBC sporting and music coverage, community news and information, and give independent filmmakers the opportunity to showcase their work. The producer for the Big Screen was Erik Burnett-Godfrey, and it was launched on Friday, 2 May 2008 by Alex Lovell, a television presenter on *BBC Points West* from Bristol. The New Swindon Company ceased to exist in March 2010. The Big Screen's schedules continued to be managed by the BBC, which in 2012, decided to withdraw its management in order to cut costs. On 13 September 2013, control of the Big Screen passed to inSwindon, the town centre Business Improvement District company, which was established in 2007 with finance from member businesses. Swindon council soon acknowledged that it did not have the necessary expertise to generate sufficient income from the project. In 2014, it contracted with a private company, b-focused, a sponsorship facilitator, sports marketing and project management organisation, to run the big screen and organise events in the surrounding area.

Blackmore, Reginald John (1904-1973) Best known for his contributions on the history of Swindon and the railway in the *Great Western Railway Magazine*, the GWR staff magazine *Swindon Railway News*, and the *Swindon & District Monthly Review*. RJB also wrote poetry for children and nonsense verse and, throughout the 1950s, made recordings at Bristol for BBC radio *Children's Hour*. His most prolific writing period was during the 1930s, although much later he continued to contribute pieces to *Swindon Viewpoint*.

Reg Blackmore's father was John Alexander Blackmore (b. Exeter, Devon, 1872). By the time he was in his late teens, John was working as a live-in 'billiard marker' on the staff of the Royal Hotel, St Peter Port, Guernsey. In 1894, back in Devon, he married Leah Farr (b. Westbury, Wiltshire, 1869), and the couple must have at once settled in Swindon, firstly in Holbrook Street but soon relocating to Armstrong Street, and where John was employed by the GWR as a railway carriage fitter. Their first child, Margaret, was born in 1896, followed in 1898 by Gladys, and Reginald completed the trio in 1904. In his early years, Reg was an avid trainspotter, regularly meeting his friends at White House bridges and staying out until after dark.

Reginald John Blackmore followed his father into the GWR Works in 1919, at the age of fifteen. Initially employed as an office boy, he eventually found his calling as a fitter and turner in No.15 carriage shop, played for its cricket and football teams, and sang with its '15 Glee Singers'. Eventually, he left this group when its activities conflicted with the times of Sunday worship. Within a decade, the general depression had so affected the Works that, finding himself out of a job, he relocated to Hull with some railway colleagues, where he found employment as a petrol pump fitter. One of his pumps was in Chatsworth House. In 1929, he married Elisabeth Madeleine Dore, the couple having previously attended Sunday school in the Railway Mission in Wellington Street, where his mother Leah was a member. RJB and Elisabeth set up home at 28 Oxford Road (now designated Stratton Road). From the early days of their marriage, they were both associated with Stratton Green Baptist Church, where Reg wrote the lyrics of choruses for children to sing at Sunday school and created the tunes, together with Gwyneth Lander, the minister's daughter. He wrote sermons and fulfilled the role of lay preacher for all of his adult life. Too young for the First World War, and too old for the Second, Reg served as an ARP warden.

He subsequently returned to the GWR Works in Swindon, where he stayed in No.15 shop until 1951, the year John Alexander Blackmore died, before taking over the running of a grocery shop at Stratton Crossroads. Two years after the death of his wife in 1953, he re-applied for work with the GWR and became a diesel brake inspector at Rushey Platt. During this time, he continued his involvement at Stratton Green and was, from 1957, an elder at Cambria Baptist Chapel. In 1962, he took early retirement from the GWR to take up the post of honorary pastor at the Baptist Church, Dolton, Devon, where he lived in the manse. When he officially retired in 1969, he relocated to St Giles in the Wood, a small hamlet near Great Torrington, where he was very active in the Baptist Chapel at nearby Kingscott. He is buried in the little cemetery beside the chapel.

Blaylock's shoe retailers, Bath Road Four generations of the Blaylock family have run one of Swindon's most enduring retailers, which is now one of the leading shoe businesses in the south of England. Robert Blaylock (1896-1955) was born at Bowness on Windermere, Westmorland, the son of a house painter. As a child, he contracted rheumatic fever and was ever afterwards to have heart problems. Despite warnings that he should do nothing manual, he was, by the age of fifteen, apprenticed to a local boot and shoe repairer. During the First World War, Robert was billeted at Chiseldon Camp, where he repaired army boots. When the war finished, he remained in Swindon, opening a boot repair workshop at 254 Cricklade Road. He was also a part-time lay preacher at Florence Street mission hall, where he met Lillian Skinner, the daughter of Daniel Skinner, who ran the mission. The couple married in 1921, moved into 158 Cricklade Road, and had seven children.

In 1928, Robert relocated his business into 5 Bath Road, Old Town, where he operated a shoe repair workshop at the rear. The landlord of No.5 Bath Road would not give him a lease; Randolph Pollard, the gent's outfitter, who was next door at No. 3, had a long lease. When the landlord of No. 5 decided to sell his property, Pollard bought it and moved in his business, transferring his lease at No. 3 to Robert Blaylock. By 1949, Robert's health was failing, and although none of his sons had wanted to take on Blaylock's, his son Robert Arthur resigned his job in the National Provincial Bank to do so. When the property came up for sale, Robert Arthur bought it, and was also able to buy the property next door, which was on the corner with Devizes Road, plus a little lock-up adjacent called The Corner Cabinet, which sold antique glassware. He expanded the business.

Robert Arthur's son David John Blaylock was also initially not of a mind to follow in his father's footsteps, but in 1974 he gave up his clerical job with Swindon Borough Council in order to continue the business. He ran it from 1988, and was joined in 1997 by his son Mark Adam Blaylock.

Blunt, Frederick Albert (b. 1975)
The cartoonist, comic artist and book illustrator Fred Blunt was born at Princess Margaret Hospital, and was the son of a Plessey maintenance engineer from the East End of London. He was educated at Lainesmead Primary School and Churchfields School. From a very young age, he had a natural ability for drawing, and his cartoons were being published in various magazines by the time he was barely in his teens. Fred undertook a Foundation Arts Course at Swindon College, 1991-93,

and attended the University of the West of England, Bristol, 1993-96, from where he graduated with a BA (Hons) in Illustration. Magazine work and illustrations for greetings cards followed, then caricatures of pop stars for animations in BBC television children's and comedy channels. He was represented by the Meiklejohn Illustration Agency in London, and by Bright Children's Illustrations, and in 2005, he became a full-time illustrator. Since then he has drawn comic strips and his portfolio of publishing houses has increased; it included children's publisher Usborne, Scholastic Press, Collins, Macmillan and Penguin Books. His 2011 show 'Doodles at the Arts Centre' exemplified the minimal but vibrant and action-packed style of drawing that is so characteristic of his work. Fred Blunt also gives tuition in illustration in Swindon schools, and carries out workshops in association with the Swindon Youth Literature Festival.

Brooks, Henry Jamyn (1839-1925) One of Swindon's earliest pioneer commercial photographers, H.J. Brooks was also the shortest-lived in the town. Born in Birmingham, he became an oil painter and set up as such in Abingdon, Berkshire, where he lodged with the widow Ann Hartwell, who had a tobacconist shop in the market place. In 1863, he married Selina Ann Couldrey (b. Abingdon, 1840). Brooks opened his 'Photographic Establishment' in 1864 at 5 Bath Terrace (which had been built in 1852 on Bath Road opposite the entrance to Victoria Street). His advertisements pointed out that his work was 'inferior to none for excellence of finish and permanence, at a price considerably below what is usually charged for first-class productions' and that he specialised in 'photographs finished in oil and watercolours'. He had a studio in the Literary Institute in Bath Terrace, where he had 'erected a glass house and arranged all the accessories, backgrounds for first-class photography only'.

Brooks stayed in Swindon for less than a year. In 1865, his business was taken over by Edward Butler, and he went back to Abingdon, where the couple's first child, Emily Beatrice, was born that same year. He expanded his business at Abingdon, and by 1869 was advertising himself as a photographer, bookseller and stationer, painter and artist colourman, and circulating library, operating from premises in High Street. By 1871, his sister, Mary Brooks, had become his assistant in the business and, as soon as Emily Beatrice was old enough, she joined the firm as an artist and portrait painter. In the 1880s, the family relocated to London, where H.J. Brooks continued as an artist and portrait painter in oils, before removing to Shelford, Essex, where he died.

Brothels see St Tropez Massage Parlour

Brunel FM radio station *Brunel FM* came about after *Swindon FM* applied for a second radio station licence in the town in 2005. This was won by The Local Radio Company, which had originated in 1996 as the result of a tie-up between the GWR Group and Radio Investments Limited. The new radio station owners intended to call it *Now FM*, but almost immediately changed the name to *Brunel FM* as a reference to Isambard Kingdom Brunel, who brought the Great Western Railway and its Works to Swindon. The station's livery was mauve and yellow. It occupied the former GWR Radio's Lime Kiln Studios at Wootton Bassett, and

launched on 2 September 2006. Later, the station relocated to the Shrivenham 100 Business Park. Two years after launch, it was sold to Laser Broadcasting, a Darlington-based organisation that owned several other radio stations. In late 2008, Laser went into administration at the High Court in Leeds, and *Brunel FM* was sold to SouthWest Radio Limited, a company that was created for the purpose. However, this went into administration in August 2009. The group of radio stations including *Brunel FM* was acquired by the Your Media Communications Group. It immediately ran into difficulties when Ofcom, the media regulator, refused to allow YMC to take ownership of the station licences. The YMC stations were closed by administrators in 2010. As a result, *Brunel FM* was bought by One Gold Radio Limited, which, by agreement with the Total Star Group of Cheltenham with which it was associated, rebranded the *Brunel FM* station as *Total Star Swindon*. When One Gold Radio split from Total Star in June 2011, it became More FM, and *Total Star Swindon* was renamed *More RadioFM*. The organisation moved back into the Lime Kiln Studios at Wootton Bassett. The licence owned by More Radio FM was acquired by Celador in April 2012, which rebranded as *Jack FM* and opened on 28 May 2012. (See also BBC Wiltshire Sound; GWR Radio; Radio 105.5; Swindon FM; Wiltshire Radio.)

Bull public house, High Street This ancient hostelry was built halfway along the east side of High Street. The premises were eventually incorporated into a run of old buildings that became Mason's grocery store and which was completely demolished in the 1960s. Its known history is complicated.

The earliest reference to the Bull is dated 1633, when it became the property of Robert Tuckey, a family that remained in High Street for generations. The exact nature of the Bull at that time is not known, except that it operated from one of two adjacent thatched cottages. These, and the land on which they stood, later belonged to Thomas Tuckey and his mother Elizabeth, and were acquired by William Wilkins, who sold them to John Smith, whose family lived next door. By 1701, Smith had converted the pair into a single hostelry, adding cellars, outhouses, barns and stables. By 1714, this property had passed to William Boxwell and his wife Judith; of Boxwell's siblings, his brother Robert was a baker; John made periwigs; Roger was a miller; and Lawrence, and his wife Margaret, to whom the Bull was assigned in 1715 by William's widow Judith, were victuallers. They leased it for a while to Richard Farmer, who also worked on the Swindon quarries. In 1747, the Boxwells sold the Bull to John Smith, son of the John Smith who had it in 1701. The Smith family continued to own the Bull until 1771, by which time John had died and his brother Thomas first leased and then sold the Bull to Seymour Wroughton, a landowner of Eastcott. Wroughton immediately leased the Bull to Thomas Smith.

Seymour Wroughton also loaned Smith £800; interest was to be paid at £4 per £100 per annum, although the sum had to be repaid by early February 1772. The penalty for failure to do so was £1,600. It was further stipulated that Smith was to insure the building and pay the rates. Thomas Smith never repaid his debt to Seymour Wroughton. He died at the end of 1772, assigning his lease in the Bull to his wife Ann, who was unsuccessful in maintaining the business. Wroughton brought a suit in Chancery against Ann Smith for his money; she was in trade as a grocer in the property next door to the Bull, and was declared bankrupt in 1779. An out-of-court settlement on all outstanding monies was made to Seymour Wroughton in 1780. Meanwhile, Thomas, the son of Thomas and Ann Smith, converted the grocery business back into the dwelling house and warehouse. In 1782, he sold this property and the Bull to London grocer Francis Kemble, and Edward Kemble, a tea broker also of London. These two, and other businessmen in the Kemble family, converted the dwelling and the Bull into the grocery trade, and although the properties were to have several owners, it was in the same grocery trade that they remained until the 1960s. (See also Bull public house, Newport Street; Kemble family of grocers.)

Bull public house, Newport Street

On the south side of Newport Street was a public house called the White Hart. Its origins may lie in the 1600s, but it is first named in 1739. In 1782, when the Bull in High Street was converted into a grocer's shop, the Newport Street property took its name. Its keeper presumably realised that the former Bull had a better reputation and it might be beneficial to take advantage of that by so renaming his business. It remained the Bull until 1881, and the names of some of its nineteenth-century keepers are known. John Wyatt (1820-22); J.W. Mayle followed by J. Wright (1830); Joseph Browning (1835-42); Henry Hawkins (1848); Sarah Hawkins (1850-51); John Palmer (1851-60) John C. Bingham (1861-71), who afterwards became a greengrocer in Newport Street; Stephen Lawrence (1874); Edmund Brown (1875); E. Barron (1878); J. Marfell followed by Henry

Lailey (1879); and John Adams (1881). At this point, the public house was renamed Railway Hotel, being very close to the Swindon station on the Midland & South West Junction Railway's line, which opened between Marlborough and Swindon on 29 July 1881. (See also Steam Railway Co.)

Bullen's Bridge In 1851, a bridge was built across the North Wilts Canal at the east end of Sheppard Street, immediately to the south of the Great Western Railway line. It has been suggested that this, an iron trellis bridge, was made in Chippenham and was shown at the Great Exhibition of that year; but it has also been alleged that the New York Iron Bridge Company was the maker. Possibly both were involved, one as the maker and the other as the modifier to fit its Swindon location. It was the penultimate bridge before the North Wilts Canal met the Wilts & Berks Canal, about three hundred yards later. It was initially referred to as Sheppard's Bridge because the land on which it stood, Sheppard's Field, had previously been owned by landowner and brewer John Henry Harding Sheppard, who desired that each of his names should be perpetuated in the streets and buildings that went up on his former property. Immediately to the east of this bridge was the Union Tavern, which Sheppard built 1840-41. For a while, the bridge was known as Union Bridge or, rather strangely, Old Union Canal Bridge, both after the Union Tavern. In 1873, the Union Tavern was taken on by Richard Bullen, and it was by his surname that the bridge came to be known.

Richard Bullen was born near Croydon, Surrey in 1831. In 1867, at Westminster, London, he married the widow Jane Annette Betteridge, née Dixon (b. Wantage, 1839), whose previous marriage to William Betteridge in 1860 had produced a daughter, Eliza Jane, in 1862. The couple settled in Newbury Street, Wantage, where Richard was occupied as a licensed victualler, and it was there that their son George was born in 1872. The following year, the family relocated to the Union Tavern at Swindon. However, they did not stay long: Jane Bullen died at Swindon in 1873; Richard Bullen was last recorded in the town in 1875. By 1880, he was living in Clapham, London, and soon afterwards took on Barnards Inn Tavern at Holburn, remarried and, c.1889, became landlord of the Three Compasses, Southwark. He died in 1907.

Meanwhile, his legacy in Swindon was not the Union Tavern, but Bullen's Bridge, where the name stuck to such an extent that it was so named on town maps and Ordnance Survey maps, and continued to bear the name until it was demolished in 1923. Its site became a footpath. The Union Tavern closed in 1958. In 2013, Richard Bullen's pewter beer tankard, inscribed 'R. Bullen. Union Hotel. New Swindon' and made in Bristol, turned up in a box of pewter being auctioned at Rochester, Minnesota, USA. The former property of a late vicar, it was bought by Rochester resident Shari Jarett. She returned it to the town and it is now in the care of The Swindon Society.

Burge & Norris see Saddlers

Butler, Edward (1810-1894) Edward Butler is an example of a competent artist who eventually added photography to his portfolio, afterwards abandoned it, and became very well known in his original areas of expertise. Born at Benson, Oxfordshire, he married early in the 1830s and set up as a portrait painter, later establishing his family home at 9 St Mary Butts, Reading. There, were born his sons Edward Butler (1833), who became a 'photographic artist'; John Butler, who became a carver and gilder; and, in 1840, his daughter Annie Burgis Butler, who would later be styled 'professor of painting and drawing'. John and Annie never married, and remained at the Reading address with their mother Harriett (b. Oxford, 1810). Around 1853, Edward embraced the new art and by 1861 was calling himself 'artist photographer, carver and gilder'.

The circumstances of Edward Butler's arrival in Swindon are unknown, but in October 1864, he was put in charge of H.J. Brooks's photographic studio at 5 Bath Terrace. When Brooks went back to Abingdon in August 1865, Butler acquired his business. However, the Bath Terrace premises were too small to facilitate the same-day, on-site processing and printing service that Butler wanted to offer his customers so, in 1866, he went into partnership with George King, photographer of Devizes Road. This arrangement continued until 1869 when Edward Butler left Swindon, returning to his family at 9 St Mary Butts, Reading. There, where he was to remain for the rest of his life, Edward Butler continued as an artist photographer for a while, but dropped photography as he gradually developed the landscape painting and portraiture for which he became well known.

Butts, The, cricket at see Tarrant's *Recollections*

Byron Street It is ironic that one of the meanest, plainest, unfinished streets in Swindon should have been named after the flamboyant poet Lord George Gordon Byron (1788-1824). Byron Street was built just south-east of Regent Circus in the mid-1870s, on a field that had come onto the market in 1869. Just 150 yards long, it curved slightly as it began to climb the hill towards Old Town, parallel with Rolleston Street. Byron Street was built up, on its west side only, with a single terrace of twenty-seven brick-built, two-storey properties; each was just thirteen feet wide. Devoid of any architectural embellishment whatsoever, except for plain window sills, and with flat frontages that pressed hard on the roadway, the terrace in Byron Street was probably the worst example of residential utilitarianism in Swindon. On the east side of the street was open ground; to the north-west was also open ground with a track that led beside the Rehoboth Particular Baptist Chapel, built 1864, into Rolleston Street. This enabled Byron Street's early residents to reach Old Town via Prospect Place. In the 1880s, a number of larger properties were built on the east side of Byron Street. In the mid-1890s, the Swindon Technical School was erected on the large piece of land remaining at the south-east end of Byron Street, which led to its back entrance, whilst the front faced Victoria Road. There was only ever one shop in the street; this was the Empire Fish Restaurant, named after the nearby theatre. The restaurant closed in 1961, by which time most of Byron Street had been pulled down to make way for a six-storey extension to the College, and a car park in front of it for which it became an exit road. The College extension was closed down and abandoned in 2006, and demolished in 2012. On the site is now the Regent Circus mixed-use development. All that is left of Byron Street is just a short stub, dwarfed by the Regent Circus development, but comprising a couple of properties that were built on the east side of the street in the 1890s.

Cannon, Charles (1824-1885)

Distinguished as being the earliest-known professional photographer in New Swindon, Charles Cannon was also a picture framer. Born at Chilton, Berkshire, in 1849 he married Sarah Pullen (b. Highworth, 1814). The couple were living in Swindon by 1850, although his occupation was unknown. He first appears as a photographer in the early 1870s, advertising himself as a landscape, architectural and portrait photographer at 49 Regent Street, the family home. Sarah died in 1876; by 1881, he was living at 30 Regent Street, where the elder, unmarried of his two daughters, thirty-year-old Sarah, was described as being her father's housekeeper. Charles Cannon died at Chiseldon, four years later.

Carpenter, Ernest (1868-1909)

The man who had plans drawn up in 1896 for what became Swindon's Empire Theatre, and had it built in 1898, was born in Islington, London. He was the son of Frederick Carpenter, a fine art publisher. From the age of fourteen Ernest added to his income as an office clerk by acting monologues and excerpts from plays in working men's clubs around the East End. In 1885, he became a professional actor with a touring company, and was soon his own touring company's actor-manager, marrying one of his players in 1891. She was Jessie Beatrice Lord, whose father John Buckley Lord was head of the Transfer Department of the Lancashire & Yorkshire Railway. Thereafter he became, in rapid succession, lessee of a theatre in Darwen, Lancashire, and the Theatre Royal, Bristol, and bought the Empire Palace at Hanley in the Potteries. Each of these was in a bad way, and Carpenter rapidly turned around their fortunes.

He sold the leases of all but the Bristol theatre, from where he organised the planning and building of the New Queen's Theatre (it became the Empire in 1907) at Swindon. It was a huge leap of faith, as the town had no previous experience of theatre. He briefly (1898-1900) also held the lease of the Bristol Empire. In Swindon, Ernest Carpenter managed to book very varied programmes of good quality, and was much admired in the town for his work ethic. He was extremely well liked personally and appreciated for his charitable deeds. At the end of the 1903-04 season, he leased the New Queen's Theatre to Alfred Manners and took over the Eden Theatre, Brighton. In 1907, he acquired the Lyceum Theatre, London, with his business partner Henry R. Smith, and died two years later. (See also Manners, Alfred James.)

Carpenter, Maurice (1911-78)

Known as 'The Poet of Gooch Street', after the Swindon thoroughfare in which he and his wife Tina made their home for a while from October 1972, Carpenter was a poet of legend and ballad. His wife, born at Bradford-on-Avon, had a degree in philosophy and Greek from Keele University. He was a sometime teacher at Pewsey Vale School, Pewsey, and was the author of *The Indifferent Horseman*, a biography of Coleridge. In 1964, he won the Poetry Society's Shakespeare Quartercentenary Prize for his work *Orpheus Expresso*, about a group of mods and rockers in Hell. The Arts Council gave him an award in 1971 for the anthology *Black Ballads and the Love Words*. Maurice and Tina were well known in Swindon for their regular poetry readings in public, particularly for the series they carried out in the big assembly room of the White House public house in Corporation Street. Whilst engaged on these, he was given an Arts Council grant to continue his public poetry readings, which paid for a slot once a month in the Studio at the Wyvern Theatre. In 1974, he relocated to Wootton Bassett.

Carpenter's Arms, Cricklade Street William Bizley, the keeper of the Carpenter's Arms, is first mentioned as such in 1848, and there is no indication that the property was in any way in trade before that. It was a stone-built, two-storey, two-bay house, with a single-bay window. William Bizley (b. Swindon, 1804) and his wife Joanna, née Sadler (b. Broad Hinton, 1805) had five children, all of whom were packed into the property with numerous boarders. At the time he opened what he firstly named the Carpenter's beerhouse, William is recorded as a carpenter (which he had always been, and hence the name, which would have been good for business), wheelwright, beer retailer, and provision dealer, all of which he seems to have carried out from the same site. By 1861, two of the Bizleys' sons, Edward (b. 1843) and Albert (b. 1847) were apprentice carpenters. William continued to run the business until 1868 when he retired to Albert Street, where he nonetheless continued to be a carpenter and wheelwright, dying later that year. The Carpenter's Arms was taken over by his son Albert. The beerhouse closed in 1873 and was soon afterwards demolished.

Castle Hotel, Prospect In 1862, Charles Barker (b. Finchampstead, Berkshire, 1831) acquired the land on which he built the Castle. By the time he was in his early twenties, Barker was an under-butler at Berrington Hall, Eye, Herefordshire, a mansion designed by Henry Holland and built 1778-83, and now in the keeping of the National Trust. He was still in his twenties when he took on the Roebuck Inn in the Market Place at Wokingham, Berkshire, and had hardly turned thirty when he came to Swindon and staked a claim on the plots of land in Prospect. He already had a son, Charles Hall Barker (b. Finchampstead, Berkshire, 1860), who eventually became the owner of the Aerated Water Works in Clifton Street. Charles Barker retained ownership of the Castle until 1884 but, by 1870, was also the live-in landlord of the Great Western Hotel in Station Road.

Meanwhile, the keeper of the Castle was Charles Benjamin Boniface, until his death in 1878, after which his wife Ann Pedder Boniface continued to run the pub. She was followed, probably after Barker sold out to the Stroud Brewery in 1884, by Robert Smith, who had arrived in Swindon, c.1875, to be employed as a boilersmith in the GWR Works. However, the most high-profile landlord of the Castle was Robert William Menham (b. North Shields, Tyneside, 1871), the son of a cabinet maker. During the 1890s, he played in goal at The Croft for a regimental football team, then played for Everton for some years, and then Wigan until 1898. That year, he joined Swindon Town F.C., and at the 1901 census, Bob Menham was described as a 'professional footballer and working men's club steward'. This was the West Swindon Club, and his failing sight was threatening to end his football career, although he did join the club's board of directors. In 1902, he took over the Castle on

Prospect, and remained there until 1928. He died in 1945.

Cellular Operations building, Peatmoor

The hi-tech headquarters and call centre of Cellular Operations, providers of cellular products and services for mobile networks, was designed by Richard Hywell Evans in glass and steel, took fifteen months to build by Tilbury Douglas Construction, cost £7 million, and was opened beside the lagoon at Peatmoor in January 2000. It was innovative in the sense that it broke the mould of call centre premises that had the reputation of being purely functional spaces, and instead provided an exceptional work environment flooded with daylight. The structural engineer was Buro Happold. The 40,000-square-foot, 9-metre-high structure was described as being 'zeppelin' shaped; it was known locally as 'the glass cigar', and was named Arclight House. Its bulbous glass extensions, running the length of the building and supported on thin tubular columns, were created out of a Miesian box. It featured a pre-cast concrete spine staircase based on the skeleton of a dinosaur, thematic toilets, fibre-optic, south-facing panels, and a north-facing, two-storey galleried break-out space. Externally, polished Caledonian boulders were placed on the ground beneath the glazed walls, and these were sculpturally uplit by concealed lighting. Arclight House won twenty prestigious design awards, including Best Large Office Building in the FX Magazine International Interior Design Awards (2000); Civic Trust Award (2001); and Business Week Architectural Record Award (2002).

In 2003, Vodaphone acquired Cellular Operations and closed down the premises at Peatmoor. Arclight House remained empty for more than four years, and in 2004 it was damaged by vandals. Baylight, a London-based commercial property developer, bought the building in 2006, plus three and a half acres of adjacent land; they applied for planning permission to split the building into three separate units, one of about 25,000 square feet, one of 11,000 and one of 5,000. It was renamed The Garden Room. 6a Architects remodelled the interior to accommodate these alterations and designed a new core to the smaller units, at a cost of £2 million. The larger unit was pre-let to the Swindon-based firm HSM. The same architects also custom-designed a motorcycle driving test centre on the land for the Driving Standards Agency, and the remainder of the development site was sold to the motor dealership, Fish Brothers. The offices have remained filled since 2007.

Cetus Buildings

In an isolated spot along the north side of the Wilts & Berks Canal, immediately east of the Whale Bridge (built 1804) across the canal, on a field called Little Medgberry, a terrace of a dozen properties was built, c.1841-42. These cottages were called Cetus Buildings or Cetus Cottages, (cetus being the Welsh word for whale) as a pun on the Whale Bridge, which had been named because of its hump-back shape. These properties were built at right angles to the track that joined Lower Eastcott Farm and Upper Eastcott Farm (at that time known just as Eastcott Farm). The back entrances to Cetus Buildings had steps at intervals leading down to the canal. This circumstantial evidence has helped to maintain the long-held view of local historians that the terrace was built by the Wilts & Berks Canal Company for bargees and other canal workers. Research carried out in 2014 by canal historian Jan Flanagan proved that Cetus Buildings was a private business venture by William Dunsford, who was one-time superintendent of the Wilts & Berks Canal, Edward Rowden (Rowden's Sun Brewery at Highworth was involved with the Wilts & Berks Canal Company) and James Crowdy. In 1841, the canal company sold land on either side of the Whale Bridge to this trio, on which they built the cottages in 'brick, stone, and slates'. Dunsford died in 1845, the same year that the twelve Cetus Cottages, said then to have been 'newly erected', were put up for sale as part of the Crowdy estate.

The 1851 census records the occupations of the cottagers (some properties were unoccupied, others had more than one worker) as:

William King, 24, coal haulier
Robert Day, 46, carter
Jacob Haines 32, agricultural labourer
Henry Hill, 29, iron drilling labourer
George Aldridge, 26, boilermaker's labourer
William Cook, 54, shoemaker
John Cook, 22, boilersmith
Elizabeth Cook, 19, dressmaker
George Smith, 16, groom
Thomas Garratt, 26, cattle dealer
Ann Weeks, 23, washerwoman
Thomas B. Newman, 22, groom

What is obvious is an absence of workers on the Wilts & Berks Canal.

At about the same time as Cetus Buildings were built, the Whale beerhouse was built adjacent, with a large yard. Here, the bargees tethered their horses. Its first keeper was Jonas Head, who was first mentioned in 1841 when he was a twenty-five-year-old beerhouse keeper of Eastcott. When he left in 1845, the Whale was taken over by Richard Dunn (b. Marston, Wiltshire, 1812). He titled himself 'publican', but at the same time was otherwise occupied as a railway platelayer for the GWR, in whose Works two of his sons were also employed. One was an apprentice engine boilermaker, and the younger was a boilermaker's labourer. Cetus Buildings became the south-western end of Medgbury Road when this was built in the late 1870s on the field formerly known as Great Medgberry. It had a terrace of thirty-two properties on the northern side, thirty-five on the southern side backing onto the canal next to Cetus Buildings, and a further eight at right angles at the east end of the street. The Whale Bridge was rebuilt in 1893; the Whale public house closed in 1962, and was later demolished.

Charlotte Corday sculpture

This life-size sculpture in white marble is in the entrance hall of the former New Swindon town hall in Regent Circus, now the reception area for Swindon Dance. The piece was given to the Borough of Swindon in the 1920s by Alderman James E. ('Raggy') Powell (1849-1930), a supporter of the arts and a considerable benefactor of the town. The sculptor was Pasquale Miglioretti (1822-81), an Italian who lived and worked in Milan, who made this piece, of which there was more than one version, 1865-67. It won him the gold medal at the Universal Exposition in Paris, 1867. The statue measures 67 inches (1.7m) high, $27\frac{1}{2}$ inches (0.7m) deep, and $31\frac{1}{2}$ inches (0.8m) wide. It shows the seated, contemplative figure of Marie-Anne Charlotte de Corday d'Armont (1768-93), who was executed for assassinating the radical journalist and politician Jean-Paul Marat (1743-93) in his bath, at the time of the French Revolution.

Chimney sweeping 1840-1855 see
Tarrant's *Recollections*

Chinese Experience, Peatmoor
The Chinese Experience restaurant was
created on a two-and-a-half-acre site beside
the lagoon at Peatmoor, West Swindon,
1989-90 by businessman Sik Jong Chan
and his partners, a group of London- and
Swindon-based Chinese businessmen. Sik
Jong Chan came from Canton, China, to
Swindon in 1961 where, five years later,
he and his first wife Yim Hing opened the
Hong Kong Fish Bar in Hythe Road. This
was Swindon's first Chinese Takeaway, and
was followed in 1971 by his New Hong Kong
Fish Bar in Manchester Road.

The Chinese Experience was designed
by Swindon company Wyvern Architects,
and its construction was inaugurated by
James Cordon (Mayor of Swindon 1988-89).
At the time of its opening, this landmark
building was said to be the largest Chinese
restaurant in the UK. It was built pagoda-
style in two storeys, with some 6,883 square
feet of space on the two floors. The roof tiles
were imported from Taiwan. The restaurant
had 300 seats, and was originally run by
Lawrence Lee, the owner of a local Chinese
takeaway. It closed in May 1999 and was
given a £100,000 facelift. Sik Jong Chan
retired in 2000, and ownership passed
to Lik Wai Hung and David Hung, who
experienced severe economic difficulties,
and in 2003 the restaurant was once again
closed. In 2004, the Chinese Experience was
taken over by Albert Tang and Tony Tang,
and given a £150,000 facelift. The same year,
the restaurant was destroyed in a fire, and
the premises were closed for some time. Sik
Jong Chan died in 2008, following a motor
accident.

The restaurant was renamed Pagoda
Palace, and was for some time run by
a Chinese consortium that went out of
business. It remained empty and rapidly
deteriorating from January 2009. Li Zin
and Jian Zhong then spent £200,000
refurbishing the building following fears
that it might otherwise be turned into
residential buildings, an office campus,
or remodelled for other commercial or
institutional use, and was reopened in
September 2010 as the Oriental Buffet. In
2012, James Young and Tony Jiang became
the owners, investing a further £100,000
and redecorating the interior in keeping with
traditional Chinese tastes and traditions.
The name was changed to Hongxin Oriental
Buffet, and the restaurant was reopened by
Ray Ballman (Mayor of Swindon 2011-12).

**Chitty, Brien Albert (1934-
2002)** Brien Chitty was the first artistic
administrator at Swindon's Wyvern Theatre
which, at the time of his appointment, was
in the course of being built. He was born
at Aldershot, Hampshire; took up acting
in 1951; learnt his craft at the Webber
Douglas Academy of Dramatic Art in
London, and was for some time in repertory
in Morecambe, Lancashire. He turned to
theatre management as a trainee house
manager with Northampton Repertory in
1957, and there met Judith Byles, whom he
married in 1960. He was later box office
manager at Golders Green Hippodrome,
London, and then spent three years as
house manager and party organiser at The
Everyman, Cheltenham. He followed this
with two years as theatre manager at the
Bristol Old Vic, and was afterwards theatre
manager at the Playhouse, Newcastle-
upon-Tyne, on behalf of the Tyneside

Theatre Trust. He and Judith lived at Holly Hall farmhouse, above the Tyne Valley at Sandhope, near Corbridge.

The Playhouse closed down in deference to the new University Theatre at Newcastle, and in June 1970 Chitty secured the job in Swindon, initially on a fixed-period contract that was to expire in May 1973. The family relocated to Goddard Avenue. Judith joined Swindon Opera and became secretary of the local branch of the National Society for the Prevention of Cruelty to Children.

In the four years he was in Swindon, Chitty worked tirelessly to establish the theatre as a cultural centre for the town, and established a wide-ranging programming policy. In 1972, he became programming director of the Wyvern, but was always frustrated in his work by financial constraints placed on him by Swindon Borough Council through the Wyvern Arts Trust, and by the lack of audience support for many of the productions that came to the theatre.

He left the Wyvern in 1974 to work with Anvil Productions, a repertory offshoot of the Oxford Playhouse Company, and developed his one-man show giving readings of Charles Dickens's work. He went briefly to the Watermill Theatre, Newbury, as interim manager, and then left the theatre world for a while to run the Kilmarnock Hotel at Torquay, followed by a public house at Somerton, Somerset. In 1980, he became house manager at the Vaudeville Theatre, London, followed by a similar role at the Aldwych Theatre. In the mid-1980s, he first broached the idea of forming a society that would commemorate the British theatre at the time of Sir Henry Irving and that actor-manager's contribution to the period. This was held over whilst he took on the Palace Theatre, Newark, Nottinghamshire in 1987, a tenure that lasted for ten years. Still interested in the catering industry, he opened a bed and breakfast establishment in Newark in 1995 with his partner Anne Burns, which catered mainly for theatrical people and antique dealers. Approaching early retirement, he founded The Irving Society in October 1996 and was its first secretary. Brien Chitty died at his desk in Newark.

Clarence Street Princes Street began to be built up in the mid-1870s, laid out between the Whale Bridge over the Wilts & Berks Canal to the north and York Place (then the north side of what was to become Regent Circus) to the south. Near the south end of Princes Street, a footpath ran off south-southeast towards Old Town, amidst the fields on the lower slopes of Swindon hill. It debouched into a track that would eventually become Groundwell Road, and opposite that point was another track that ran up the hill to the east of, and parallel with, the wider thoroughfare that would one day be called Victoria Road. By 1885, this was known as New Road but was not made up or populated, except for 100 yards or so at the top of the hill. The footpath at the bottom, and the track opposite that climbed the hill, were destined to remain as such until 1892. Then, the whole of the footpath and part of the track — about 215 yards in total — were widened and named Clarence Street. Princes Street had been named after Prince Albert Victor, Duke of Clarence and Avondale (1864-1892), the infamous 'Eddy'. It seems likely that Clarence Street was named after the same person because it was effectively a southwards continuation of Princes Street, and because Albert, who was Edward VII's eldest son, had just died. Clarence Street was never a residential street. In 1898, the New Queen's Theatre was built on its corner with Groundwell Road; the County Court building was erected 1904 on the east side; and the Methodist Central Mission Hall was built on the west side in 1907-8. Today, Wessex Court, a large property of residential apartments, stands at the north-east end of Clarence Street.

Clarence Street School, Euclid Street

Clarence Street School is now Grade II listed. When it was opened as a mixed junior (Higher Elementary) in 1897, on the corner of Clarence Street with Euclid Street, there were no properties whatsoever in the former, and just a single terrace of four houses on the south side of the latter which, at that time, was no more than about fifty yards long. On the north side of Euclid Street, where the Swindon Borough Council Offices (the Civic Offices) were to be built 1937-38, was the tree-lined Princes Street Recreation Ground. Beyond that, to the east, there were unbroken fields, except for an extensive brick and tile works. Residential Swindon was about to expand into this area, and Clarence Street School was built at a cost of £12,091 to take some of the children from this expansion. It was the last school in Swindon to be built under the auspices of the Swindon School Board before the Education Act of 1902 (the Balfour Act) came into force, which abolished local school boards and attendance committees, and replaced them with Education Committees.

The architect of Clarence Street School was William Drew (b. Highworth, 1838), surveyor and land agent, who lived at 22 Victoria Street in Old Town. He arranged the classrooms on either side of a central hall that ran the whole width of the building. It was a large building, of two and three storeys, intended to accommodate 840 children, although it opened with half as many, but had around 1,000 at its most crowded. Externally it was a tour de force in red brick with a fanfare of stone dressings – highly decorative Dutch gables, string courses, vertical drop pilasters, door and window surrounds and jambs, segmental arches, plinths and finials. It was multi-gabled with some half-hipped roofs, had tall, slender chimney stacks, decorative panelling, a riot of windows, and topped by an open cupola.

The first headmaster was George Walters (b. Worcester, 1861), a gardener's son who went into teaching. In 1890, he married Mary Moss (b. Swindon, 1851). She was a widow who in 1866 had married James Moss from Portsmouth, where their first child was born in 1871. By 1874, they were in Swindon when their daughter Florence was born, and James was working as a railway boilersmith. Mary Moss married George Walters in 1890, and, when he was appointed to Clarence Street School, Florence Moss was also appointed as a pupil teacher. In 1904, an infant school for 314 infants was added at the rear, at a cost of £3,285, and the following year the mixed junior school was segregated into boys and girls, each having a separate entrance. These changes left George Walters as overall headmaster and in charge of the boys, whilst Miss C.J. Stiles was appointed the first girls' mistress, and Miss L.M. Kent looked after the infants. George Walters continued as headmaster until the outbreak of the First World War, when he was succeeded by John James Stafford, formerly the master at Gorse Hill School. Miss Kent left, c.1924, and was replaced by Miss H. Ingram. Clarence Street School became a junior mixed school again in 1946. The school closed in the 1980s, and was afterwards used as offices by Swindon Borough Council.

Clifton hotel, Clifton Street, The

At the same time as speculative builders were covering each side of Clifton Street with terraces of two-storey houses in red brick, Arkell's brewery was negotiating with James Hinton for a piece of land on the east side of the street, where the firm intended to build a pub. This was The Clifton hotel, which opened as an off-licence in 1879 before acquiring its full on-licence in 1881. It was a good move. Radnor Street was being built adjacent to the north at the same time, and this whole area was at the centre of the fastest building spree Swindon had known; within a year, sixty-six properties had been built in Clifton Street and, for the most part, were lived in by railway employees and their families. The Clifton hotel was probably named after the steep embankment formed behind it by railway excavations, but the more attractive explanation is that Clifton Street may have been named after that area of Bristol, and the pub prefers to illustrate its name with a picture of the suspension bridge there. Its landlord, by the mid-1880s, was Henry Jefferies, and Samuel Ward had taken over by the end of the 19th century. The Clifton is allegedly haunted, there having been reports of poltergeist activity and a wandering nun. However, there is no more real evidence of this than there is for the one-time presence of a priory hereabouts, with which the nun is popularly associated. (See also Clifton Street.)

Clifton Street

Building began in Clifton Street in 1879, on land that had hitherto been part of J.H. Sheppard's extensive Kingshill estate. As the street was built up, it included grandiose names like Clifton Villas, Gordon Terrace, Harvey's Buildings, Kingsdown Terrace and Suburban Buildings; there were also individual properties with pretentious names such as The Manse, Elim House and The Laurels. Within another two or three years, some three hundred houses were put up thereabouts. Early in the 1880s, Primitive Methodist services were being held in Clifton Street on the premises of John Green, a coach builder, and in 1882 the Primitive Methodists built a little red brick chapel in Clifton Street. This was enlarged eight years later to accommodate 360 people, by which time the demography of Clifton Street had begun. Funding was found for the Primitive Methodist Chapel to build an associated Sunday schoolroom. The chapel was subsequently demolished.

By the mid-1880s, there were a number of people living in Clifton Street who were classed as having private means, and the street was no longer so full of railway labourers. People such as George Difford, Swindon's deputy registrar of births, deaths and marriages, John Marcus Watts, who was secretary to the Swindon Water Company, and Ellen Mitchell, who ran a registry office for servants, were giving it an early respectability. Small businesses were establishing in the street (William Coker, William Smith and Charles Pearce, grocers; John Wall, shopkeeper in Gordon Terrace; Elizabeth Coxon, dressmaker; James Spackman, slaterer and plasterer). By the close of the 19th century, just over 180 houses had been built in Clifton Street, and although railway workers continued to predominate, these properties were no longer all let to factory workers; many GWR and other employers' clerks and chief clerks made their homes there. The assistant superintendent of the Swindon Post Office, Frederick W. Snell, lived in Clifton Street at the turn of the century, and other occupations were represented at the same time; there was a sanitary inspector, an architectural draughtsman, several teachers and music teachers, mechanical engineers, accountants and photographers.

Clifton Street School The tenure of the second triennially-appointed Swindon School Board (1880-83) was marred by counter-productive internal politics, distrust of personal motives, and disagreement over whether a much-needed new school should be sited in Old Town or New Swindon. In 1882, Ambrose Lethbridge Goddard offered to sell the board a site in New Town, but it declined, eventually leaving the problem with the third board, which was elected in 1883. This board comprised railway engineer James Holden (chairman); William Henry Stanier, the GWR stores superintendent (vice-chairman); John Hulme Preece, secretary of the Mechanics Institution; the jeweller and watchmaker Hubert John Deacon; Hon. and Revd Maurice John George Ponsonby, vicar of St Mark's church; Revd Henry George Baily, vicar of Christ Church; Samuel Cornish Randell, railway accountant; A.M. Hack; and the department store owner Levi Lapper Morse. Free of the previous board's internal wrangling, they took up Goddard's offer.

By the early 1880s, a new school was needed for boys, girls and infants from the developing residential area around Kingshill. The third board's first venture, named Clifton Street School, was something of a misnomer, being placed between William Street (which had been built up in 1878) and Radnor Street (a development of 1879). The architect for the school was William Henry Read of Bath Road, and the builder was Thomas Barrett of Newport Street. It was built on two levels, the Radnor Street elevation being twenty feet higher than that of William Street, to accommodate 235 boys, who entered via William Street, and 153 girls and 200 infants, who went in at the higher level of Radnor Street. The cost of the land and the building totalled £6,457, and Clifton Street School opened in 1885. The first headmaster for the boys was George Pressey, who lived at Hillside House, Clifton Street; the girls' headmistress was Susan Ann Wright; and Jersey-born Mary Anne Le Manquaise of 101 Clifton Street was head of the infant school. She remained in charge until resigning in 1919. The segregation continued until 1939, and in 1945 it became a mixed infants' and junior school. It closed in 1984 and was converted into office accommodation.

Cock Robin, Cavendish Square The first public house to be opened in the rapidly developing Park North and Park South local authority housing estates was named after a former nickname of the Swindon Town Football Club. The pub sign was a huge robin. It was part of the Cavendish Square mixed development of retail, residential and social, and was owned by the then recently formed (1958) West Country Breweries of Cheltenham. Whitbread acquired the brewery in 1963, the year the Cock Robin was opened amidst a number of unattractive walkways within the shopping precinct. It included a 2,400-square-foot ballroom. The first landlords were John and Rita Chetter from Wolverhampton. Cavendish Square gradually deteriorated and became the focus of undesirable and illegal activities, and by the end of its life the Cock Robin had acquired a bad reputation. It closed in 2003, and the increasingly derelict premises were soon broken into and became a dangerous play area for local children. Concerns were raised in 2006 when children were seen running around the flat roof of the building. The following year, it took thirty-five firefighters and six fire engines to extinguish a fire on the property started by arsonists. What remained of the Cock Robin public house was demolished in 2008.

College Street This roadway was laid out, and built up on its north side (no properties were built on the south side), between 1873 and 1877. It was to accommodate the Great Western Railway Company's girls' and infants' school, and ran east off Regent Street, just south of the Golden Lion Bridge on the Wilts & Berks Canal. The street ran parallel with the canal and then turned to the north, running straight down to the south bank of the waterway. College Street, which was 300 yards long, was so named because of the school (although it was never a college), next to which there was a terrace of three houses, followed by the aerated water works factory, then a terrace of eight properties with bow windows. There was a terrace of five houses, also with bow windows, on the leg that inclined towards the canal. The rear of all the premises in College Street ran down to the canal bank. (See also Aerated Water Works; College Street School.)

College Street School This institution has a unique place in the history of education in Swindon. It was built under the School Sites Act, 1852 by the Great Western Railway Company in 1873, as a school for infants (who were accommodated in classrooms on the ground floor) and girls (who were taught on the floor above). The building cost £2,500. It was long and low, with a façade of four bays on each side of a central, gabled, projecting two-storey porch with room above, and with projecting wings at either end, which were also gabled. A triangular date stone was placed above the main entrance.

By the time the Swindon School Board was formed in 1877, it had become impossible for the GWR's schools to accommodate the children of the rapidly growing New Town, and the company also had plans for turning its boys' school in Bristol Street into more profitable business premises. In 1879, Swindon School Board accepted College Street School for girls and infants on a twenty-one-year lease, nominally costing £5 per year. The quid pro quo was that the board would build a school for boys, which it did in nearby Sanford Street. In 1898, College Street became a Higher Grade School for girls, which it remained for the next five years, and it became a junior school for boys and girls in 1946.

Plans made in the 1950s to redevelop that part of the town meant that College Street School was abandoned, with a view to demolition. However, under the provisions of the 1852 Act, the whole site reverted to its original owners. It had to be purchased from British Rail before demolition could take place in 1961 to make way for The Parade shopping centre. Shingler Risdon, the architects of The Parade, and the developers, Oddenino's Limited, had the 1873 date stone reset into the wall of a building on the site of the former school. (See also Sanford Street School.)

Commonweal School, The Mall

Founded as a secondary school for 410 students, Commonweal was designed as a two-storey building by the Wiltshire County architect T. Walker and built, 1925-27, by the firm of R.J. Leighfield, on land sold by Fitzroy Pleydell Goddard, Lord of the Manor of Swindon. It was opened by Thomas E. Loveday, vice-chancellor of Bristol University. The frontage to the Mall was 430 feet, and the width of the building was 331 feet, with an entrance of Portland stone. There were separate quadrangles, each 100 feet by 50 feet, for boys and girls. It made up its initial complement of students by taking pupils from the secondary school in Euclid Street and that in Victoria Road, which shared the Technical College building. Commonweal's first headmaster was T.A.M. Hartley, previously an assistant master at the Technical College, who retired from Commonweal in 1932. He was succeeded by Dr C.E. Jones, who remained in charge until 1953. In 1965, following the phasing out of the Eleven Plus examination, which decided whether pupils should continue their education at a grammar school or a secondary modern, Commonweal became a senior high school. In 1983, it lost its Sixth Form and became a comprehensive school for younger pupils. Its academy status was awarded in 2012 and it thereafter gained further status as a Performing Arts Academy. The Sixth Form was reinstated, and its new building, on what had previously been the staff car park, was officially opened by solo Atlantic rower Debra Searle on 2 October 2014.

Coronation Music Stores

The first retail outlet in Swindon to sell recorded music, phonographs and gramophones was Seaton's Coronation Music Stores, situated on the corner of Victoria Road and Clarence Street, opposite the Empire Theatre. The corner premises were no. 13 Victoria Road, and no. 12 next door was also incorporated into the music stores. Immediately before these premises were converted in 1901, no. 12 was occupied by Charles Williams, whose firm built the Empire Theatre, and who had a shop window at street level. William Jolliffe, the borough rate collector, occupied no. 13, a substantial corner property with a large, canted bow window to the ground floor.

The proprietor of the Coronation Music Stores was Arthur W. Seaton (1858-1925) who, for a short period before the place was named in 1902 to coincide with the coronation of Edward VII, had managed a music warehouse on the same site, selling pianos, organs and sheet music. Seaton had an interesting history. He was born in Dunkirk, Kent, the son of schoolmaster William Seaton and his schoolmistress wife Louisa. During the 1860s, the family came to Rodbourne Cheney, where William and Louisa continued in these occupations while, by 1871, at the age of just thirteen, Arthur William was already an office boy in the GWR iron works. A decade later, William Seaton had become a labourer in the iron works and Arthur William was working for the railway company as a blacksmith. That was still his occupation when, at Bristol in 1888, he married Elizabeth Lamb Popplestone (b. Ashburton, Devon, 1863). By the time of their marriage, Elizabeth's twenty-three-year-old brother Albert, who had left school to become a tailor's assistant, was a tailor and draper in Bristol. Over the next few decades, he would become a master tailor, a clothing manufacturer, wholesale clothier, and an employer in the city.

Importantly, for Arthur W. Seaton, Albert Popplestone (1865-1934) lived and worked in Swindon during the 1880s, so it is feasible to suppose that Arthur met Elizabeth during this time.

The financial arrangements regarding the purchase and conversion of Nos. 12 and 13 Victoria Road in 1901 are not known. However, for the next few years, part of no. 13 was also the Swindon branch of A. Popplestone & Co., tailors. The bow window at ground level was removed, one was built at first-floor level (possibly to let in more light to facilitate tailoring activities), and the whole of the downstairs was converted to shop premises, having picture windows to Victoria Road and Clarence Street, with an angled doorway on the corner between. The whole was given a moulded cornice with a decorative ironwork cresting above the name 'A.W. Seaton's Music Stores'. No. 12 remained largely unchanged, except that its name became 'Coronation Music Stores'. Across the roof tiles of no. 13 was written, in huge capital letters, 'CORONATION MUSIC STORES. A.W. SEATON'. What Seaton had for sale was also writ large on the Clarence Street elevation, where it could be read by patrons exiting the Empire Theatre, and especially those with new songs on their minds.

Crucially, Seaton's music stores also sold the relatively short-lived Neophone Company's new invention, the vertically cut, papier mâché recorded disc for playing on phonographs. With a playing time of ten minutes per side, these were effectively the first long-playing records; it was cutting-edge technology for the time. One of his advertisements read: 'A.W. Seaton, who first introduced the gramophone and phonograph in Swindon. Noted house for pianoforte and American organs. From all the leading manufacturers. At lowest prices for cash or easy terms. New pianos from 15 guineas. Organs from 5 guineas. Six month's music lessons free. Twelve month's tuning free. Pianos removed, packed and warehoused. Terms moderate. Second-hand pianos and organs taken in exchange. Gramophones from 30/-. Phonographs from 15/11. Neophones from 30/-. Records of every description'.

Elizabeth Lamb Seaton died in 1907, and Arthur William gave up the Coronation Music Stores and relocated with his children to Bristol where, by 1911, he was working as a salesman for a gas fitting company. Both of the Swindon premises that made up A.W. Seaton's Coronation Music Stores, 1901-1907, are extant.

County Ground, Arkell's stands

In 1896, the year that Swindon Town Football Club took up residence at what was then called the Wiltshire County Ground, its committee entered into an agreement with Thomas Arkell, brewer, to loan them £300. They wanted the money to finance a spectators' stand beside the football pitch. Thomas Arkell (1839-1919) was the eldest son of 'Honest John' Arkell (1802-1881), the Kempsford-born founder of the brewery at Kingsdown in 1843. In 1896, the football club's committee included the following:

Samuel Henry Allen (b. West Bromwich, 1868) railway clerk. *Sam Allen joined the football club's committee in 1895. In 1902, he became officially the club's secretary and then effectively the club's manager, which dual position he held until retiring from the latter in 1933. He was awarded the Football League's Long Service Award in 1941, but continued as* secretary until his death in 1946. In 2013, his dilapidated, overgrown grave in Radnor Street cemetery was rediscovered, and Swindon Town Football Club historian Dick Mattick began a successful campaign to raise sufficient funds for it to be restored. Johnson & Daltrey of Royal Wootton Bassett, who had also contributed substantially to the cause, carried this out, and the grave was rededicated in 2014.

George Montagu Butterworth (b. Deerhurst, Gloucestershire, 1859), solicitor and land agent. The son of Revd George Butterworth of Deerhurst, GMB was educated at the Gentleman's School, Leamington Priors, run by a clergyman. He was then an articled clerk to a solicitor at Westbury on Trym, and in 1884 his father married him to Catherine Lucie Warde (b. India, 1862) at Paddington, London. She was a suffragette. The family came to Swindon in the 1880s, where they lived firstly at Brunswick Terrace, Bath Road and later at 8 High Street. During this period, he financed a number of building ventures, had five children, and built up a staff of seven, including a butler. He became head of the firm of solicitors Butterworth, Rose & Morrison, with offices at 6 High Street, and was variously clerk to the Swindon magistrates, superintendent registrar, clerk to the commissioner of taxes, secretary of the Swindon Chamber of Agriculture, and secretary of the North Wilts Conservative Association. He died at Dorking, Sussex, in 1941.

Humphrey Hayward (b. Brinkworth, Wiltshire, 1852), sawmill foreman. Probably an employee in the GWR Works, but nothing else known.

William Barnes Keylock (b. Swindon, 1872), railway clerk. Probably the son of former GWR pattern maker William Keylock, who in the 1890s was landlord of the Baker's Arms public house in High Street (Emlyn Square), New Swindon.

William Henry Lawson (b. Stratton St Margaret, Wiltshire, 1848), railway clerk. The son of William Lawson, a clock and watchmaker who set up in business in Newport Street soon after WHL was born. In the 1850s, the family returned to Stratton St Margaret and split up, with some of the clockmaker's children living with himself and his wife, and two more living next door with her parents. WHL left school and went into the GWR, where he remained. By the 1870s, he was lodging at 34 Regent Street.

George Major No details known.

Albert Henry Noble (b. Gloucestershire, 1862), railway clerk.

George Plumley No details known.

William Reynolds No details known.

Ernest Clement Skurray (b. Swindon, 1865), corn dealer, miller and motor dealer. In 1893, ECS's father Francis built the flour mills and wharf, off Princes Street, which operated until 1924 beside the Wilts & Berks Canal. ECS was forward thinking; he embraced electricity and was pre-eminent in bringing it to Swindon, and then foresaw a future for motor transport. He combined the business of miller with that of motor engineer close to the Whale Bridge.

Thomas Smith No details known.

Henry William Thomas (b. Swindon, 1861), beer retailer. Before Swindon Town Football Club made its headquarters at the County Ground, these were at the Eagle Tavern, Regent Street, which was run by HWT.

Charles Williams (b. Swindon, 1849), builder or (b. London 1872), builder.

Both of these, father and son, were living and working in Swindon at this time. The father built the Empire Theatre in 1898, and both were involved in the building of the County Ground Hotel, on land that the father had owned, and in which the son was to become the first landlord. Both, therefore, would have been aware of the football club just a few yards away, so the Charles Williams on the committee could have been either. (See separate entry in this book under County Ground Hotel.)

Thomas Arkell loaned £300 to this committee under an agreement dated 2 October 1896. The money was to be repaid out of the income from admittance charges to the stand (and the agreement ensured that the lender had the first call on these, up to and including the amount of each instalment, plus interest). The agreement specified that the first payment would be made the following June, and thereafter one instalment of £60 in January of each of the following four years, together with annual interest of £4. The committee also had to agree that, during the period of repayment, the stand would not be removed from its original position without Thomas Arkell's prior permission. In 1971, the earlier involvement by Arkell's was commemorated when a new two-tier Arkell's Stand was built on the north side of the football pitch, financed by the brewery, which has supported the club since 1896, and which continues to sponsor the stand.

County Ground Hotel, County Road

This is the unofficial headquarters of the supporters of Swindon Town Football Club. It stands next to the County Road entry towards the club's ground, and, during the season, the flags that fly on its front elevation are printed with the club's crest. Inside, various examples of this emblem loom large on the walls. When the public house was built, it stood in some isolation to the west of the town. The only other building in County Road was a lodge next door, wherein lived the caretaker of the County Ground complex (then a recently laid-out cricket ground with cycle track and adjacent football ground). A man named Charles Williams owned the land on which the County Ground Hotel was built.

Charles Williams I (b. Gloucester, 1815) was a builder, carpenter and joiner. His son, Charles Williams II (b. Swindon, 1849), also a builder, was the man who constructed the town's New Queen's Theatre in 1898. His son, Charles Williams III (b. London, 1872), was likewise a builder, although not for long. In 1896, he married Winifred Cratchley in Swindon. Winifred and her sister Annie Louisa Cratchley were the daughters of Fred Cratchley, one-time landlord of, among other pubs, the Lord Raglan in Cricklade Street, the Union Tavern, Sheppard Street, and the Volunteer in Bridge Street. He was soon to retire and go to live in King William Street, and then Hythe Road. Prior to Winifred's marriage to Charles Williams III, both girls were employed as barmaids at the Volunteer Inn, Bridge Street. Charles and Winifred began their married life at 146 Princes Street. It was Charles Williams II who sold the land by the County Ground to Arkell's, brewers of Kingsdown, and it is not unreasonable to suppose that he and Charles Williams III also built the County Ground Hotel. It opened in 1897.

Immediately, Charles Williams III moved in as the pub's first landlord. In 1899, he and Winifred had a son, born at the County Ground Hotel, whom they named ... Charles

Williams. When Charles Williams II retired, he and his wife took up residence with their son and his family at the hotel. However, in 1908, Charles Williams III was granted a divorce from Winifred on the grounds of her alleged adultery, at the County Ground Hotel, with Henry Postlethwaite Coulton. The hotel was used as the headquarters of The Swindon Athletic Club from 1921. Charles Williams II died there in 1922, and Charles Williams III continued as landlord until 1924 when he was succeeded by Henry Albert Bates. W. Witts had it for a while in 1926, before Bates returned the following year, and remained there until M. Turton took over in 1933. E.T. Hamilton succeeded him in 1934, and F.S. Fox was in charge in 1948.

On the outside of the County Ground Hotel is a terracotta date stone that includes the likeness of Queen Victoria (1897 was the year of her Diamond Jubilee) set among the national emblems. Although there has been a considerable amount of internal remodelling, particularly in 1921 and 1954, some original features have been retained, including several windows with painted glass.

Coventry House, High Street see Tarrant's *Recollections*

Cross Keys beerhouse, Bridge Street This part of what was to become Regent Street was still insufficiently built up by the late 1840s to be any more than an eastern continuation of Bridge Street, and that was when and where the Cross Keys was established. Ironically, the site was next to a Roman Catholic chapel. Initially, it was kept by Ellen Horne (b. Stanton Fitzwarren, 1808), a widow, living at the time with her

three children at Eastcott, and trying to make ends meet by taking in lodgers. At home, she also accommodated two GWR workers and two charwomen. By 1855, the Cross Keys had been taken over by James Edward Toe (b. Swindon, 1822), a boot and shoemaker who lived at 16 Westcott Place and had previously been at the Artillery Arms. He simply added 'beer retailer' to his list of accomplishments. By 1860, he also had a workshop at 13 Market Place (later to be named Emlyn Square). He gave up the Cross Keys c.1864, and the beerhouse closed early in the 1870s in the occupancy of William Theobald (b. Lyneham, 1837) and his family. By that time, it was numbered 23 Regent Street. Thereafter, for a time, it was a common lodging house. The Regent Arcade was later built on this site, and then the Arcadia Cinema.

Cross Keys, Wood Street No. 27 Wood Street, revamped and remodelled, opened as Baker Street bar and restaurant in 2010; from 2002, it had been Picklejohn's public house, owned by Picklejohn's Leisure. Baker Street was named after the singer-songwriter Gerry Rafferty (1947-2011) song of the same name, which was released in 1978. However, for much of its existence in the hospitality business, No. 27 Wood Street had been the Cross Keys public house. It originated with the business of pastry cook and fruiterer that George Pimbury had established at 6 Wood Street by the 1840s. This business was taken over later in that decade by Joseph Pimbury (b. Minchinhampton, Gloucestershire, 1808) who, at Minchinhampton in 1836, married Elizabeth Warden (b. Woolthorpe, Herefordshire, 1801). They had one child, Harriett (b. Stroud, 1839). By 1851, Joseph was employing a baker and an errand boy in his Wood Street business. He gave it up, c.1869 and, by then widowed, took on a small farm of thirty-four acres at Rodborough, near Stroud, where his daughter Harriett was housekeeper. Joseph Pimbury died at Dursley in 1873.

When Joseph gave up his Wood Street pastry cook business, it was acquired by Henry Lay (b. Highworth, 1815), who married Eliza Judd (b. Faringdon, Berkshire, 1822) and had set up in the 1830s as a confectioner and baker in London Street, Faringdon, moving a couple of decades later into Market Place, just around the corner. Henry remained at Faringdon but had plans for the expansion of the Swindon branch. He obtained a Refreshment House Licence, and thereafter offered a range of services at 6 Wood Street. These included 'wholesale and retail confectionery, manufactured by machinery on the premises', wines, ale and stout, and tea and coffee. He established dining and luncheon rooms, and catered for wedding breakfasts and ball suppers.

In 1873, Henry Lay relocated this business to 27 Wood Street, premises that had previously been occupied by George Osmond, chemist, and his family. He divided the downstairs in half, with a counter for confectionery on one side and a bar for refreshments on the other. This dual arrangement continued for several decades into the 20th century. Henry Lay died at Faringdon in 1879, and the business at 27 Wood Street, Swindon, was taken over by one of his sons, Albert George Lay (b. Faringdon, 1850). By 1885, it was listed as 'refreshment rooms and confectioner', run by Henry Lay's widow, Eliza. Meanwhile, Albert George Lay took on the refreshment rooms at the newly opened Midland & South West Junction

Railway's station, off Newport Street. By 1903, he was advertising the Wood Street business as that of confectioner, and wine and beer retailer. This continued until the early 1920s, when the establishment was renamed Lay's Restaurant. By 1923, it had been taken over by Sydney John Lawrence, who owned pleasure boats at Coate Water and had a bakery in Victoria Road. He converted the Wood Street business back to a wine and beer retailer, and thus it remained.

Dodson, Zephaniah (1847-1931) Dodson was born at Basford, Nottinghamshire, the son of a lacemaker, Samuel Dodson, who named Zephaniah's sister Zilla. In 1875, in Reading, Zephaniah married Sarah Albinia Lane (b. Doulton, Somerset, 1845). The family moved to Swindon in 1869, where they lived in Eastcott Lane. That year, Dodson went into partnership with the photographer George King, whose studio was in Devizes Road, as Dodson & King. The latter died in 1872, and Zephaniah Dodson struck out on his own. He opened as an 'artist photographer' at 58 Prospect, naming the premises The Prospect Studio. 'Life-like portraits can now be guaranteed in any weather', he boasted, and that 'parties (could be) waited upon at their residencies when required'. His premises also offered a private waiting room for ladies. By 1877, customers could also buy from him walking sticks, tobacco, pipes, pouches and cigar cases. He also gave a pipe repair service. In 1883, he was appointed sole agent in Swindon and district for the wholesale and retail of fireworks. He made much of the fact that this was the result of an appointment by 'the pyrotecnist [sic] to Alexandra Palace and the Royal Yacht squadron'. He also listed the variety of events for which the residents of

Swindon might care to commission firework displays, and where he might also give added value by taking photographs. Also in 1883, he moved his business premises to 58 Regent Street, New Swindon. Variously, over the next decade or so, he had premises at 19 and 28 Regent Street and in Sanford Street. Zephaniah Dodson retired from photography in 1895, and became an agent for parcel delivery companies at his home, 39 Eastcott Hill.

Dog public house This was an alehouse on the west side of Cricklade Street. Its origins are unknown, but it might have existed in the early 1600s. It is mentioned in a document dated 17 May 1731, whereby Hannah Spencer leased to William Vilett, a Swindon land and property owner and merchant, 'two messuages etc. (formerly one messuage called 'the Dog') in Cricklade Street'. It stood opposite the White Horse. (See also White Horse beerhouse.)

Dolphin, Rodbourne Road There were no houses northwards between the Rodbourne Lane railway crossing and the old village of Rodbourne Cheney when, 1872-73, Arkell's brewery built the Dolphin Hotel in isolation on the west side of the road. As a public house, it could not rely on local trade. It would be four years before Linslade Street and Guppy Street were completed, and another six years would pass before Jennings Street was added in 1883, and Thomas Street a year later. Five years later, Morris Street was built, followed by Charles Street and Hawkins Street in 1890, and speculative builders began to join up the geographical dots around the Dolphin with brick-built terraces. Between 1889 and 1907, Percy Street, Redcliffe Street, Drew Street,

Montague Street, Rose Street and Deburgh Street changed the face of the area, and gave the Dolphin a regular local clientele.

That notwithstanding, Arkell's showed how shrewd they were in not simply opening a small beerhouse, but a large building that was an inn from the start, ready to accommodate visitors to the GWR workshops. Indeed, the project devolved on the proximity of the Works, and was situated to take advantage of the Rodbourne Road entrance, just across the road. A lot of the workforce used this gate. Some were men who walked the mile or so from Rodbourne Cheney village and beyond. Others found it more convenient, depending on where they toiled in the sprawling Works, to come up from Westcott Place or the streets to the north-west of the railway village rather than the High Street (Emlyn Square) entrance. Still more walked all the way from Stratton St Margaret via Gorse Hill. Their thirsts had to be slaked.

Right from the beginning, the Dolphin was intended as a place of some importance. In what later became the pub car park, an 'enclosed quoit ground with lawn adjoining' was laid out, and this area was further developed as a pleasure garden, where weekly dances were held outdoors until the First World War. The inn's first keeper was Robert Bishop, who was granted occasional special licences that allowed him to open at four o'clock in the morning on railway 'Trip' days. Bishop left in 1879 to run the Great Western Hotel, and was replaced by Thomas Hayward (b. Kempsford, Gloucestershire, 1847), a former carpenter and joiner. Hayward's advertisement of 1884 declared that his outdoor grounds were 'Affording special facilities for unobtruded Enjoyments', no doubt in earshot of the

'Harmonic Meeting ... held every Friday and Saturday evening' in the 'large new room' that had been added. He took early retirement in 1900, moved to Goddard Avenue, where the family lived on their own means, and was replaced at the Dolphin by Alfred Edward Morgan (b. Festiniog, Wales, 1851).

Drew, William (1838-1905) One of William Drew's last commissions was to design the houses for a street that was built in Rodbourne in 1907, and which bears his name. Drew is almost forgotten now, but he was also a designer of schools in Gothic style in the town, of which his biggest and most flamboyant was Clarence Street School. He is likely to have been involved in the designs of Euclid Street School and Lethbridge Road School, and certainly designed Gorse Hill School with Local Board surveyor William Henry Read, with whom he was closely associated.

William Drew was born at Highworth, the son of Edward Drew (b. Marylebone, London, 1799) and his wife Dinah (b. Shaftesbury, Dorset, 1809). Edward was a carpenter, and three of his sons, including William, took up the same occupation. William went to London to work, and was in lodgings there in Markham Street when, in 1866, he married farmer's daughter Mary Jane Busson (b. Lydiard Tregoze, 1843) at St Luke's, Chelsea. The couple returned to Highworth, setting up home and business in the high street, where their first child was born in 1867. Another five children were born there before the family relocated to 4 North Street, Swindon, in 1876. Also in the 1870s, William Drew began to promote himself as architect and surveyor, and became an early Member of the Society of Architects after

its formation in 1884. At North Street, three more children were to be added to the family, which also accommodated Mary Jane's widowed mother. By 1891, William, Mary, and their youngest child were living at 22 Victoria Street in Old Town, and from there William Drew continued his practice until his death. Mary Jane died in 1914.

Of their sons, George Drew became a painter and decorator, and Frederick Drew went to London, where he lived in the household of his maternal uncle and occupied himself as a house painter. Edward Drew and William Busson Drew were architects and surveyors, the former becoming a partner in his father's business, and the latter setting up on his own account in Swindon.

Drill Hall, Church Place In 1860, when England feared that Napoleon III of France would launch an invasion, a group of about 250 GWR employees formed the Eleventh Wiltshire (New Swindon) Volunteer Rifle Corps. Its first, but short-lived, commander was Capt. William Frederick Gooch, and the men − 'the finest and most able-bodied in the country' − were organised into three companies, with a brass band and 'an efficient fife and drum band'. They marched and practised warfare around an area immediately to the south of High Street, New Town (Emlyn Square) on which, in 1862, an armoury and drill hall was built for them. In 1871, this building, with adjacent cottages, was annexed by the GWR for its accident hospital, and what was then called a 'drill shed' was built to take its place at the north-east corner of the company's cricket field (The Park). An armoury was established nearby in Taunton Street. The drill hall premises comprised some 8,000 square feet, and cost about £1,500, of which the GWR contributed all but £300, which came from the Corps and 'other sources'. From the outset, it was also intended to use the drill hall as a school for girls, pending the custom-built accommodation that eventually proved to be College Street School, because the existing GWR schools were at that time full to capacity. The drill hall was in the charge of Drill-sergeant John Rice (late of H.M. 43rd Regiment) and Colour-sergeant D. Phillips, who lived on the premises. By the mid-1870s, when William Dean was its commander, the Corps had two companies of 150 men; in 1878, they were described thus: 'comprises 200 men, of whom 174 are efficient!'. There were twenty-five men in the band. In the 1880s, a gymnasium was established in the drill hall, under the auspices of the Swindon Gymnastic Society.

Duck, Son & Pinker music shop In 1921, the Bath firm of Duck, Son & Pinker took over that of C. Milson & Son, and that year established itself in the latter's former premises at 9 Fleet Street, Swindon. The firm was named after William Duck (1820-1892), a one-time hairdresser in Bridge Street, Bath, who opened his first piano shop at 2 Pulteney Bridge in 1848; his son Edward George Duck (1855-1910), who was taken into the firm in 1878; and William's one-time piano tuner Thomas Joseph Pinker (1844-1887), who was killed in a yachting accident. In Swindon, DS&P at first sold pianos and sheet music from the ground floor of its double-fronted premises in Fleet Street. Eventually, it relocated to corner premises at 15 Bridge Street, Swindon, when pianos and other musical instruments occupied the downstairs showroom, and sheet music and recorded music were sold

from the floor above. In 2006, the firm closed the downstairs, retreated to the first floor, and sub-let its former showroom to Subway, the fast-food outlet. This led to problems of access to the upper floor under the Disability Discrimination Act, 1995, and there were difficulties in conforming to local authority fire regulations. Unable to finance the necessary alterations, Duck, Son & Pinker in Swindon closed on 17 February 2007. The firm, although in trading difficulties, continued to operate in Bath from 9-12 Pulteney Street, financially supported privately by its managing director, Leslie Fudge (1921-2010), who also had other business interests. Following his death, Duck, Son & Pinker was no longer viable, and closed down in 2011.

Duke of Wellington This public house was established on Eastcott Hill in 1869 by brewer John Arkell, closed in April 2011, and was afterwards converted to private residential accommodation. Before it was a public house, the premises comprised a pair of terraced houses built speculatively in brick by Swindon builder Henry Caiger of Belle Vue Road. The pair of two-bay, two-storey houses were almost at once acquired by Arkell, who converted them to retail trade in less than six months. He opened the pub under the Beerhouse Act, 1830, which had been passed by the Duke of Wellington's Tory government. Under this Act, anyone could brew and sell beer on payment of two guineas for a licence. The rationale for this legislation was that if more people made beer and retailed it, the price would come down, thereby encouraging drinkers away from stronger liquor such as gin. Arkell opened the Duke of Wellington public house just before this Act was repealed by the Wine and Beerhouse Act, 1869, thereby ensuring that, as it was an established public house, a licence would be granted thereafter. The pub was reputed to have had the smallest bar in the town.

Duncan and Mandy's Website

From the moment it was set up in 2000, Duncan and Mandy's online, pictorial record of Swindon and North Wiltshire churches and churchyards immediately became a hugely valuable resource for local historians and family historians. Its compilers were Duncan Glendower Scott Ball (b. Swindon, 1959) and his wife Mandy Patricia, née Lea, (b. Stratton St Margaret, 1962). The pair married in 1981. Duncan's family came to Swindon when his great-great-grandfather, born in Lincolnshire, and a one-time metropolitan police officer, eventually transferred to Swindon and lived in a cottage in Wanborough. Duncan's great-grandfather was Harry Tydeman, half of the well-known Swindon building firm of Tydeman Brothers, which, at the beginning of the twentieth century, had premises in the town in Edgeware Road and Cow Lane. Mandy's family came to Swindon when, in the mid-1940s, her maternal grandfather walked to the town from South Wales hoping to secure a job at the GWR Works. He had been a coal pit worker, much concerned with the safety of the miners and vociferous enough in this regard to earn the displeasure of the pit authorities. He lodged at Westcott Place, got a job at the Works, and moved his family from South Wales into a house in Gordon Road.

The seeds for their website were sown by Duncan and Mandy's interest in their own family history. This was followed by their involvement in *Moonraker*, an online

sharing site dedicated to the history and genealogy of Wiltshire. The pair began by photographing churches and the contents of churchyards in 1998, and by 2013, Duncan and Mandy's Website had upwards of 45,000 images of ecclesiastical buildings, and the individual memorials and gravestones associated with each. The early pictures were taken with print film. Later, the couple replaced these images with digital shots, and found, in many cases, the tombstones had considerably eroded in between. This rate of erosion underlined just how important Duncan and Mandy's Website will be to future historians. The couple configured their website to include the names on the photographs, a location index, and a name-search facility to help visitors to the site locate those pictures that might be relevant to their enquiries.

Edgeware Road

This roadway effectively linked Sanford Street with Regent Street. It was built up in 1877 by speculative builder H. C. Smith of Edgeware Road, London, who in Swindon erected a terrace of fifteen properties. When the street was built, there was still open land to the east, as far as the back gardens of the terraces that lined the west side of Princes Street. When Islington Street was built in this space in 1893, at right angles to the north of Edgeware Road, the latter was extended by seven properties to meet it. The alleyway between the back gardens to the east of Islington Street and those to the west of Princes Street became Cow Lane. The breadwinners of almost all the families who moved into Edgeware Road when it was first built were Great Western Railway Works' employees; by 1900, the heads of the families in these twenty-one properties included two railway carriage builders, one wagon builder, one engine driver, three engine fitters, one boilermaker, two railway smiths, one railway storekeeper's assistant, one railway horse box builder, one porter, and four widows of former railway Works' employees. The rest of the street comprised the families of one grocer, two builders, and a musician at the Empire Theatre.

A number of the later buildings in Edgeware Road were the properties of Tydeman's 'builders, housefitters, decorators, plumbers, sanitary engineers, and undertakers', who also moved into a building in Cow Lane. Henry W. Tydeman (b. Calne, 1868) opened his business at 1 Edgeware Road in the 1890s, and advertised it on the side of Bourne Villa, the property next door on the corner with Sanford Street. This was a three-bay, two-storey, brick-built house, double-fronted with canted bay windows, which was put up for Thomas Powell, minister of the Primitive Methodist Church in New Swindon. Tydeman's house, before he took it on, had been a grocer's shop. St Paul's church was built in Edgeware Road in 1880-81, and a vicarage adjoining in 1884. These were demolished in 1963, at about the same time as the rest of Edgeware Road came down so that the area could be redeveloped, leaving only space on the site for St Aldhelm's chapel of ease, which was opened in 1966. (See also Hunter's furniture store.)

Edwards, William Vaughan see Ironmongers in Wood Street

Engineer's Arms, Emlyn Square
In 1854, an octagonal covered market was built adjacent to the Mechanics' Institute in what was then known as High Street,

New Swindon. Initially, the take-up for its stalls was not good, but one of the early stallholders was William Mace 'chinaman', who had set up in stalls 16, 17 and 18 by 1858. Mace (b. Gravesend, Kent, 1803) had previously been a 'dealer in earthenware'. Shortly afterwards, Mrs E. Taylor took them over, and called them her 'china warehouse'. In c.1860, she relocated to stall no. 12, where she established her 'fancy warehouse', and the stalls from where she previously ran the business were acquired by Jane Taylor, beerhouse keeper. These premises became known by the dual name Engineer's Arms and The Hole in the Wall, the latter being ascribed to the hatch on the outside of the building through which off-sales could be obtained. In 1862, John Edwards was the beerhouse keeper of this establishment, followed by Jane Edwards, who was there until the place was closed down in 1872.

Engineer's Arms, Wellington Street This four-square, stone-built, three-bay, two-storey property with basement was built by the Wilts & Berks Canal Company in the early years of the 19th century, hard by its waterway, and was clearly intended to stand out. From the early 1840s, it was run as a beerhouse by William Smith, who was also a carpenter. He was still there in 1848, but the premises were recorded as being empty at the time of the 1851 census. It passed into the hands of the GWR, and at some point during the 1850s it became known as Elm Villa, Spur Lodge or The Spur. William Jaggard, ticket collector for the GWR, lived there with his wife and five children. By 1871, when the house was called Elm Villa, GWR Works' manager Samuel Carlton was the tenant, with his wife and six children. It was advertised for sale by auction in 1873, but remained unsold, and Carlton subsequently relocated to Clifton Villa, one of the GWR's villa-like houses beside the railway works. By the 1880s, Elm Villa was the home of James Hughes, the manager of Compton's Clothing Factory, his wife and a servant. It then went back into the drinks business, albeit non-alcoholic, when the occupant was John Frederick Jefford, aerated water manufacturer, and his large family. According to pub historian David Backhouse, writing in *Home Brewed*, between 1905 and 1919 the premises were owned by a brewery, which used the cellars as a store, and it was afterwards acquired by the Preater family. These dates may be doubtful because by 1917, and throughout the 1920s, it was run by Annie Foss as Elm House Commercial Hotel. She had previously run the Wellington Hotel in Gloucester Street with her late husband Samuel B. Foss, and had afterwards been living on private means at 58 Wellington Street. Swindon Borough Council bought the property c.1960 and subsequently demolished it.

Euclid Street School Built for the Swindon School Board on the south side of Euclid Street, opposite the Princes Street Recreation Ground in 1897, this was originally designed as a day training centre for pupil teachers being admitted to board schools in the town. Built of red brick with yellow terracotta dressings, the property was smaller and more conservatively decorated than the flamboyant Clarence Street School of the same date, further to the west on the opposite side of the road, but was nonetheless in keeping with it. It presents a symmetrical and mostly two-storey elevation to Euclid Street of effectively eighteen bays. Decorated gabled sections are tied together by a single-storey central section with a pierced parapet, and flanking elevations to the east and west include recessed entrances at street level. The gabled sections are forward of the flanking entrances, and the single-storey part is forward of the gabled sections. The yellow dressings include string courses, decorative arches, keystones, caps on the three-stage buttresses, plinths and finials. On the roofs are two spirelets.

The old school boards were swept away under the Education Act of 1902, and, in 1904, the building became a Higher Elementary School for pupils aged ten to twelve. Three years later, twelve-year olds were taken on instead, for a period of three years schooling. In 1919, the school in Euclid Street became effectively an overspill venue for the Swindon College in Victoria Road, and teaching was offered at the same levels at both. The first master at that time was Arthur James Dicks, who lived at 177 Victoria Road, and who continued in the post until 1930. The school became Headlands Secondary School in 1943 and relocated in 1952 to the newly built Headlands, off Cricklade Road and Headlands Grove, which was given grammar school status. Thereafter Euclid Street was used to relieve overcrowding in other Swindon schools. This continued until 1964, when it reverted to training for teaching, this time specifically for mature students who wanted to enter the profession because of a need to change jobs. In the 1990s, it became the Swindon School of Art, which had until then been at the Swindon College in Regent Circus, and which continued in Euclid Street until 2006. The Euclid Street School building, together with the headmaster's house and workshops at the rear, were given Grade II status in 2001. The building was sold in 2006, and has since been converted to residential apartments.

Even Swindon School, Hughes Street, Rodbourne

A mixed school, built by the Rodbourne School Board, was opened in 1880 on the corner of Hughes Street and Rodbourne Road. It accommodated 520 boys and girls, and 200 infants. Henry Day was the headmaster of the former, and the headmistress of the latter was Clara Ellison, who lived at 2 Westcott Place. The site was a large one, enabling a separate infants' school to be built adjacent, which opened in 1884. Six years later, Rodbourne was taken into the borough of Swindon; the schools at Even Swindon were taken over by the Swindon School Board, which immediately set about enlarging the school with additional classrooms and a hall, which were opened in 1891. The sprawling school was built of brick with stone dressings. Twenty-two- year-old Henry Day had been appointed assistant master at the GWR's Bristol Street School in 1878, under James Alexander Braid, and relocated to Even Swindon School when it opened, remaining there until his retirement in 1919. In 1880, he married Sarah Arabella Thomas, the daughter of William Thomas, a Swindon beerhouse keeper living in High Street (now Emlyn Square), New Town, and his wife Arabella, and the couple set up home at 51 William Street. (William's premises eventually became the London Stout Tavern, later renamed The Glue Pot.) Even Swindon School was enlarged in 1894 to take another 210 pupils, at a cost of £8,097. By the 1890s, the Days were living at Brendon House, Ashford Road. When Day retired, a plaque was attached to the school, which read: 'Erected by old scholars on the retirement of Mr H. Day, the first headmaster of this school 1880-1919, as evidence of appreciation of his meritorious services'. Sarah died in 1936, and Henry died in 1941.

Even Swindon School became a junior mixed school in 1946, which closed in 2007 when the pupils were transferred and the site was taken over by the Primary Care Trust. This closed down in 2012, after which the premises were targeted by vandals and became the focus of anti-social behaviour, culminating in a fire that destroyed part of the building in February 2013. It was demolished in December 2013.

Fairclough, Harry Stanley (1894-1965)

Born in Glossop, Derbyshire, H.S. Fairclough (known always as Stanley) was the son of Walter Peake Fairclough (b. Codnor, Derbyshire 1858), a self-employed professor of music and organist, and his wife Mary (b. Charlesworth, Derbyshire, 1865). Stanley was one of five siblings; his father died in 1941 at Bradbury's hairdressing shop, High Street West, Glossop. Stanley studied music in his own town and also became a self-employed professor of music. He came to Swindon in 1920 to teach music through evening classes at the Technical College, Victoria Road, and at Euclid Street School, soon adding Commonweal School to his portfolio. Using pupils from his evening classes, he founded the College Musical Society in 1926, and this became the Swindon Choral Society. Stanley married Muriel Iris Brackpool at Portsmouth in 1929, and the couple settled at 41 Westlecot Road, where he continued his music teaching. The society he founded changed its name to the Swindon Musical Society in 1947, and Stanley continued as its musical director until his death at the Victoria Hospital. When the Wyvern Theatre opened in 1971, one of the rooms there was named after him, in commemoration of his services to music in the town. On 25 January 1975, his widow unveiled the memorial plaque that marked it. Eventually, the plaque was removed, and the room became known as the 'Blue Room'.

Ferris, Frederick J. G. (1931-2013) Swindon's first and only town crier was appointed in 1997 by the Borough of Swindon, and continued in the job until his death. Fred was a native of Swindon, the third child of Frederick G. Ferris and Florence E. Jones, who married in 1927, and was brought up at Pinehurst. He served with the Wiltshire Regiment, and worked for the Bristol Tramways & Carriage Company (which became the Bristol Omnibus Company in 1957, and after 1993 was the Stagecoach firm), as a conductor and driver, and was an inspector by the time he retired. He was married twice: in 1953, to Rita O. Griffin, and to Gwyneth M. Johns in 1980. Fred had eleven children. In 1997, Swindon Borough Council decided that a town crier would be a good way of publicising the town, but had not thought through exactly how the appointment could best be used. Fred was given just one official job in the first three years, although he came to be much in demand at private functions. In 2000, he was promoted by the Swindon *Evening Advertiser* to publicly advertise the town's Business Expo at Blunsdon House Hotel, but official functions still failed to materialise until the matter was taken up in mid-2002 with Stan Pajak, that year's mayor.

Even so, Fred Ferris took his job of town crier very seriously. Always smartly turned out, he broke with tradition among town criers by wearing a uniform of black and green, with gold piping to the lapels and cuffs of his greatcoat. His top hat had a green ribbon around it and included a badge bearing the likeness of a locomotive. He wore a wing-collar with a black cravat, and a badge bearing the words 'Station Master'. Locally, he was known as 'Mr Shiny Shoes'. The whole livery ensemble, vaguely that of a Victorian stationmaster, was emblematic of Swindon's railway history. It won him the Town Crier's Association's title of Best Dressed Town Crier more than a dozen times. He achieved the Best Content of Cry Award in 2011. In 2012, he was the recipient of the prestigious award, the Loyal Company of Town Crier's Badge of Honour, presented to him by John Robinson at a meeting of the Swindon Borough Council. Fred was a standard-bearer for the Royal British Legion, and a vice-president of Swindon's Pegasus Band, which played at his funeral.

Forward Swindon Set up by Swindon Borough Council on 10 March 2010 to replace The New Swindon Company, which was then abandoned, the regeneration organisation Forward Swindon had a much wider brief than had its predecessor. Although council-funded, Forward Swindon was set up as a limited liability company, with a board made up largely of representatives of the private sector. Its brief was to encourage and facilitate economic growth and property development in Swindon, encourage business investment and generally enable economic and build regeneration of the town. In 2013, its Masterplan for Swindon was agreed, dividing the town into five areas: Town Centre, Railway Southside, North Star, County Ground, and Old Town. It was also the co-ordinator of the extensive Kimmerfields (formerly Union Square) commercial scheme, a collaboration between Home and Counties Agency, South-West Regional Development Agency and Swindon Borough Council, being developed by Muse Developments. (See also New Swindon Company.)

George, The By the late 1700s, this property was a stone-built cottage situated in the hamlet of Eastcott. It probably opened as a beerhouse soon after the Beerhouse Act, 1830 was passed, and developed its trade from the early 1840s, situated as it was on basically a track that connected a hamlet, Upper Eastcott Farm and Lower Eastcott Farm, with the retailers of Old Town on the Hill. It appears to have been called The George at least from this period, although it is not clear whether that devolved on the monarch of the day, the legend of George and the Dragon, or the name of the beerhouse keeper who, in the 1840s, was George Bishop. He was a former agricultural labourer who was then described as 'beer retailer and cowkeeper', and remained there into the mid-1850s. Then, the place was taken over by Charles Hurt, who was similarly described, and who had to compete with at least three more beer retailers on Eastcott Hill.

As the railway village developed and New Swindon began to emerge, the old track, which became Eastcott Hill, also became a favoured route for the new population. The George was in a prime position, just as the roadway began its ascent. Henry Wicks took over c.1865. The property was owned by brewer John Henry Harding Sheppard until 1872, when it was acquired by Cripps & Co., the brewers of Cricklade Street, Cirencester. In c.1880, the landlord of The George was Henry Sharps Lewis, who had previously been a GWR boilersmith, and the pub was still being run by his wife Eliza in the late 1890s.

In the 1890s, Cripps & Co. became the Cirencester Brewery Company. In 1937, they were taken over by H. & G. Simonds of Reading, who were merged with Courage in 1960. Thus, the history of The George was inextricably bound into this sequence of acquisitions. It closed as part of the Enterprise Inns' estate in April 2011, although there was an attempt to revive it that summer, just ahead of Enterprise Inns' confirmation in August that the property was for sale. In spring 2012, a group of volunteers, including employees from Swindon businesses and unemployed people working with the Princes Trust, renovated the vandalised building for Wizard Education, turning it into an education centre for children with behavioural problems and learning difficulties, a drop-in centre, and a focus for people looking for work experience.

Gilbert's Hill This was the name of a large, narrow field sited among a number of others, on land between The Sands (Bath Road) in Old Town and the course of the Wilts & Berks Canal, below Swindon hill. By 1870, the area had hardly been encroached upon; Old Town had been extended northwards only as far as Lansdown Road, and west into Prospect Place. The western side of these fields was bordered, from 1870, by the line of Cambria Bridge Road. At about that time, a speculative builder put up some houses on Gilbert's Field between Cambria Bridge Road and Eastcott Hill, thereby starting what became the Gilbert's Hill estate. Initially this did not amount to much, and was by all accounts slow to attract buyers, even after the site had been taken over and further developed by the United Land Company of London.

The whole estate devolved on just two streets, Dixon Street (where the first fourteen properties to be built were known as 'Gilbert's') and Stafford Street, which were built parallel to each other amidst the fields, and were named in 1873. Many of the early properties were built by the Gorse Hill Brick & Tile Company. Except for these two roads, the whole area remained open fields until 1880 when a municipal cemetery was laid out, at what was then effectively at the southern end of Cambria Bridge Road. This we know today as Radnor Street cemetery. By 1900, some 200 properties had been built in Stafford Street and Dixon Street.

Gilbert's Hill School Brightwen Binyon, architect of Ipswich, designed the Gilbert's Hill school for the Swindon School Board. The board had bought the land from the United Land Company of London, whose residential development on land it owned in the Eastcott area had fallen sufficiently short of expectations for the Company to try to recoup part of its outlay by placing a premium on the price of the land. Negotiations, and the impartial intervention of local board surveyor and valuer William Read, secured the site in Dixon Street for £295. The school was built at a cost of £2,100 by George Wiltshire, and was opened for infants on 8 July 1880. Its capacity was 280, and its first headmistress was Mary Tammage, an experienced board teacher who had previously worked in Bristol. From 1890, Gilbert's Hill School also accommodated girls.

Gilling's English Butter Factory
Henry Gilling (b. Bagley, near Wells,

Somerset, 1867), the son of a farmer, came to Swindon in his early twenties. He lodged at 34 Fleet Street and was occupied as a grocer's assistant at a time when the premises next door, at 35 Fleet Street, were a grocer's shop run by the widow Moore. In 1894, he married Minnie Louisa Pearce (b. Hambrook, Bristol, 1867) at Barton Regis, Gloucestershire; this is the earliest year in which he was documented as a grocer in his own right, having taken over 35 Fleet Street, where he was operating as Gilling & James, grocers. His partner was most probably Joseph Hillier James (b. Upton, Berkshire, 1850), baker and confectioner of 46 Regent Street, the son of a grocer and baker at Upton. By 1899, there was to be another Gilling & James shop at 20 and 21 Fleet Street.

By 1901, Henry Gilling was described as a farmer dairyman. The family had moved to 15 Transfer Terrace, the end property in a terrace at the north end of County Road and, at the time, the only buildings on the west side of the thoroughfare. He had opened his extensive brick-built creamery and butter factory next door, on the corner with Station Road. Gilling extended the residential accommodation along the upper storey of the works, which he labelled 'THE BEST ENGLISH BUTTER FACTORY IN THE DISTRICT', and upon which he advertised his other products: 'Gilling's Creamery, best quality corn, meal and feeding cake at lowest prices'. By then, Henry and Minnie had their children living there: daughter Dorothy (b. Swindon, 1896), and son Norman Henry (b. Swindon, 1900), who would later go into the family business. Also living on site were a number of the employees, including their clerk, two butter makers, three milk delivery assistants, their dairy shop assistant, and a general servant. Gilling's had a number of horse-drawn carts and covered wagons, and some handcarts, which were used for making house to house deliveries. Each handcart carried a churn of milk, into which householders dipped their own jugs as the delivery boys passed along their streets. The larger carts and wagons were used to supply the Gilling & James shops.

At the end of the 1890s, Henry Gilling also acquired the fourteen-room Wharf House in Drove Road, formerly called Canal House, built by the Wilts & Berks Canal Company for its clerks and superintendents. It was most likely that he changed its name to Fairholm, and it was from where he continued to trade as a cattle feed merchant. At this time, the nearby wharf was called Gilling's Wharf. Two more children, Arthur (1903) and Lionel John (1905) were born there. The family stayed at Fairholm for many decades; Minnie died there in 1919, and Henry Gilling, in 1936.

Gorse Hill School, Avening Street Gorse Hill was incorporated into the borough of Swindon in 1890; before then, it was part of the parish of Stratton St Margaret. In 1878, the Stratton St Margaret School Board opened its school for boys (160), girls (160) and infants (130) in Gorse Hill. The architects were William Henry Read and William Drew of Swindon; George Wiltshire, also of Swindon, built the school and the nearby teacher's house. The development cost £4,700. Until 1884, Avening Street was called School Street. The first headmaster of Gorse Hill School was Henry Wager (b. Tetbury, Gloucestershire, 1844), who had lived for many years at Long Newnton before taking up residence at the school house in Gorse Hill, and the

headmistress was Emma L. Clark (b. Bath, 1851). The school opened with two pupil teachers for the infants, two more for the girls, and an assistant to the headmaster, J. Williams, who was in charge of the boys.

Gow, David Godfrey (1924-1993) Born in London, into a family whose ancestors had composed and performed Scottish fiddle music, David Gow became a prize-winning student at the Royal College of Music. He taught music in London and Oxford, and became involved with the Open University from its formation in 1969. The following year, he was appointed lecturer in music at Swindon Technical College. In 1972, he formed the Swindon College Wind Orchestra. Gow continued to teach at the college, as well as composing prolifically for choir, orchestra, and instrumental ensembles; individual brass, wind and stringed instruments; concert bands, choirs and chamber music. He retired from the College in 1986, and continued to compose in retirement. (See also Swindon Concert Band.)

Grant, Edwin (1839-1896) By the mid-1860s, the provincial market was expanding for cartes de visite and cabinet portraits, and Grant then came to Swindon to take advantage of its potential among the town's expanding gentry and businessmen. Born in Dalston, Middlesex, he was brought up in Mile End, London, where his father was a solicitor's managing clerk and his mother was a music teacher. By the time he reached his twenties, Edwin Grant was boarding with a school governess at Bethnal Green and was employed as a photographic artist with the London Stereoscopic & Photographic Company. It had recently changed its name from the London Stereoscope Company, under which it had been formed in Oxford Street in 1854 by George Swan Nottage (1823-1885), who became Lord Mayor of London in 1884. Edwin Grant came to the Swindon area following his marriage in 1861 to Elizabeth Rachel Sydney Davis (b. Bishopsgate, London, 1844). They settled into 19 Gloucester Street, Faringdon, and remained there until 1875 when they relocated to Prospect, Swindon. His new photographic studio was at 63 Prospect Place, and Grant made much of his former connection with the London company. Over the next decade or so, he advertised at other addresses in the town, principally 2 Cambria Villas, Prospect Place and Newport Street. The family left Swindon in the late 1880s and were latterly living at Upton Park, Essex.

Grapes Hotel, The The hotel was built in Faringdon Road (but usually described as being in Cambria Place) in the 1860s by Simonds (a brewing firm which started in the 1700s in Reading). The earliest-known licensee was Samuel Rowles, a former porter with the Great Western Railway Company. He lived in Oxford Street, Gloucester and took up the tenancy of The Grapes in 1863, at the age of forty-four. It was soon afterwards acquired by James Kempster, a former fishmonger. He died in 1871, and his second wife, Ann, continued the tenancy. Early in the 1880s, it was taken over by John Blackford, a one-time butcher who had a stall in the octagonal market house when it opened beside the Mechanics' Institute in 1854. Simonds became H&G Simonds Limited in 1885, and The Grapes was wholly owned by them until 1960 when they were taken over and incorporated into Courage Barclay Simonds Ltd. In August 2012, the public house hosted a reggae weekend put on by Michael Carty, a Jamaican and, as MC Ranks, a presenter on Swindon 105.5 community radio, in celebration of the island's fifty years of independence. The following month, The Grapes, then owned by Enterprise Inns Limited, based at Solihull, closed down. The property was sold and, in 2013, was converted into fifteen bedsits.

Great Western Photographic Company This was the first photography business in Swindon that was not named after an individual. It seems to have been formed in 1879 for the specific purpose of buying William Short's photographic business and naturalist activities at 15 Wood Street, which it gave as its address, and his stock of negatives, which totalled some 12,000. The company stated that it could supply copies of any photograph taken by Mr Short since 1865. As well as offering the usual kinds of portrait, landscape and architectural photography, it also advertised 'microscopic objects magnified and photographed; transparencies prepared for the magic lantern'. Its naturalist department 'carried on as heretofore' with 'animal and bird stuffing, and taxidermy in all its branches'. The Great Western Photographic Company produced just one known advertisement, dated 1880. By the following year, it had disappeared without trace, and 15 Wood Street was taken over in 1881 by Henry Cook, baker and confectioner.

Greyhound public house, Westcott Place This public house stood beside the Wilts & Berks Canal, adjacent to the rear of properties in Westcott Place. It may have been in business since the 1830s; if so, it preceded the residential development there that took place from the mid-1840s. Rather than becoming a focus for this development, it must have been rather obscured by the line of the houses, which included The Falcon public house, built in 1849 as part of Falcon Terrace. It failed to survive competition from this and several other pubs in the area: the Greyhound in Faringdon Road, a few hundred yards to the east, opened in 1847; the Duke of York, which opened on the western end of Falcon Terrace c.1850; and the Wild Deer, close by at the west end of Westcott Place, which had been in business since the 1840s. In 1851, the keeper of the Greyhound in Westcott Place was Robert Alexander; it was George Parsons when it closed later that decade.

Grose jewellers The founder of this longstanding Swindon jewellery business was Alfred Grose (b. St. Austell, Cornwall, 1868), the son of Joseph Grose, a butcher and innkeeper. He was landlord of the New Inn at St. Austell. Alfred was educated at Prospect College, Shebbear, Devon. (This, a Methodist, independent day and boarding school, now called Shebbear College, was founded in 1829.) By the time he was in his early twenties, Alfred was boarding in Sadler Street, Wells, Somerset, where he was assistant to a silversmith. In 1899, he married Edith Ashbee (b. Margate, Kent, 1872), the daughter of George Ashbee, a master baker. The couple came to Swindon, c.1900, where they rented living and business premises at 18 Regent Street from the Morse family, in which Alfred established his business as 'shopkeeper, watchmaker, and jeweller'. Next door was the Arcadia picture house, and Alfred and Edith used to listen through their wall to the sound of the piano being played therein to accompany the films. Their

children were born over the shop, and one of these, Kathleen, recalled how she would always hide under the covers whenever the trams (the service started in 1904 and continued until 1929) went past, so that people sitting on the top deck would not see her in bed. The trams made everything in the house rattle, and the clocks in the window display downstairs shook so much that they often fell off their stands. That notwithstanding, Edith arranged the shop window, often winning the annual Swindon window-dressing competition.

Being a jeweller's shop, the premises had a spy hole in the front door so that the beat policeman could look through on his rounds. One day, the police told the jeweller that they had received information of an exact date and time, the occupants being away, when Grose's jewellery shop was to be burgled. The police would be waiting to apprehend the thief. On the night before, the beat policeman, peering through the spy hole, saw a scene of devastation. The thief had come a day early; he had taken slates from the roof, descended into the attic, knocked a hole in the ceiling, dropped into an upstairs room, taken up floorboards, and let himself into the shop, taking care to position a grandfather clock so that he could go back the way he came. The police, who knew the identity of the thief, went straight to his house, where he was apprehended at his kitchen table in the act of taking off the jeweller's labels. Alfred Grose died in 1924; Edith continued the business, which was eventually taken over by their eldest son, Joseph Donald Grose (b. Swindon, 1901). Edith died in 1957, and the shop closed in the 1970s.

Guggenheim family of photographers Julius Nicholous Franz

Guggenheim (1821-1889) was born at Pest, a district of Budapest, Hungary. By the early 1850s, he was working in Thanet, Kent, as a tutor to the children of Isaac Myers, the private chaplain to the British-Jewish philanthropist and Jewish rights campaigner Sir Moses Haim Montefiore, Bart., (1784-1885). He relocated to Henley-on-Thames, Oxfordshire, where he opened a photography business and shop at West Street in the 1850s and, in 1859, married Elizabeth Walklett (b. Oxford, 1831). Their first child, Joseph Francis Guggenheim, (b. 1860) was born at Henley-on-Thames, as were their next two children, including Jules Sigismund Guggenheim (1863-1938). In 1865, the family removed to Oxford, where the third of Julius and Elizabeth's seven children, George Gustave Guggenheim (1866-1929), was born. Jules Sigismund Guggenheim and George Gustave Guggenheim were both to become photographers. Meanwhile, Julius Guggenheim continued to operate a prosperous photographer's business from 56 High Street, Oxford, where the family lived with three servants. Elizabeth died in 1875; in 1877, Julius Guggenheim married Agnes Ann Hart (b. Gravesend, Kent, 1855), with whom he had a further six children. Agnes died in 1931, having survived her husband for forty-two years.

By the 1880s, Jules Sigismund Guggenheim and George Gustave Guggenheim were both working as assistant photographers in their father's business. In 1888, Jules married Mary Ann V. Harding (b. Swindon, 1866); they immediately set up home at 54 Regent Street, Swindon, from where he worked as a photographer, and where their two children were born, before she died in 1899 aged just thirty-three. Jules removed with his two children to 14 Regent

Circus. There, as well as continuing as a photographer and picture dealer, he also opened a 'fancy repository' and sold artists' materials. In 1902, he married Kathleen Eleanor Clarke (b. Swindon, 1883).

At this time, his Swindon business was tied up with one in Birmingham. His brother, George Gustave, had married, in 1890 at Wolverhampton, Gertrude Elizabeth Cowern (b. Wolverhampton, Staffordshire, 1872). After living for a while in Tunbridge Wells, Kent, where he had a photographic business and maintained an open house for artists and photographers, they relocated c.1893 to 14 Allen Road, Wolverhampton, where they lived with their seven children and two servants. The Swindon business and the Wolverhampton business were both styled 'Guggenheim and Company' until 3 April 1902, when the partnership was dissolved by mutual consent. Jules thereafter maintained his business in Swindon independently of the Birmingham business, which continued to be run in the name of Gertrude Elizabeth Guggenheim. She survived her husband for seventeen years, and died in 1946. Jules Sigismund Guggenheim retired from photography c.1915, and when he died in 1938, he was living at 145 Faringdon Road, Swindon.

GWR Radio *GWR Radio* came into being when *Wiltshire Radio,* operating out of Lime Kiln Studios, Wootton Bassett, changed its name immediately after merging with Bristol's *Radio West* in 1985. Three years later, in 1988, *GWR Radio* launched *Brunel Classic Gold. GWR Radio* continued to broadcast, changing its name in 1988 to *GWR FM.* It was the sponsor of Swindon Town Football Club during the 1989-90 and 1990-91 seasons. The following year, now part of the GWR Group, it re-launched as *New GWR FM*. In 1997, in an attempt at standardisation within its several local stations, the GWR Group launched The Mix Network, and in 2003, its subsidiary, *Now Digital*, began a local DAB service that covered Swindon. The GWR Group merged with the Capital Radio Group in 2005, whereupon the Mix Network was rebranded The One Network by the new organisation, GCap Media. Three years later, this organisation was taken over by Global Radio. The name of GWR Radio, which had persisted throughout all these changes and mergers, was finally lost. It was rebranded *Heart Wiltshire* from 23 March 2009. (See also BBC Wiltshire Sound; Brunel FM; Radio 105.5; Swindon FM; Wiltshire Radio.)

Hemmins, Henry (1857-1941) In 1871, Henry Hemmins was apprenticed for five years to Oxford photographer Henry William Taunt. His father, Thomas Hemmins (b. Woodstock, Oxfordshire, 1822), a one-time hairdresser and latterly Oxford college servant/messenger, was required to give his permission as the lad was under fifteen years of age. The family lived at 21 Ship Street, Oxford. Henry, who was born at Eton, Buckinghamshire, was destined to spend the whole of his working adult life as a photographer. By 1881, he was married and living at 15 Bullingdon Road, Oxford, with his own photographic business, and a young son, Francis Henry, who was also destined to become a photographer. The family came to Swindon in 1882, living at Grosvenor House, 16 Victoria Street, from where he advertised the business of Hemmins & Howell, portrait and landscape photographers. They offered special terms for college, school, and club groups, and advertised 'old photographs copied with the greatest care' and 'architectural drawings carefully copied'. Nothing is known of Mr Howell, and by 1885 Henry Hemmins, 'late Hemmins & Howell', was in business on his own from the Victoria Street address. 'Instantaneous Photography' was the boast of Henry Hemmins, who was using the latest technology to reduce exposure times. He continued to operate in Swindon until 1927, and died fourteen years later at Harrow, Middlesex.

Hempleman-Adams, David Kim (b. 1956) Although claimed by Swindon, the polar explorer, mountaineer, author and businessman had a short association with the town. He was born at Moredon, the son of Michael D. Hempleman and Merle E. Orchard, who married in 1956, was named David Hempleman, and attended Moredon Infant and Junior Schools. In 1965, his parents divorced, and he moved away from Swindon. When his mother married Anthony J. Adams in 1971, David Hempleman changed his surname to Adams, finally settling on Hempleman-Adams in 1980.

High Street 1840-1855 see Tarrant's *Recollections*

Hop Inn, Devizes Road No.7 Devizes Road has been in trade since about 1915, when David and Sarah Richman opened Richman's grocery stores there. During the 1970s, it became an unlicensed sex shop, which was part of the national sex shop estate owned by David Sullivan, businessman, philanthropist and one-time joint chairman of Birmingham City Football Club. It remained as 'The Private Shop', until its owners, thinking their business would be better served on the internet, put the property up for sale, and prospective purchasers were required to view whilst the sex shop was still operating. The building was bought in 2007 by property developer Pete Grooby. Initial plans for it to be incorporated into the adjacent Arts Centre fell through when Swindon Council failed to find the cash, and No. 7 Devizes Road remained empty whilst Grooby considered converting the ground floor to two shop units. He then drew up plans to convert the premises into a contemporary pub. This coincided with Jason Putt deciding to go into the trade in Swindon after being made redundant from his job as a development manager in sales. For thirty-five years, Jason's parents had been in pub management in Monmouthshire, and in Bristol, where they had the King William Ale House. Together with his wife Karen Griesel, they added their input to the remodelling and refurbishment of the interior, which was carried out by local builder Paul Piper, and the Hop Inn opened on 3 October 2012.

Horder, Sir Thomas Jeeves (1871-1955) The man who was to become one of the country's most eminent physicians was the third son of draper Albert Horder (b. Donhead St Mary, Wiltshire, 1831) and his wife Mary Ellen, née Jeeves (b. Bampton, Oxfordshire, 1839,) who married in 1865. The family lived over the drapery business they ran in Shaftesbury, Dorset, until 1872, when they set up in High Street, Swindon in a property immediately to the south of the drive onto the Goddard estate. The shop bore the surname of its founder for just over a century, eventually closing in the 1970s. Thomas Horder was educated at Swindon High School, and then privately, outside the town, from 1886. At the suggestion of the family's doctor, he began to study medicine, and later joined the staff at St Bartholemew's Hospital, London, where he spent much of his career. In 1902, he married farmer's daughter Geraldine Rose Doggett (b. Newnham, Hertfordshire, 1873). He was physician to British monarchs Edward VII, George V, George VI, and Elizabeth II, two prime ministers, and one party leader. Thomas Horder was knighted in 1918, and created 1st Baron Horder in 1933.

Horsell Street The site of much of Horsell Street lies beneath the approach to the Regent Circus development and its food store supermarket, which opened in 2014. Until the 1890s, this area was known as Frewin's Field, a tract of land immediately south of Lower Eastcott Farm and the field that was subsequently developed and became Regent Circus. In 1891, the New Swindon Local Board approved plans to build 550 houses, mostly around Rolleston Street and Eastcott Hill, on part of which was Frewin's Field, which had lately been in the ownership of the Rolleston estate. The developer of part of this land was William Crombey (b. Durham, 1824), a former engine driver, who lived at the Park Inn, William Street, run by Ann Elizabeth Harvey. By the time he died in 1891, the year Crombey Street was built, and named after him, he had a considerable shareholding in the Midland & South West Junction Railway.

In 1890, Crombey joined with builder John Horsell, who had been the New Swindon Local Board's Assistant Overseer in the 1880s, to lease land from the Rolleston estate on which they built the Rolleston Arms (on the corner of Commercial

Road and Curtis Street). John Horsell (b. Swindon, 1848) was the son of Charles Horsell, a slater, plasterer and turner who lived in Albert Street, but John was brought up in Newport Street by his grandmother, confectioner Louisa Long. For a while, after his marriage, he lived at 1 Victoria Street, Old Town. Once the Rolleston had been built, Horsell and his family lived there and ran the place from the time it opened until c.1905. Also in 1890, Horsell laid out Horsell Street, between Eastcott Hill and Rolleston Street, and built the terrace of seven houses on the south side. These were followed by a terrace of eight houses on the north side. John Horsell died in 1907. When the Bristol Omnibus Company had its offices in Regent Circus, Horsell Street became known as the place where some of its fleet was parked up overnight. Part of Horsell Street was demolished in the late 1950s to make way for the technical college extension of 1961, and what was left disappeared to accommodate the further extension of 1969-70 and its associated car park.

House, George (1816-1903) When
George House retired at eighty-four years of age from his job as an engine maker and fitter at the GWR's Swindon Works, just three years before he died, he was officially the country's longest-serving railway employee. When the company's line was laid down between Maidenhead and Swindon, 1838-40, House, who was then a labourer, helped in building it. He also laboured in the construction of the first workshops at the Swindon Works, before himself taking a job 'inside', initially also as a labourer. By the late 1840s, he was living in Britannia Place, a dogleg of an alley, with a short terrace of small houses that had just been built, off

Devizes Road, Old Town. House, his wife Elizabeth and their two small children lived in one of these, with two lodgers. He became an engine fitter shortly afterwards, and by 1851 had moved into 4 Taunton Street, close by the Works, where he was to remain for the rest of his life. Taunton Street was built c.1845, so it is possible that just as George House and his family were most likely the first people to inhabit the house in Britannia Place, so too did they go into a new-build in Taunton Street. The remaining seven of their nine children were born there. By the time he was eleven years old, George's firstborn, also George, was employed in the GWR Works as a 'rivet boy'. During his time as a GWR worker, George House was involved in setting up the GWR Medical Fund, and actively supported the company's juvenile fête, which was held annually in the nearby park from 1868. A widower for the last twenty-five years of his life, he was looked after firstly by his daughter Emma (b. 1861), and then her sister Elizabeth (b. 1858). After his death, George's exceptional service was commemorated in a portrait of the man, commissioned to hang in the Mechanics' Institute building in Emlyn Square.

Howe, Revd Newton Ebenezer
(1849-1925) The great Victorian scandal in Swindon involved Newton Ebenezer Howe, vicar of Christ Church (1887-1890, and 1894-1900). Admitted adulterer, and convicted of obtaining money by false pretences, for which he went to prison, Howe from the outset outraged the sensibilities of his parishioners, and was much disliked. His case made not only the local press, but appeared in a whole raft of regional newspapers, and was even reported abroad. It put Swindon on the map.

Newton Ebenezer Howe was born in Greenwich, the seventh child of schoolmaster and author Thomas Howe and his wife Mary. He attended Magdalen College, Cambridge. In his early twenties, he was living with his brother, Thomas Hasloper Howe, a fellmonger, and his wife, in Heavitree, Devon, where he described himself as a 'student of philosophy'. He was a deacon at St Albans in 1879 and, in the same year, was appointed curate at St Saviour's church, West Ham, London, where he stayed until 1882. That year, he married Susannah Henrietta Wigzell in Halifax, Yorkshire, and became rector of Luckington, near Chippenham. Five years later, the couple arrived in Swindon, where Newton Ebenezer Howe quickly established a reputation for being regularly absent from his parish, which prejudiced the cause, in the late 1880s, of raising sufficient funds to build a new vicarage. There were also rumours of financial difficulties, and allegations of a more personal matter in his private life.

These centred on his relationship with Marion Ormond (b. Swindon, 1868). She was the daughter of William Ormond, the Swindon solicitor who was also secretary and treasurer of the Society for the Promotion of Christian knowledge. The family lived at The Limes, Devizes Road. Marion was a young Sunday school teacher who, in the late 1880s, began a relationship with the married Revd Howe. His parishioners were scandalised when the pair were discovered walking together 'in secluded places' in the woods, he with his arm about her waist, and kissing each other. In the face of public outrage, Howe ceased to take any services in the parish after 17 June 1890. He admitted this affair later that year when charged before an Ecclesiastical Court at Bristol,

pleading guilty to 'improper familiarity with a young lady member of (his) congregation, of lewd and indecent behaviour towards her, and of soliciting her chastity on more than one occasion'.

The Court suspended Howe 'from office and benefice' for three years, after which he was allowed to return to Swindon. During his absence, his place at Christ Church was taken by Curate-in-charge, Revd Charles Frederick Goddard. In the meantime, Marion Ormond almost immediately went to work at a convalescent home in Thatcham, Berkshire. Afterwards, she took up nursing, and was by 1901 living in Harley Street, London. She remained a spinster. William Ormond died in 1908, leaving £51,000. When Marion died in 1942, she was living at Old Haslings Hotel, Warninglid, Sussex. Probate was granted to her sister Louisa, wife of farmer Christopher Henry Ware, and she left £18,000.

Following his suspension by the Ecclesiastical Court, Howe left Swindon, and was next located, still married but living on his own, at Liscard, Wallasey, Cheshire. At some point, he went to the Isle of Man 'engaged on clerical duty'. There, at Douglas in 1891, he met and befriended Mary Stringer Roskell (b. Douglas, Isle of Man, 1852). At the time, she was living with her father, Joseph Roskell (b. Liverpool, 1813), variously a merchant, a clerk in the local Packet Office, and a grocer, and her mother, Eliza née Stringer (b. Bridgnorth, Shropshire, 1814). Joseph died in 1892, and Eliza died in 1894, events that strengthened the ties between Mary and the vicar. These continued after he had been reinstated at Swindon, where she often stayed at the vicarage, and where she took up permanent residence in 1898. This situation prompted the Swindon churchwardens to have Howe prosecuted for adultery under the Clergy Discipline Act. It was alleged that he and Roskell stayed together at Oxford, St Leonards, Brighton and Walmer.

Mary Stringer Roskell was 'a lady of independent means'; she never took up any occupation, never married, and all her life was looked after by a servant. At Howe's trial in 1900, she told the court that the vicar's interest in her affairs, following the death of her parents, was at her instigation. Susannah Howe said that she consented to Mary Roskell living at the vicarage, and that she believed her husband to be innocent. Lord Coleridge, who defended him, said that the case had only come to court because of his admitted improper conduct with Marion Ormond, a decade before. Presiding over Bristol Consistory Court, Judge Ellicot agreed. He failed to understand how there could be adultery if Howe's wife Susannah was living with him on the same premises. He thought that 'money, not immorality, was the keynote of the case'; Howe could not afford to lose her (as a paying guest) and had 'gone out of his way to show her attention and make things pleasant'. All charges against Howe failed. However, he was shortly to be on a charge from which he could not escape.

In July 1900, Howe obtained £10 in cash from Swindon grocer Henry George English in return for a cheque for that sum, which Howe knew would not be cashed. He was arrested at Llandrindod Wells, where he was in the company of Mary Roskell, and charged with obtaining money by false pretences. English claimed that Howe had assured him that he was due a large amount from tithes and had several cheques to present to his bank. (At the time, the living was sequestrated, and the tithes were being paid to the registrar of the diocese. Howe had only a few shillings in his bank account and no cheques were paid in for some time afterwards.) Several witnesses evidenced that Howe's cheques to them had not been honoured. He was bailed, but was immediately rearrested for an outstanding amount of £19, owing to Edwin J. Morris, coal dealer of 50 Devizes Road. This time, he paid up. At his trial at Salisbury Assizes in October 1900, there was a hung jury in the matter of obtaining money by false pretences, but things went differently at the re-trial at the Winter Assizes at Devizes in 1901.

Before Mr Justice Day, the vicar admitted to telling untruths in letters about dishonoured cheques. In summing up, Day said he 'could only regard it as a benefit to the public at large, to his diocese, and to the benefice in which the prisoner had laboured, to be rid of his services'. He also criticised the Ecclesiastical Court for allowing Howe to resume his former duties in Swindon after three years. Newton Ebenezer Howe was given a twelve-month custodial sentence with hard labour, which he served in Devizes goal. Meanwhile, Mary Stringer Roskell lost no time in distancing herself from Howe. By early 1901, she had taken up residence in Bognor Regis, although she was later to relocate to Oxford, where she died in 1933. Howe, having been committed to prison, was replaced at Christ Church, Swindon, by Canon Edmund Walter Estcourt.

Humphreys hairdressers see Tarrant's *Recollections*

Hunter's Furniture Store, Regent Street Arguably, the best piece of late

Victorian architecture extant in Regent Street is that bearing the name W.W. Hunter, on the corner with Edgeware Road. It is slim, gabled, of three storeys and with six bays to Edgeware Road; it is built of red brick with limestone dressings; and has decorative mouldings, plain string pilasters, plinths and finials. There are large picture windows at street level and to the first floor, and pairs of windows in the bays to the second floor. It was built 1891-92, opened as a furniture store in the latter year, and remained in the Hunter family until the 1940s. Afterwards, it was Woodhouse & Son's furniture showrooms, was later a branch of Laura Ashley, and has since been in occupancy of several other businesses. The Society of Merchant Venturers, Bristol, bought the building in 1989 for £1.8 million, and sold it in 1997.

The property was built for William Wallace Hunter, who was born in 1864 at Dalston, Middlesex. By the time he was seventeen, he had left the family home and was domiciled in Sutton, Surrey, working as a 'lathe tender'. In 1886, he married Mary Ann Mitchell (b. Shingle End, Sandwich, Kent, 1863), whose father, a commercial boatman, lived at the coastguard station in Worth. Within two years of their marriage, William and Mary were in Swindon, living in Victoria Road, where he was described as a 'general dealer'. Their children, all born in Swindon, were Reginald Wallace (b. 1888), Ralph (b. 1890), and William Samuel (b. 1895). In 1891, the family relocated to 24 Regent Circus, where they lived in rooms above the shop that he opened as a furniture dealer, and remained there until the custom-built property was opened in Regent Street in 1892. The business prospered, and at some point in the 1890s, they moved home to Wallace Lodge, Bath Road. Of their children, William Samuel was killed in action in 1916; Ralph became a motor engineer; and Reginald Wallace followed in the family furnishing firm.

William and Mary retired to Weston-super-Mare, where they lived at 'Sandridge', Clarence Road East. He died in 1936 and she, in 1945, by which time their children were described as being 'retired house furnishers'. The Swindon building, still proudly proclaiming the name of its founder on its Regent Street and Edgeware Road elevations, remains a visual delight.

Ironmongers in Wood Street

Henry Bristow was recorded as a Swindon blacksmith in 1697. In 1771, Ambrose Goddard leased a shop and messuage in Wood Street to William Bristow, blacksmith. This is the earliest mention of premises that continued to be occupied and developed in the ironmongery trade for the best part of two centuries. By 1830, William's son Sadler Bristow was running his business as an ironmonger and blacksmith from there. He died in 1845, and the premises were taken over by William Vaughan Edwards and Frederick Thompson, who styled themselves 'wholesale, retail, and general furnishing bar iron and glass merchants'. In the mid-1840s, these men lived next door to each other in Prospect Place.

Frederick Thompson (b. Tewkesbury, Gloucestershire, 1812) was only briefly a partner in the enterprise. He married Barbara Ann Brown in Bristol in 1849, and the couple lived with Benjamin Patey Tregenza (b. Bedford, 1832), who was apprenticed as an ironmonger to F.J. Thompson in 1851. The Thompsons were at Prospect until c.1857 when they relocated to Bristol, where they thereafter lived with his parents (Frederick's father John Thompson was an ironmonger's assistant). With Thompson gone, the firm in Wood Street became Edwards, Ironmongers. Meanwhile, Tregenza had courted Elizabeth Mills (b. Wootton Bassett, 1834). The couple married at Cricklade in 1860. He gave up the ironmongery trade and they moved to Cumberland, where he became a commercial traveller, representing a Sheffield manufacturing firm until his death in 1885. Elizabeth died in 1931.

The senior partner in the Wood Street business of Edwards and Thompson, William Vaughan Edwards (b. Brecon, 1823) was described in 1851 as 'an ironmonger employing twelve men and apprentices as smiths' in Wood Street. He was then a single man, living in Prospect with one servant. The following year, he married Jemima Wansbrough (b. Bristol, 1823) in her home town, and brought her to Swindon to live at what was later numbered 2 Prospect Place. Also in 1852, presumably mindful of the prospective value to his enterprise of any business it might bring, Edwards became a director of the Swindon Market Company. This was formed that year, with the aim of demolishing old stables and warehouses in the Old Town market square, and building a market house that could also accommodate the County Court and Petty Sessions for the Division of Swindon, which had hitherto been held at the Goddard Arms Hotel. The market building, which came to be known as the Old Town town hall, was opened in 1853.

In 1861, William Vaughan Edwards took into partnership William Parker Suter (b. Retford, Norfolk, 1832), self-styled ironmonger, smith and iron founder. He too lived in Prospect with his wife Jane née Mousir (b. Grantham, Lincolnshire, 1831), whom he had married at Banbury in 1856, and daughter Emily (b. Banbury, 1858). The firm of Edwards & Suter was described as 'wholesale and retail ironmongers, iron and brass founders, oil, colour and glass merchants'. The partnership in Swindon, where William and Jane had two further children, survived into the late 1860s, when Suter took his family to Dudley, Worcestershire, where he set up as an ironmonger employer on his own account. He was still employed as such in 1886 when he died at Banbury.

Following the departure of Suter, the firm in Wood Street, Swindon became Edwards & Co. William Vaughan Edwards ran the business, and opened a branch in New Swindon at 1 Faringdon Street. Bristow's old yard had by then become the site of the Castle Iron Works. This was expanded over the next decade or so; at its height, it comprised some thirteen buildings spread around the perimeter of a yard behind Wood Street, on the north side, and covering an area of over 13,000 square feet. On its street-side were two shop frontages, one on each side of an alleyway that led straight into the manufacturing area of the business. At this time, the Castle Iron Works and its three shops were employing nineteen men and four boys.

By the 1870s, Edwards was also employing Edward Bays, who would later take over the ironmongery business. Edward Bays (b. Woodbridge, Suffolk, 1848) was the son of Thomas Grain Twight Bays (b. 1811), a hatter and freemason, and his wife Susannah Maria née Sharpe, who had married at St Helen's, Bishopsgate, in 1841. Edward's brother, Thomas George Bays, also became a hatter, and in 1889 was given the freedom of the City of London. T.G.T. Bays died in 1873 at Woodbridge, Suffolk, just after his son Edward made his first appearance in Swindon.

Edward Bays was educated at the Royal Masonic Institute for Boys, which had been set up at Wood Green, London in 1857 to educate the sons of needy and deceased freemasons. He is first recorded in Swindon in 1871, lodging with the widow Margaret Sheppard and her son William at 8 Bath Buildings, Bath Road. He is described as an ironmonger's assistant, as is Sydney Charles Fry (b. Bath, 1852), a fellow lodger. Fry was to remain in ironmongery, but not in Swindon; he soon relocated to Merthyr Tydfil, Wales to live with his father, George Carey Fry, who ran the Temperance Hotel. In 1876, Edward Bays married Eliza Pratt (b. Bristol, 1848) at St Andrew's, Holborn. She lived at 33 Viaduct, and her father, then deceased, had been a refiner. At the time of his marriage, Edward Bays had relocated to Prospect Hill, Swindon, working as an ironmonger with William Vaughan Edwards at the Castle Iron Works. Edward and Eliza settled at 34 Prospect; by 1881, they had three children, and Edward was described as an 'ironmonger's shopman'. He was soon to be given the title 'ironmonger'.

About this time, Edward Bays became a partner in the business with William Vaughan Edwards, forming Edwards & Bays at what had by then been numbered 22 Wood Street. Meanwhile, by 1881, Arthur Joseph Rye (b. Earthlingborough, Northamptonshire, 1856) had been employed to live at 1 Faringdon Street and manage the New Swindon shop there. Rye's schooling had been at Spalding, Lincolnshire, in the hands of Baptist minister and schoolmaster John C. Jones, M.A. His appointment at the Castle Iron Works' New Swindon branch coincided with his marriage, at Swindon

in 1881, to Emily Bockingale Greenaway (b. Ramsbury, 1861). William Vaughan Edwards died in 1884, although the firm continued for a while to bear his name.

In 1885, the shop was relocated to 40 Faringdon Street, and the Ryes shortly afterwards set up home at 55 Commercial Road. The arrangement with Rye continued until 1892 when he too was taken into partnership, and the firm became Edwards, Bays & Rye. It maintained the Castle Iron Works and two shops in Wood Street, and a shop at 40 Faringdon Street. One of the Wood Street shops majored on general ironmongery, and the other specialised in gardening equipment. The circular-headed entrance to the Castle Iron Works was distinguished by having the name 'BAYS & Co.' picked out in an ornamental nameplate; it was made in cast iron and set into the round-headed arch that formed the entrance to the works, beneath a plain keystone with floral decoration in the spandrels. There were flat pilasters on either side of the entrance, with corbelled-out heads. The Rye family was at 2 Devonshire Villas in The Sands (Bath Road), by which time four children had been born to them, when Emily died in 1901. The following year, A.J. Rye married Adelaide Lucy Langfield (b. Newbury, 1868) in Kensington, London, and left the Castle Iron Works business, setting up on his own as Arthur J. Rye, ironmonger, in the Faringdon Street premises. The business continued much as ever in Wood Street, although, by the 1920s, Bays & Co. was also advertising itself as a builders' merchants.

Arthur Joseph Rye later went into partnership with Thomas Henry Blackwell, forming Rye & Blackwell, and the pair added premises in Farnsby Street. Rye died in 1919, at his home, 100 Bath Road,

Swindon, leaving in excess of £17,000 to his wife, who died at the Westlecot Nursing Home, Bath Road, in 1922. Edward Bays died on 10 August 1922 in Swindon, leaving just under £13,000, and Eliza Bays died in Swindon, on 22 January 1927. Edward Bays junior (b. Swindon, 1879) became an ironmonger in the business, and died in 1964 at Cheriton Nursing Home, Devizes Road.

Jennings Street School This large three-storey building with heavy gables, built of brick with stone dressings such as lintels, string courses, keystones, corbels and flat pilasters, was opened on a corner site in 1904. It accommodated 198 infants and 580 older boys and girls. Its first headmaster was Frederick King (b. Ilminster, Somerset, 1865), who had previously been headmaster of Lethbridge Road School (opened 1891), when he lived with his family in Springfield Road. They moved to 130 County Road when he took up the appointment at Jennings Street. The headmistress was Jessie E. Handley (b. Worcester, 1879), a spinster who lived with her unmarried sister Kate M. Handley (b. Worcester, 1876), who was headmistress of Ferndale Road School (opened 1907), at 20 Queen's Terrace, Station Road. Jennings Street School became a secondary modern school in 1946. Eighteen years later, it was amalgamated with Westcott Secondary Modern School, both sites becoming Westbourne Secondary Modern School. The Jennings Street part was closed down, and later demolished in 1967. Even Swindon Community Centre, built on part of the site, was opened in 1990.

Kemble family of grocers About halfway along the east side of High Street stood the Bull, a public house first mentioned in 1633, but of unknown origin. During the 1700s, the Smith family owned it, and some adjacent land, where, by the 1770s, Ann Smith carried on the trade of a grocer. The Smiths lived in the property next door to the pub. Ann Smith was declared bankrupt in 1779, and the properties and land, which had previously been the subject of a still unresolved suit in Chancery, were in 1782 put up for sale by Ann's son Thomas Smith, through the Court of Chancery. The successful purchasers were Francis Kemble, grocer of Swithin Lane, Cannon Street, London, and Edward Kemble, a tea broker of Bow Lane, London.

Edward Kemble relocated at once to Swindon, where he re-established the grocery business, leaving his eldest son Nash Kemble to carry on the London end of his operation. The premises had been remodelled from a grocer's shop into a residential house, and Kemble turned it back into a shop and warehouse. In 1798, Nash, together with Joseph Kemble and Joseph Travers, bought the Swindon business. Edward returned to Bow Lane, installing at Swindon his eldest son William, with James Embling. In 1800, Edward Kemble leased the Swindon property to Joseph Kemble, who had also been working at St Swithin Lane, but who soon afterwards went to live at Great Staughton, Huntingdonshire, leaving the Swindon grocery business in the charge of James Kemble. In 1803, James Crowdy bought from Edward Kemble the land that had for so long been associated with the two properties, together with some land that Edward had previously acquired at the end of Dammas Lane from John Tarrant, a Swindon mason.

Joseph Kemble of Great Staughton still held the lease on the High Street property wherein James Embling was still trading as a grocer, and this he assigned to John Kemble, and grocer William Gerring of Shrivenham. Gerring was an enthusiastic freemason and a member of the Swindon Group of Yeomen Cavalry. In 1818, in the company of other freemasons, he obtained a warrant to establish a lodge, called the Lodge of Emulation, at the Goddard Arms Inn.

The grocer's shop and warehouse were retained until 1811, when the premises were bought by Richard Angel Nobes, a plumber and glazier. In 1812, Thomas Goddard bought these premises and the Bull next door, on behalf of the Goddard estate. James Crowdy died in 1808, but the adjacent land remained in his family until 1830, when his daughter Elizabeth Henrietta Crowdy sold it to Ambrose Goddard, and thereby it was also incorporated into the Lord of the Manor's estate. (See also Bull public house.)

Kempster & Son music shop

William John ('Jack') Kempster (1914-1986) was born in Swindon, the son of a GWR shunter. Jack also joined the railway and became a signal box operator, and was thus employed at Challow, Berkshire, when he met Pamela Evans (b. Wantage, 1924), the daughter of the family with whom he was lodging. They had a piano, which he played, and which was the catalyst for his interest in the piano as a musical instrument. Jack and Pamela married at Wantage in 1943. Jack was transferred to the signal box at Shrivenham station and, in 1945, the family (their first daughter was born at Wantage) moved into a flat in Manchester Road, Swindon. Jack had by then qualified as a piano teacher.

Almost at once, Jack Kempster answered an advertisement for a pianist for dancing in Trowbridge, and the family (their son Jeffery Howard Kempster having been born at Swindon in 1946) relocated there to Silver Street Lane, where they were surrounded by farms. In Trowbridge, Jack ran a small band and played as one of The Jolly Waggoners country-dance band. He also taught piano, bought old pianos that he then reconditioned and sold on, and had an arrangement with Ushers to maintain the pianos in their public houses. All of this suggested to him that there might be a decent living to be made in the piano market, and Swindon could be just the place to exploit it. In 1952, the family came back to Swindon and bought a residential property at 98 Commercial Road. While Jack set about converting this into business premises, Jeff went to College Street School. The conversion caused so much disruption that Jeff was sent to live for the duration with his father's parents in Swindon, and his sisters found themselves domiciled with their grandparents in Wantage.

At first, the business was called The Music Shop, and sold sheet music, brass instruments, harmonicas and accordions. Soon '78s' were added, the shellac records that preceded vinyl discs, and amplifiers. Whilst he was a pupil at Commonweal School, Jeff helped out in the shop on Saturdays, as would his sister Penny. Jack repaired and renovated pianos in his workshop at the rear. Throughout the tail end of the traditional jazz revival period of the 1950s and '60s, Jack Kempster's shop had the reputation of being the only place in Swindon where followers of the genre could be assured of finding recordings of sometimes the most obscure bands. The business was renamed Kempster & Son (The Music Shop) and when Jeff effectively took over in 1976, it was styled Kempster

& Son, as it has since remained. The record department was downstairs, where Jeff continued the policy of providing commercial records and many more specialist titles, and musical instruments were sold upstairs. When national chain stores began offering big discounts on records, Kempsters could not compete, so closed its record department in 1986.

Kimmerfields By 2006, there were plans to regenerate an area of Swindon between the railway station, the town's head post office in Islington Street, and the police station in Princes Street. This area was to be remodelled as a commercial and business centre called The Exchange, a name supplied by Forward Swindon, predecessors of The New Swindon Company. The chosen developers were AMEC Developments and its business partner Morley Fund Management, but this fell through. In 2008, the name of the project was changed to Union Square, and the deal was signed in that year between Muse Developments, Swindon Borough Council, and the New Swindon Company. A grant was to be supplied by the Home & Communities Agency.

The £350 million development, scheduled to start in 2010 and take a decade to complete, provided for shops, restaurants and cafés, but principally up to 16,000 square feet of office space, 450 homes, sheltered housing accommodation, and an 850-spaces car park. Muse Developments won a 'Property Deal of the Year Award' for the plans in 2009, but the financial recession and resulting Government spending cuts immediately slowed down the project. In 2013, Muse Developments changed the name of the development from Union Square to Kimmerfields. The half-baked rationale

for this was that design changes meant that the site was no longer square; that before the railway came to Swindon the area was covered in fields; it was on a band of kimmeridge clay; and a name change would avoid confusion with other Union Square projects being undertaken in the UK.

Work started on the first part of this scheme, on the former police station site, in 2012, and was completed in 2014 at a cost of £6.2 million. It comprised the car park, and forty-five assisted-living apartments called Kimmerfield Court, carried out by Swindon Borough Council and the housing group Green Square. Both are six-storeys-high and were built by John Sisk & Son Ltd.

King, George (1834-1872) The earliest known of Swindon's pioneering commercial photographers was born at Hastings, Sussex. By 1850, he was living with his widowed aunt, Sarah Tuck, in Short Hedge (part of what is now Devizes Road), who was described as a 'landed proprietor'. The sixteen-year-old King was already working as a photographer from her address. In 1866, he went into partnership with Edward Butler to form the photographic firm of Butler & King. Their business premises were at 8 Devizes Road, and remained there when Butler left in 1869 and King formed Dodson & King with Zephaniah Dodson. This partnership continued until 1872 when King died, aged just thirty-eight.

Kitto, Richard (1917-1999) In 1973, the Foundation for Alternatives in Urban Development set up a centre at Lower Shaw Farm, West Swindon and appointed Dick Kitto as the first warden. Brought up in London, Kitto had, after wartime service, enjoyed a creative and bohemian life in

Devon and Cornwall before spending two decades in education, mostly at Dartington Hall School in Devon. He already had a reputation as an organic grower, writer and educationalist, and this attracted him to Stan Windass, author of the *Where Do We Go From Here?* series of books, who lived near Oxford and was a key member of the Foundation. Once installed at Lower Shaw Farm, and with the help of Alexandra Merivale, Dick Kitto initiated courses in organic gardening, energy conservation, alternative medicines, and various forms of counselling and education. The Foundation had many high-profile patrons, and foremost thinkers of the time came together at Lower Shaw Farm to debate energy supply and conservation, land usage, health, food and education. There were regular meetings on these and related topics, aimed at discussing big issues and finding new solutions.

Dick Kitto was a large man, always in a state of perpetual excitement, always questioning, and bubbling with enthusiasm. Visitors who were invited to Lower Shaw Farm might stay for a week or a whole season. In 1976, he held three workshop camps there, each lasting two weeks. As a result of one about health, Dr Tom Heller moved to Sheffield, where he set up a cooperatively run medical centre in Durnall. Kitto was also involved in community matters; he founded Swindon Pulse, the organic retail cooperative, revitalised the Rural Settlement Movement, and helped to facilitate Education Otherwise, producing a newsletter for people who wanted to educate their children at home. Under his regime, Lower Shaw Farm became a host farm for Willing Workers on Organic Farms (WWOOF), and whilst he was there, he wrote and published *Composting: The Cheap and*

Natural Way to Make Your Garden Grow. He left Swindon in 1980, and continued to write books and magazine articles. (See also Pulse Wholefood Cooperative.)

Lansdown, Thomas Smith (1822-1895) In 1866, Lansdown designed and built his own home, Fairfield Lodge, Bath Road, in heavy Gothic style. He had a brief period as a Swindon architect and surveyor, during which time he designed the schoolroom adjacent to the Baptist Church in Fleet Street (1868), converted the GWR's 'barracks' on Faringdon Road into a church for the Wesleyan Methodists (also 1868), and The Great Western Hotel in Station Road (1870).

Lansdown was born at Broad Hinton; in 1847, he married Jane Hunt (b. Lyneham, 1817) at Wootton Bassett, although the couple were not resident in Swindon before the mid-1860s. By then, he was styled as architect and surveyor, and nurseryman and florist, the grounds adjacent to the east of Fairfield Lodge being laid out as a nursery. In 1877, he leased land on Swindon quarries from Ambrose Lethbridge Goddard, for the purpose of quarrying and lime burning. Two years later, he was adjudged bankrupt, and relocated into 1 Brunswick Terrace, Bath Road. Jane died in 1887; in 1889, Lansdown married the widow Rachel Organ, née Cook (b. Horton, Gloucestershire, 1825). They set up home at 18 King William Street, and Lansdown dropped all references to his former business life, advertising himself only as a stone quarryman. He never had any children. Meanwhile, Rachel's son by her first marriage, George Organ, had been left an interest in the Swindon quarries, and had come to live in the town with his family at 1 North View Cottages, Okus Road. After

Lansdown died, Rachel went to live with her son, where she died in 1899, leaving George Organ, quarry owner, £1,933. (See also Organ, George.)

Lethbridge Road In 1876, Ambrose Lethbridge Goddard (1819-98), his son Ambrose Ayshford Goddard, and James Copleston Townsend began to sell, by individual lots, sections of their land immediately to the west of Devizes Road. A.L. Goddard was Lord of the Manor of Swindon, his son was then a captain in Her Majesty's Regiment of Grenadier Guards, and Townsend was a Swindon solicitor who owned The Croft and lands thereabouts. The lots made up what was then described as 'an intended road', which became Lethbridge Road. Its name commemorated A.L. Goddard's mother, Jessie Dorothea née Lethbridge (1797-1843). The sale of the land carried the condition that the purchaser of each and every lot should within three years of completion 'erect, build and complete good and substantial houses ... to the satisfaction of the vendors and their surveyors'. In this way, c.1879-81, twenty-five houses were built on the south side of Lethbridge Road, and a further six were built on the north side. The developer of each plot of land built his property in such a way that the result in each case had the appearance of a terrace, but close inspection of the architectural detailing still clearly reveals the limits of each purchaser's building within the scheme.

Lethbridge Road, Clifton House
The last house to be built in Lethbridge Road was Clifton House, a small, three-storey villa composed of red bricks, with a roof of Welsh slate, on the corner with Devizes Road. The land on which this was built was purchased in 1881 from Ambrose Lethbridge Goddard, Lord of the Manor of Swindon, by Joseph Williams, a joiner and builder. He apparently made the purchase for his son, 'as a token of (his) love and affection'. The son was Frederick James Williams, also a builder, who erected Clifton House on the corner site soon afterwards. F.J. Williams made his own bricks at Wroughton, impressing his name in the frog of each. By 1891, he had given up the building trade and relocated to Oxford, where he became a licensed victualler. That year, he sold Clifton House to his unmarried sister Florence Mary Williams, who obtained a mortgage from the Swindon Permanent Building Society. In 1904, she married plumber and gas fitter Herbert John Dismore at the Congregational Church, Victoria Street. She thereafter re-mortgaged Clifton House several times, and let it as apartments, but remained in ownership until 1932. The property changed hands at least seven times over the next thirty years, and in the 1960s was the Swindon Driving Test Centre. Afterwards, the ground floor became derelict and was boarded up, although the upper floors were still lived in. Its current owner (2014) bought Clifton House in 1984, and converted it into an office and residential mix.

Lethbridge Road School When Lethbridge Road School was built across the western end of Lethbridge Road (1890-91), it backed onto the main Swindon quarries and had another quarry site immediately to the north of it. Not for several years would anything be made of its surroundings, but then the Town Gardens, which opened to the public in 1894, were created on part of it.

The front elevation of the original building is symmetrical and has great charm. It lacks the flamboyant decorative touches of Clarence Street School and is more homogeneous than Euclid Street School, with both of which it is contemporaneous. Lethbridge Road School effectively presents eleven bays and two storeys to its east-facing front. It is built of red brick with yellow and red terracotta dressings, and decorative motifs with large gabled sections at each end, each forward of the central section. In between are narrow, equally spaced, pedimented sections, each separated out by brick pilasters. There are decorative date stones in the pediments and decorative panels inset at intervals between the two levels. The other main decorative motifs are moulded stone string courses, hood mouldings, terracotta keystones, brick friezes and cornices. Little entrances marked 'Girls' and 'Infants', at the south end, are beneath little stone pediments with scroll brackets.

When Lethbridge Road School opened in 1891, the Swindon School Board appointed Frederick King (b. Ilminster, Somerset, 1865), who was living in Swindon by the late 1880s, as the school's first headmaster. He was the son of a tent maker. At the time, his home was 9 Springfield Road. With him were his wife, Elizabeth Sarah (b. St Pancras, London, 1864), whom he married in 1891 and who was a schoolmistress, and his brother John King (b. Ilminster, 1874), who was a pupil teacher. Frederick King's staff at Lethbridge School in 1891 included Sarah Ann Rance (b. Charing Cross, London, 1862), the schoolmistress. She was a 'second class certificated mistress, of the Home and Colonial Training College' who had previously taught at the school for infants in Newport Street. King's other staff were Lilian Rodwell (b. Leiston, Suffolk, 1869),

the assistant mistress, and first-year pupil teacher Alice Robinson (b. Worcester, 1879). Originally a mixed school for girls and boys between the ages of seven and fourteen, infants were admitted from 1892. Sarah Rance left c.1894 when she was appointed head teacher at Gorse Hill Infant School, and was replaced at Lethbridge Road by Miss A. Gover. Frederick King remained at Lethbridge Road until 1904 when Jennings Street School opened and he was appointed the first headmaster there. He was succeeded at Lethbridge Road by W. Anderson who, with Miss Gover, ran the school for several decades into the twentieth century.

In 1935, the infants moved out of the main building and into wooden huts, which were still in use in the 21st century. Lethbridge Road School became a mixed junior school in 1946. A new part was built adjacent to the north in 1999. In 2001, infants and juniors merged, and the resulting primary school gained academy status in 2011.

Limmex Corner see Tarrant's *Recollections*

Little London Mission During the 19th century, the area around Albert Street and Little London was at the centre of Old Town's red-light district. In 1902, a small rectangular hall was built in rough, randomly laid stone in Church Road, which linked Albert Street and Little London. Its roof was made of sheets of corrugated tin, and it had two square-headed windows to the roadway, and a small window with a depressed arch above the canopy over the doorway at the western end. A small metal cross was placed on the western apex of the roof, and the building was opened as the Little London Mission. Inside, it had a plain interior with a curtained rail in front of the altar, a harmonium to one side, and wooden chairs for the congregation. Sunday services were held there, and a Sunday school, until the place closed down in 1949. Four years later, it was sold to Pope Brothers, builders, of 13 Cricklade Street, whose yard abutted to the east of the mission building. The builders used it as a paint store. Part of this building survives in 2014, including the metal cross, which is still in situ.

Little London, thatched cottage
The last thatched cottage in Swindon was no. 4 Little London, named 'The Old Thatch'. It was built in about 1700, and was believed firstly to have been in the occupancy of that branch of the Lawrence family who were long-time glovers in the town, and thereafter belonged to their descendants. The earliest glover Lawrence of whom there is a record was Benjamin Lawrence, who was engaged in the trade in Swindon by the end of the 17th century. Railway labourer John Lawrence and his wife Elizabeth, who were both born in 1829, lived in this house. Their son, Alfred Lawrence, also lived at no. 4, and died in 1945 at the age of ninety, having been a bellringer at Christ Church for seventy-seven years. The last owners were Edward Liddiard and his wife Ivy née Gibbs, who believed she was a descendent of its first occupier.

Locomotive, The, Fleet Street
This public house, currently the Mailcoach, occupies the rear portion of what were premises of the same name fronting Fleet Street. Prior to the whole building being called the Mail Coach, when wine bars were in vogue, the front part was named the Wine Knot, and a separate bar called the Mail Coach was operated at the rear. The place

was built at the end of the 1840s by Richard Pearce Smith (b. Hinton, Somerset, 1791), when that section of Fleet Street was known as Bleat Lane. Its exact date is unknown because Smith had for some time been carrying on the business of 'beer retailer' close by, calling his business 'The Locomotive'. He bought the land for his new enterprise in 1848, and transferred the name when it was opened at some point early in the 1850s. He died in 1858, and the Locomotive was taken over by Elizabeth Jeffcoate (b. Frome, Somerset, 1820), herself recently widowed, whose husband Edward had run the Cricketer's Arms in High Street during the 1850s. The Locomotive was taken over from her in 1862 by Robert Shelley, who was the landlord until 1869, when George Smith (b. Bristol, 1823) took it on, and was succeeded c.1882 by Mary Ann Smith (b. Bristol, 1827), who was by then his widow. She kept the Locomotive until 1889 when it went to George Greenwood (b. Cirencester, 1837). Walter James Greenwood took over in 1894, and was still there into the twentieth century. By 1911, the licensee was Sydney James Strange (b. Kentish Town, London, 1874).

Lord Raglan, Cricklade Street: George Trout Nothing is known for certain of Trout's life before his arrival in Swindon, except that he was married; neither he nor his family can be traced on any censuses thereafter. (There is, however, slight circumstantial evidence that suggests he may have been a former stone-cutter (b. Street, Somerset, 1826) and if so, in 1856 he married Jane Pitman (b. Street, Somerset, 1816) at the Register Office in Wells.) However, he was in Swindon by 1863, which was when he took over the Lord Raglan from Thomas Jennaway (b.

Bucklebury, Berkshire, 1821), who had been the keeper of the beerhouse, then known as the Carrier's Arms, for the previous couple of years. In 1863, Trout brought James Davis and Charles Edwards before Swindon magistrates, charged with stealing his dog. Edwards was a bricklayer, a long-term lodger at the beerhouse. The thieves were found guilty and each sentenced to three months in Devizes prison.

This was an early indication of the litigious nature of George Trout. Between 1864 and 1867, he regularly brought his customers before the Swindon bench of magistrates, for non-payment of monies owing to him at the Lord Raglan or for causing a nuisance there. This could not have endeared him to his patrons, and may well have been one of the reasons why he was not successful in the venture. In 1864, he brought Francis Yeates of Stratton St. Margaret into court for being drunk and refusing to leave the Lord Raglan. Yeates had been a pedlar and was given the option of a 17/6d fine or fourteen days in prison. Daniel Beasant, agricultural labourer, who had been a resident at the Lord Raglan since Jennaway's time, was given the option of a ten-shilling fine or incarceration for seven days when Trout had him before the magistrates for similar offences, later the same year. And so it went on. James Iles was presented with an outstanding debt to Trout of 2/6d; Charles Horsell, slaterer and turner of Albert Street, had failed to find 7/6d; Henry Woolford had accumulated 14/- unpaid; George Mazowitch was 4/6d in arrears; William Perrymen owed 13/6d to Trout; Henry Wilson owed 14/6d; John Shipway, a bricklayer who was eventually committed to the lunatic asylum at Devizes, had an outstanding debt of 8/6d; and

George Gade was in arrears to the tune of 14/1d. Those with the larger debts, or those with smaller debts but who hardly had the finances to settle them, were allowed to pay in two equal instalments.

In 1866, George Trout was again in court, charging Thomas Gates, fishmonger of Little London, with violently assaulting him. Trout had decided to supplement his income by going into the fish trade. Gates, who had until then been a frequent visitor to Trout's establishment, took exception to this sudden competition. Thereafter, they frequently quarrelled, to the point where Trout threw out his business adversary and told him not to return. It did not help that Gates, by then drunk, tried to return and had to be ejected by Trout's wife. The next day, Gates waylaid Trout in an alley, and the two set about each other in front of witnesses. What brought the pair into court was that Trout charged him with unprovoked assault, during which he had to make his escape 'with a severe kick under his eye and another on his leg'. Gates was convicted, fined five shillings for the affray, with 8/6d costs, and ordered to keep the peace for six months.

While Trout was chasing others for unpaid debts in the courts, he was being pursued by the local authority for not paying his rates. He already had a court order against him for this, which he had refused to pay, when in 1867 William Hartley of Prospect Place, accountant by profession, clerk to the Wilts & Berks Canal Company and collector of rates for the Old Swindon Local Board, hauled him before the Swindon magistrates. Trout pleaded the 'inlegality' [sic] of the original order, but his claim failed and he was ordered to pay all costs. At about this time, he was thinking of embarking on a completely different venture.

In 1867, Trout leased from Ambrose Lethbridge Goddard 'land on or near the Quarries', on which to build. Historians have suggested that George Trout's intention was to build dwellings and a slaughterhouse there, and this appears to have been done, at least in part. In 1870, he quit the Lord Raglan and advertised: 'To be let a beer and lodging house in Swindon. Can make up forty beds. Trade from four to five barrels weekly. Apply to George Trout, the Lord Raglan'. In 1871, George Trout was declared bankrupt. (See also Quarries, The: Trout's Folly.)

Major, George (1814-1883) George Major (b. 1776) came from Bristol to settle in Swindon sometime between 1814 and 1819. He was a stonemason, and lived with his wife Mary and their firstborn, also George Major, in Newport Street. The first directory listing in which the stonemason is named is that for 1830, by which time three more of his remaining four children had been born. The last, John Major (b. 1831) also became a stonemason. In 1844, George Major (Jnr.) married Sarah Lye (b. Hungerford, 1821), the daughter of a draper. The couple, who were to have no children, lived in Horsefair Street (which became part of Devizes Road) with a servant. By 1851, George (Jnr) was a builder employing thirty men. The following year, he was commissioned by the directors of the Swindon Market Company to build its market house, which had been designed by Swindon architect Sampson Sage, in Market Square, Old Town. This he did in 1853, and is the building for which he is most remembered in Swindon. For a while, he lived in Quarry Road and worked part of the Swindon quarries. In the 1860s, the family relocated to Seaford, Sussex, where George Major was occupied as a surveyor for the rest of his life.

Manchester Road Until the late 1880s, a lane ran between the Queen's Arms Hotel (built 1841), in an isolated spot close to the railway line, and the Whale Bridge (built 1804) to the south over the Wilts & Berks Canal. In places, it was little more than a track, its primary function being to service Lower Eastcott Farm, which was about halfway along it. By the early 1870s, New Swindon, expanding eastwards from the railway village, had reached this lane with the building of Haydon Street and Mill Street, by the Swindon firm of Henry Merrin and John King (which partnership was dissolved in 1872). Haydon Street was named after James Haydon, a GWR Works manager, and Mill Street is thought to have been named after a mill associated with Lower Eastcott Farm, although there is no evidence for this.

Mill Street, west of the lane, developed in Manchester Road. Initially, it comprised eighty-one properties, in four terraced blocks. In the late 1880s, the lane itself was widened and named Corporation Street, and blocks of terraces were then planned for the whole of the area to the east of Corporation Street. This whole area had been part of the extensive Rolleston Estate, which was only then becoming available for purchase and development. The first of these properties, a terrace of eight buildings on each side of the road, was put up as an extension of Mill Street. That might have continued to be the name of the road as it progressed towards the County Ground, where the cricket pavilion and running track were built in 1893, and to where Swindon Town football club relocated three years later.

The sports site gave impetus to extending Mill Street east of Corporation Street. The first two of the planned blocks were completed on either side of the road, c.1897-1900: in all, forty terraced properties. This brought the thoroughfare as far as present-day Gladstone Street, at which point, in 1898, Strong & Co. of Romsey built the Eastcott Hotel to cater for the residential developments that were filling the area between the railway line and the canal. The early work on the Mill Street extension was carried out by Maxwell & Tuke; the business was run by the latter's son Francis William Tuke, since the deaths in 1893 of both founders, James Maxwell and William Charles Tuke. This firm had its headquarters in Manchester, so the part of Mill Street east of Corporation Street was incorporated into the new road, and from 1897, the whole thoroughfare was named Manchester Road. It was completely built up by 1902, with almost each run of terraces having a little corner shop. Between 1904 and 1929, the road was laid with tramlines, and a passing loop, for the tram service that operated between Clappen's Corner and Gorse Hill.

Manchester Road, No. 66 The former grocer's shop at 66 Manchester Road (in 2014, a slot machine and games parlour called 'Club Little Vegas'), is remarkable for its former quarter of a century as a grocery time capsule. For more than twenty-five years from the early 1980s, it remained closed, whilst its female owner, Edna Brain, lived the life of a recluse within its walls. The same display of packets from that time remained in the windows, gathering ever more dust and becoming increasingly faded in the sun, and much the same could be said of the thin stock of merchandise within. Its story began in the 19th century.

Ellen Opie was born in 1862 in St Stythians, Cornwall, the daughter of a granite worker. William George Eley was born at Highworth, also in 1862. The couple married in 1886, and the following year their daughter Elizabeth Grace Eley was born, when William was an assistant storekeeper in the GWR Works at Swindon. They set up home at 124 Chapel Street, but relocated to 101 Cricklade Street sometime after 1901, and were there when William died in the GWR hospital in 1910. Almost immediately, Ellen opened as a grocer, working from this address. In 1909, Elizabeth Grace Eley married Joseph Henry Wheeler (b. Swindon, 1886), who had been employed as a clerk at the GWR Works since 1901. This is an example of son following father in the Works, as Joseph Henry's father Joseph was also a clerk there. Joseph Henry and Elizabeth had one daughter, Edna Grace, and they lived with Ellen at 101 Cricklade Street, where the women continued to run the shop together. Joseph Henry Wheeler died in 1918.

In 1929, Ellen Eley and her daughter Elizabeth Grace relocated to 66 Manchester Road, a brick-built, mid-terrace house. They put in the ground-floor shop with its central doorway, flanked by small display windows, and set up the sign 'E. Eley' on the front elevation. In 1937, Edna Grace Wheeler, Elizabeth's daughter, married Albert George Brain, (b. Ealing, London, 1910). Ellen Eley died in 1940, and her daughter continued to run the grocer's shop at 66 Manchester Road on her own until 1950, when it was taken over by Albert and Edna Grace Brain. Elizabeth Grace continued to live there with her daughter and son-in-law (she died in 1974). When Albert died in 1983, Edna immediately shut the shop and retired upstairs, where she remained until she died in 2003. Between Albert's death and the reincarnation of the premises as a slot machine and games parlour, a generation was born, grew up, and had their own children, whilst the contents of the display windows of No. 66 Manchester Road, and the products on the shelves in its interior, remained frozen in time.

Manners, Alfred James (1870-1926)

In 1904, Alfred Manners, a baker, retail confectioner, and the proprietor of a dining room in his home at 104 Victoria Road, Swindon, leased the town's New Queen's Theatre from Ernest Carpenter, the man who had planned the property, had it built, and owned it. Manners and his family had been in Swindon for just four years.

Born in Kensington, London, Alfred Manners travelled extensively as a young man, notably in China and America. In 1892, at St Pancras, London, he married Ellen Eliza from Longparish, near Andover, Hampshire. The couple had five children: Esther, who was known as Dolly (b. Longparish, 1893); Alfred James (b. Paddington); and Winifred (b. 1901), Elsie (b. 1902) and Reginald Charles (b. 1906) – all in Swindon. His tenure at the theatre was marked by his willingness to be available at all times, in which he behaved almost like a traditional actor- manager. His numerous appearances on stage, when he spoke directly to audiences, brought him in such regular contact with patrons that he soon became a familiar and well-liked figure around the town. He revamped the theatre, organised special bus and train services for patrons, was instrumental in launching and running numerous charitable appeals, and in soliciting donations for the Victoria hospital. In 1907, he changed the theatre's name to The Empire, decided to give up the lease, and left in the face of a public outcry imploring him not to do so.

Six months later, he was back in charge of The Empire and continued to attract an extremely wide range of quality drama and musical productions of all kinds whilst maintaining his charity work. He also became lessee and manager of the Garrison Theatre, Tidworth, in 1909. In 1913, he bought The Picture House in Regent Circus and renamed it The Ideal Picture House. When the First World War broke out, Manners and his daughter Dolly put on big fundraising events at The Empire in support of servicemen overseas, and special theatre shows for their wives and families at home. In 1914, Dolly Manners established what was at first called the 'Christmas Pudding Fund', aimed at raising sufficient money to buy gifts of food for Swindon servicemen abroad. This became the 'Soldiers' and Sailors' Christmas Gift Fund', by which, annually, the lads benefited from a gift parcel and an especially printed card bearing a patriotic verse, and stirring words of comfort and support from the Manners family.

Lighter entertainments were preferred after the war, and Manners programmed less challenging plays, comedies, musicals, and revues to meet this demand. He was also responsible for remodelling and refurbishing the interior of the theatre on several occasions. In 1925, he sold his interests in The Empire and relocated to Christchurch, Hampshire. The following year, his son Alfred was drowned when he fell overboard from the ship taking him to a new life of tobacco growing in Rhodesia. This had a devastating effect on Alfred Manners, and he died later that year.

Mela This is a Sanskrit word used to define a wide variety of cultural, religious or commercial meetings, or fairs. The first

Swindon Mela, a celebration of South Asian arts and crafts, music, dances, and food was held on 2 August 2003 in the Town Gardens, Old Town, and has since been a one-day annual extravaganza. The precedent for using this site, which is Grade II listed by English Heritage and is centred on the existing bandstand stage on The Bowl and the central area of the park, were the concerts of world music and dancing that were held there, supported by the University of Bath in Swindon. An immediate cultural forerunner, also held in The Bowl, was a Bhangra concert, which featured Indian food. The Swindon Mela is sponsored by local companies and organisations, and is put together by a voluntary management committee.

Methodist Central Hall The Methodists acquired a site in Clarence Street, next to one of its minister's houses, and Revd W.J. Chant set about organising fundraising for what was called a new central mission hall. The architect was William F. Bird, of Midsomer Norton, and the hall was constructed in brick, with Monks Park freestone facings, by Tydeman Brothers of Swindon, working under the auspices of Revd Ralph Pritchard. The first stone was laid on 17 April 1907 by the Lord of the Manor, Major Fitzroy Pleydell Goddard, Justice of the Peace and High Sheriff of Wiltshire, using a silver trowel presented to him for the event. Goddard placed a cheque for five guineas on the stone, and a bottle was laid in a cavity beneath it with the names of the circuit ministers in it, and copies of the *Swindon Advertiser* and the *North Wilts Herald*. At the same time, a stone was laid to the memory of the recently deceased Alderman James Hinton (1842-

1907), who had been a generous supporter of the movement.

The hall was built fronting Clarence Street, with its rear admitting onto Regent Circus, and included space for 1,050 people to be seated, and the building had ten classrooms and offices. It was all heated by a system of hot water pipes, installed by James Lott & Son of Swindon. The place was soon called the Methodist Central Hall, and became well known for its men's mission, The Swindon Brotherhood, its Young Men's Club, and its Swindon Brotherhood Football Club. A Brotherhood Cup was instituted and competed for in the Borough League, but the club itself folded when many of its number were required for service during the First World War. The hall was enlarged in the 1960s, when it was used as a venue for public concerts. It became the venue for the Bournemouth Symphony Orchestra in Swindon until the Wyvern Theatre was opened in 1971, and the orchestra reluctantly relocated there. That was also the year in which the Methodist Central Hall closed. Soon afterwards badly damaged by fire, it was demolished in 1985.

Monopoly, Swindon edition In March 2013, it was publicly announced that Swindon was to have its own version of the popular board game, which was first published in 1934, with the town's landmarks being substituted for those on the conventional board. Townspeople were asked to nominate venues and property landmarks they would like to be illustrated, local charities to be featured, and suitable subjects for the 'Chance' and 'Community Chest' cards. The Swindon edition of the board game was launched at the town's STEAM Museum on Friday, 11 October 2013. It was made by Winning Moves of Praed Street, London, under licence from Hasbro with whom it had held licence agreements since 1995. At the launch, Dan Taylor, head of custom games at Winning Moves, gave away Monopoly money; Swindon's Pegasus Brass Band played, a five-foot replica of the board was displayed, and the game was played. A new playing piece, the likeness of a cat, was introduced for this edition. The selling price was £24.99.

Moran's Electrical and Radio Shop Walter John Moran, electrical and radio engineer, opened his shop at 153 Victoria Road, Swindon in 1923. When it closed, sixty-eight years later in 1991, it was still being run by his children, Trevor and Eileen. Walter John Moran (b. Eastbourne, Sussex, 1882) was the son of a cabinet maker, and his wife who was a lodging house keeper in the town. His father died in 1899, by which time Walter John was a gas fitter in his hometown. In 1906, he married Alice Beatrice Hickman in Eastbourne, and within two years they had relocated to 2 Brunswick Street, Swindon, and he was working as a self-styled electrical wireman. There, Eileen was born in 1910, and Trevor was born in 1923. Eileen went into the business in 1927, and Trevor followed in 1939, although his career in the shop was interrupted by military service during the Second World War. Walter John Moran became chairman of the Swindon branch of the Electrical Contractors' Association. Eileen and Trevor took over the business when he died in 1964.

Moran's shop premises remain on Victoria Road, with its tall windows separated by narrow, plain muntins, its chamfered, recessed porch and doorway next to the door leading to the flat above where Eileen lived. Its interior was remarkable in that its fixtures and fittings never changed from the moment they were installed, even though the stock was kept up to date – electrical goods, light fitments and lampshades displayed in the windows and hung from the ceiling. Such was its reputation, other retailers of lampshades and electrical goods in Swindon would readily suggest Moran's on Victoria Road if goods were not available in their own branches.

Morgan, Mary (b. 1933) Since she answered an advertisement for the job in *The Oldie* magazine in 2007, placed by tour operator Canterbury Travel, Mary Morgan has been the world's official 'Mother Christmas'. She is the 'partner' of Santa Claus in Lapland, to whom thousands of children write, at the venue to which many are taken by aeroplane and coach in the weeks before Christmas. Each November and December, Mary spends six weeks deep in a forest in Lapland, where it is very dark and freezing cold.

Born in Birmingham, Mary Morgan came to Swindon in 1970 when she was appointed as the first public relations officer for the Wyvern Theatre, which opened in 1971. Before that, the one-time variously telephone systems draughtswoman, beauty consultant and cosmetics salesperson had run the Boat and Bottle public house, beside the river at Thorpe St Andrew, near Norwich, Norfolk. In 1970, although she had no previous experience in the theatre world, she became public relations representative for the Belgrade Theatre at Coventry, after responding to an advertisement in the *Coventry Evening Telegraph*. In Coventry, she was also involved with the Samaritans.

Her success in filling the Coventry theatre helped her to land the Swindon job, where for five years she was a powerhouse in public relations. She left in 1974, having been inspired to make a career out of charity work following a meeting with Mother Teresa of Calcutta. Mary joined Help the Aged, working in Swindon and the Midlands, and eventually in Canada and America. She began working for Help the Aged in Ottawa, where she was concerned with explaining the problems associated with growing old to children in schools, and then opened an office for Help the Aged in New York. She has also lived in Haiti, but returned in 2003 to live permanently in Swindon. She has since continued her charity work with the Prospect Hospice, and is a volunteer at Royal Wootton Bassett Museum and at West Swindon public library, where she takes children's literacy groups.

Mortimer, Edmund Walter 'Monty' (1905-1985) In 1932, on his kitchen table in Whiteman Street, E.W. 'Monty' Mortimer invented what became the world's first automatic record changer to be made commercially available to record player manufacturers. At the time, he was working for Garrard Engineering and Manufacturing Company in Newcastle Street. Born at Rendcomb, Gloucestershire, Monty was the son of a groom, Joseph Edmund Mortimer (b. North Cerney, 1879) and his wife Alice née Brayne (b. Eynsham, Oxfordshire, 1877), who married in 1905 at Cheltenham. Monty was also born at Rendcomb. By 1911, the family was in Swindon at 10 Shelley Street. Joseph worked in the town, first as a groom, and later as a boiler cleaner at the GWR Works, latterly becoming a railway carriage frame builder. Monty left school in 1919, and

in 1921, the year that his father Joseph died, he was accepted into Garrard as a precision engineering apprentice. He made one of the earliest radio sets at the start of the 1920s, and until 1939 held an experimenter's radio licence for manipulating models by radio control. Much of his spare time was spent in building working scale models or aeroplanes, locomotives, traction engines, hot air engines and tramcars. Of particular relevance to Swindon was his one-sixteenth scale model of Swindon Corporation Tramways tram No.6, recreated in every detail to the original 1902-05 plans of Dick Kerr & Co. of Preston, the original makers of the vehicle.

Monty continued as a Garrard apprentice until 1926, and the following year was asked to develop an electric motor to replace the conventional spring wound gramophone motor. In 1931, he married Lily Frances Dorothy Easley (b. Swindon, 1903), a GWR wagon painter's daughter, and the couple moved into Whiteman Street. At the start of the 1930s, there were only three automatic record changers on the market. Only one of these was British; they were all expensive and not generally available to gramophone manufacturers. At his home, Monty set about designing what became the RC1, Garrard's first automatic record changer; he used a simple lathe that cost £2/15s, which was driven by an electric motor from his wife's Singer sewing machine. He invented a unique record changer, in that all the motions required for the pickup arm derived from one cylindrical cam. The machine could accommodate ten-inch or twelve-inch records, eight at a time; it could also repeat any record, and it switched itself off when the last record had played.

The prototype of this hugely important

development in the turntable industry, having been built in the kitchen in Whiteman Street, was delivered to Hubert V. Slade, managing director of Garrard at Swindon, wrapped in a copy of the *News of the World*. Garrard's agents filed patents for it the next day; Monty was put in charge of production, assembly, and testing of the RC1. The first production model was assembled at 2 a.m. in the morning, and just seven hours later, the chief engineer of RGD Birmingham, one of the country's leading radiogram manufacturers, arrived to take delivery. Monty's invention was first announced at the British Industries Fair of 1932. Thereafter, the RC1 was in production for two years before the RC1a was introduced, which allowed a mixed pile of ten-inch and twelve-inch records to be played automatically.

Monty continued to invent record playing and associated mechanisms, for which he took out twenty-four different patents during his working life. By 1961, he was Garrard's research engineer, and was latterly the company's technical sales manager. He retired in 1971, and the following year, he was made a Fellow of the Audio Engineering Society of New York. Monty Mortimer and Lily's son Brian Edmund Mortimer (b. Swindon, 1939) joined Garrard as an apprentice in 1955. He married Vera Kathleen Reeves (b. Wallingford, 1942) in 1963. She too, worked for Garrard, and was the firm's first beauty queen. The company introduced quality control in 1970; Brian became the quality control manager and held the position until 1982, when the production line was relocated to Brazil. Edmund Walter Mortimer and Brian Edmund Mortimer, father and son, have the distinction of spanning unbroken employment over Garrard's sixty-three years in Swindon.

Nash family and their sweet shops The retail confectionery business that William Nash established in Swindon in the 1870s eventually had several shops and, run by members of the same family, continued for the next century. In 1863, William Nash (b. Badbury, Wiltshire, 1840) married Elizabeth Hunt (b. Broad Hinton, 1842), and the couple lived for a while in London and relocated to Swindon in 1866, where they set up at 2 Havelock Street. William was a labourer in the GWR. The couple had several children. The eldest, Edmund William (b. Lambeth, London, 1866) was, by the age of fifteen, a labourer in the GWR Works. The other children were all born in Swindon: Clara Ann (b. 1867); Thomas E. (b. 1869); Elizabeth M. (b. 1871); Ada Mary (b. 1877); Asenath Martha (b. 1879); and Lily Amelia (b. 1881). At some point in the 1870s, William left the railway's employment and relocated to 32 Bridge Street, where he began making and selling sweets. He took on an assistant for his confectioner's shop, Martha Hunt (b. Broad Hinton, 1852).

The business was successful enough for William's son, Edmund William, to also leave his job with the GWR, and take over as a sugar boiler at 32 Bridge Street. In 1887, Edmund William married Myra Beasent (b. Lydiard Millicent, 1868) in a double marriage with his sister Clara Ann, who was espoused to William Edward Long (b. Studland, Dorset, 1866), a GWR Works' boilermaker. Edmund and Myra's first child was Francis George F. Nash (b. Swindon, 1886), who would become a blacksmith's striker in the GWR Works. Then came Rosie Maud Nash (b. Swindon, 1889) and Winifred Nash (b. Swindon, 1892). William Nash left the business at 32 Bridge Street in the care of Edmund, and in the 1880s he opened a new confectionery shop at 64 Regent Street, where he also employed two shop assistants. By 1899, William's wife Elizabeth had opened sweet shops at 10 Wood Street and 48 Victoria Road. By 1901, William Nash had decided to retire, and went to live at 150 Goddard Avenue, with his wife and three of their children, Francis G.F., Asenath Martha, and Lily Amelia.

Ada Mary Nash and Lily Amelia were together as confectioners in the Bridge Street shop by 1901. In 1902, Ada Mary married Henry James Henley (b. Jersey City, America, 1864, but of Bristol parentage). He was a coal merchant, but she continued as a confectioner, running the sweet shop at 32 Bridge Street. Also in 1902, Lily Amelia, who was by now running Nash's sweet shop at 167 Rodbourne Road, married Frederick John Hughes (b. Marylebone, London, 1879), who was a machine planer in the GWR Works. Their first two children were Alan Geoffrey Hughes (b. Swindon, 1905) and Doris Edna Hughes (b. Swindon, 1910). In the Swindon Society's collection, there is a photograph of Nash's sweet shop in Rodbourne Road, taken c. 1910, which shows Lily Amelia and her daughter Doris posing in the doorway. It became famous for its ice cream and its bags of sweets known as 'penny big lots'. Asenath Martha Nash became the confectioner at the sweet shop at 150 Goddard Avenue. In 1904, she married Frederick George Dowse (b. Swindon, 1882), who had begun his working life with the GWR as a slipper boy. It was a double marriage with Rosie Maud Nash and William George Wilkins (b. Bridgwater, Somerset, 1874), who was a GWR passenger train shunter. Frederick Dowse was a GWR rail motor conductor, working at Frome, Somerset, when he was taken ill, and he died in 1906, just two years after his marriage.

His wife continued to run the shop in Goddard Avenue.

By 1911, Clara Ann Long née Nash had also been widowed and had taken on the shop at 10 Wood Street, where she lived with her two sons Cuthbert H.W. Long (b. Swindon 1895), a frame maker in the GWR Works, and Dennis H.D. Long (b. Swindon, 1904). Thus continued the confectionery businesses that William Nash had established, and helped his children to develop. The last of Nash's sweet shops was at 32 Regent Circus, where it continued to trade until the 1970s, and was one of the last places to stock Kunzle cakes. In 1980, Ken White painted a mural beside Cambria Bridge depicting Ada Mary Nash and Lily Amelia Nash in the doorway of the shop at 32 Bridge Street.

Nationwide building, Piper's Way The Nationwide Building Society was effectively 146 years old when its £50m landmark headquarters was opened on 15 April 1992, by its then chairman, Sir Colin Corness. It was initially called 'Croft Centre', but this was later changed to 'Nationwide House'.

The Society can trace its origins back to the Provident Union Building Society that was established at Ramsbury, Wiltshire, in 1846. Mergers began to take place, but it was those that followed the opening of the Southern Co-operative Building Society in 1884 that led directly to Nationwide when, in 1970, the Co-operative Building Society changed its name to Nationwide Building Society. In 1987, it merged with the Anglia Building Society, and was briefly Nationwide Anglia before returning to its former name in 1992. By then, it had been in Swindon for eighteen years, and had enjoyed great success.

Nationwide opened an administrative centre in Princes Street on 29 October 1974; it was then the third-largest building society in Britain. More properties were taken on as its activities expanded, and by the late 1980s it was working out of six sites around the town. This, and the popularity of the Nationwide FlexAccount banking services, made it desirable for the company to centralise on a custom-designed headquarters. The freehold of 28.5 acres was purchased from Thamesdown Borough Council in January 1989. The building was designed by Holford Associates, and built in just ninety weeks, from April 1990, by Taylor Woodrow Construction Southern Limited, with the help of ten specialist sub-contractors. It was built around a steel frame, and clad externally with powder-coated, white aluminium panels. Some 22,000 tons of concrete, 3,200 tons of steel, and 3.2 acres of glass went into its construction. It also had 349 miles of cabling (excluding data and telephone) and 4.8 acres of carpeting.

The Society provided a number of facilities for its staff at the new headquarters. These included aerobics, an alternative therapy suite, cricket pitch, football pitch, gymnasium, hairdressers, an internet café, netball, perimeter jogging track, a pool, restaurant (expected to provide 1,100 meals each day), rugby pitch, shop, sports pavilion and table tennis. In the adjacent grounds, which are divided from their surroundings by a ha-ha to prevent animals from encroaching, Nationwide planted 70,000 trees, and Thamesdown Borough Council added another 24,000. The focal point of the grounds is a lake, with a one-acre surface area and three fountains.

New Swindon Company, The This organisation, also known as the Swindon Urban Regeneration Company, was set up in 2002 under a Government initiative to regenerate town centres. At the time, it was one of only twelve such undertakings. It was part-owned by Swindon Borough Council, the Homes and Community Agency, and the South-West Regional Development Agency, and involved local businesses, the National Trust, the Swindon Redevelopment Agency, and English Partnerships, the national equivalent of the Regional Development Agencies. Its brief was to concentrate on the centre of Swindon, and one of its first moves was an open invitation to residents of Swindon to say what they wanted in the town. Only two hundred people (of an estimated population of 200,000) did so, proving what the company described as 'apathy' and a 'poverty of aspiration' among the town's residents.

The New Swindon Company divided the town centre into four sectors: Station Gateway (around the railway station), the Heritage Quarter (taking in Emlyn Square and the Mechanics' Institute), the Retail Core (incorporating the Brunel Centre) and the Commercial and Cultural Quarter, around Regent Street. On 8 July 2004, it unveiled a £1 billion scheme for the revitalisation of New Swindon's town centre, which included 100,000 square metres of retail and leisure development, 90,000 square metres of new office space and 3,000 new homes. In 2008, it contracted Capita Architecture to draw up a strategy for remodelling the area between the former college in Regent Circus and the magistrates' court in Princes Street. The company was largely ineffective and was heavily criticised by the general public, members of the Borough Council, and organisations such as the Swindon Civic Trust, which put forward its own proposals for the regeneration of central Swindon. The New Swindon Company was closed down on 31 March 2010, and was replaced by Forward Swindon. (See also Forward Swindon.)

Niblett & Co., aerated water manufacturers One of the most evocative images of Swindon's historic businesses in the town's photographic archive is that of Niblett & Co. It was taken in 1890 and shows their premises on the corner of Cheltenham Street and Milford Street. A large group of children, clearly in their best clothes, and possibly on their way to an outing via the nearby railway station, are positioned around Niblett's, possibly to suggest that they are about to take with them bottles of the firm's mineral water. Niblett & Co. had taken over these premises, until then a butcher's shop, in c.1882.

The members of the Niblett family involved in this enterprise came from the Stroud and Cheltenham areas. Charles Niblett, the 'founder', was born in Painswick in 1817. By the time he married Selina Hunt (b. Stroud, 1828), he was a 'ginger beer manufacturer', probably based in Stroud. The couple set up home in Albion Street, Cheltenham, where Charles was variously described as a 'confectioner' and 'soda water manufacturer'. One of their sons, Alfred Niblett (b. Cheltenham, 1856) was, at sixteen, his father's assistant in the firm, and eventually became foreman of the Cheltenham works. In 1873, Charles went into voluntary liquidation as an 'aerated water manufacturer and fruiterer'.

Meanwhile, Henry Haycraft, a surgeon in High Street, Stroud, living next door

to a chemist and druggist, employed John Niblett (b. Kingscote, Gloucestershire, 1830) as an assistant surgeon, c.1850. The latter occupation held more appeal for John who, by the time he married Mary Ann Peacey (b. Stroud, 1831) in 1854, was himself a chemist and druggist in the town. They had three children: Frederick John (b. Stroud, 1856), Amy Kate (b. Stroud, 1858) and Norman Edward (b. Stroud 1860). This last named child never knew his father because John Niblett died in 1859. Mary Ann continued the business of chemist and druggist, with David Smith (b. Newton, Montgomeryshire, 1835) as her assistant and shop manager. The couple eventually married. None of John and Mary Ann's children went into the pharmaceutical side; both boys opted for the mineral water business, which they would develop in Stroud.

By the time he was twenty-five, Frederick John Niblett was in charge at Stroud, describing himself as 'a mineral water manufacturer and an associate of the pharmaceutical society of Great Britain'. Norman Edward joined him as a 'mineral water manufacturer'. Since Charles Niblett was no longer operating in Cheltenham, it would effectively have been the Stroud Niblett & Co. that came to Swindon in 1874. Then, Charles Niblett, only recently in liquidation, appears to have been installed as a fruiterer, and then grocer and seller of aerated water at 7 Faringdon Street. He remained there for about three years. About five years later, Niblett & Co. took over the corner shop at 20 Cheltenham Street, declaring itself at Stroud and Cheltenham on the windows, but labelling its bottles 'Stroud and Swindon'. It remained at the Cheltenham address until a final move to Lagos Street in 1902, and ceased trading in Swindon c.1910, when the manager was Henry Niblett (b. Stroud, 1873), who lived at Swindon in Southbrook Street. The Lagos Street premises were taken over by John Russell Bown (b. Stratton St Margaret, 1863), mineral water manufacturers. The firm of J.R. Bown stayed in the Lagos Street premises until 1959, when mineral water manufacturers Leese Ing & Co. acquired the building. From the 1980s, the premises had various retail uses, but the building was gutted by fire in February 2013.

Noad family see Tarrant's *Recollections*

Norman, Nigel (b. 1942) The originator of the extensive Swindon Music Scene website and the group Rockers Re-United was born at the Cheriton Nursing Home, Springfield Road. He was the only child of a bank manager; the family lived in Avenue Road, and he went to Lethbridge Road infant and junior schools before attending Commonweal Grammar School from the age of eleven. By the age of seven, he had begun piano lessons with Dora Cutler in Croft Road, and by the mid-1950s was being taught by Alvin W. Hext at 81 Avenue Road. Hext was a former band musician who introduced Nigel to a range of different musical styles. In 1960, he joined a strict tempo dance band called The Rhythmics, playing piano. Then he met Justin Hayward (later of The Moody Blues fame), who was playing in a rock band called The Offbeats, changing from strict tempo to rock 'n' roll in order to join him. The Offbeats played a summer season at the Springfield Theatre, Jersey, incurring the displeasure of Dr Harold Craig, the headmaster at Commonweal. Dr Craig lived at Aldbourne. His doctorate was in

nuclear physics, and he took up his position at Commonweal when he was discharged after the Second World War with the rank of Lieutenant Commander.

Shortly after the Jersey episode, Nigel Norman (bass and vocals), Justin Hayward (lead guitar and vocals), Tony Cole (rhythm guitar) and Jeff Bull (drums) formed The Whispers, a very successful, local rock band that supported many of the top professional bands of the day. In 1965, Justin Hayward left to develop his own career; The Whispers changed their name to All Things Bright and went to Germany, where they played in clubs and at American military bases. By the age of twenty-four, Nigel Norman had stopped gigging, and started on a career in banking, computer systems and mobile telephony. He eventually became a self-employed consultant in the mobile telephony industry, operating worldwide until his retirement in 2005. Afterwards, he concentrated on researching the history of music in Swindon, and making the information available online. (See also Rockers Re-United; Swindon Music Scene)

Oddfellows Arms, Cricklade Street When, 2007-9, Ward Homes created a residential development on a brownfield site off Cricklade Street in Old Swindon, they called it The Old Quarter. Two distinguished buildings, fronting the street, were incorporated into this development, namely no. 42 of 1729, which John Betjeman described as 'one of the most distinguished town houses in Wiltshire', and a double-fronted, gabled, and part-timber decorated, tile-hung property, a little to the north. The latter had once been two dwellings, one of which had a beerhouse attached. It progressed in the licensed trade from the late 1840s, and was known to the early Victorians as The Plume of Feather; later Victorians knew it as the Oddfellows Arms. In the 21st-century redevelopment, an underground tunnel was discovered alongside it, leading towards High Street, and the property was renamed Betjeman House. John Compton, a gardener and later seedsman, seems to have lived on part of the premises by the late 1840s, and probably kept the beerhouse as The Plume of Feathers. During the 1850s, it came into the hands of William Bizley, formerly a carpenter and wheelwright, who ran it as a shopkeeper (in what trade is unknown) and beer retailer. It became the Oddfellows Arms during his occupancy, and so remained.

Oddfellows Arms, North Street

This establishment is named only in the 1861 census, although its exact location is uncertain. It appears to have been run by John Dyer (b. Purton, 1828), a carpenter and joiner. Afterwards, Dyer and his family relocated to Prospect Place, Hammersmith, London, where he carried on the trade of 'house joiner', and where his son William John Dyer later set up as a staircase builder.

Oddfellows Arms, Queen Street

This beerhouse is associated with Stephen Cox (b. Aldbourne, Wiltshire, 1808), who was a labourer in his home village until sometime in the 1850s. He then relocated to Queen Street, Swindon, which was built about the middle of that decade, and became a milk seller. There is no suggestion that he also sold beer from these premises prior to the 1871 census. It seems likely that the Oddfellows Arms came into being during the 1870s when Cox made his beerhouse out of two adjacent dwellings. Also likely is that

by the time the property was sold in 1886, it had already closed for business, gone into private hands, and was, much later, demolished. Stephen Cox took up farming at Stratton St Margaret.

Okus, No. 1 see Organ, George

Old Locomotive beerhouse The

exact date of building is unknown, but this canal-side beerhouse was part of a little run of properties put up probably at the same time in the early 1840s by landowner John Henry Harding Sheppard, on one of whose fields the beerhouse was constructed on the west side of the North Wilts Canal. The associated dwellings were called 'Sheppard's Cottages'. The Old Locomotive belonged to the Wilts & Berks Canal Company, which had acquired the North Wilts Canal in 1822. A drawing of that part of the canal, allegedly done in the 1840s, shows the beerhouse to be a tall, two-storey building with external chimneystacks, hard by the canal bridge. In 1842, its keeper was S. Manning, of whom nothing is known. He was followed by Samuel Lay (b. Bradwell, Buckinghamshire, 1803), who was styled 'publican', although he was also a railway haulier. So too, was his successor, Charles Irestone (b. Grove, near Wantage, Berkshire, 1817), who had lived in one of the adjacent cottages with his family during Lay's tenure. By 1864, Irestone had been succeeded as 'beer-seller' by William Hall (b. Gloucester, 1837). By the mid-1870s, the beerhouse keeper at the Old Locomotive was John H. Matthews (b. Keevil, Wiltshire, 1837). The Great Western Railway Company demolished the beerhouse after they purchased both the building and the surrounding land in 1888, in order to widen the bridge and generally expand the railway works.

Organ, George (1856-1928) No. 1 Okus Road is a fine, late Victorian villa, on the corner with Goddard Avenue. It dates from 1900, when the roadway that led along the northern edge of the Swindon quarries began to be built up at its western end, in an area hitherto known as The Sands. The property was called North View by George Organ, the man for whom it had been built, presumably named after North View Cottages, Okus, where he had lived with his mother Rachel Lansdown. No. 1 Okus Road may well have been the result of her bequest to him.

There are three key players in the story of George Organ. One is Rachel Cook (b. Horton, Gloucestershire, 1825) – George's mother, daughter of farmer James Cook; another is her sister Sylvester Cook (b. Kingswood near Wotton-under-Edge); and the third is Thomas Smith Lansdown (b. Broad Hinton, 1822). Rachel Cook married Henry Organ in 1852, and their only son George Organ was born in 1856. Henry died in 1859, and for a while Rachel took on the running of her father's farm, although he was still alive. In 1851, Sylvester Cook married Edward Lansdown (b. Wootton Bassett, 1828), a carpenter and joiner who latterly became a builder in London. Their daughter was Clara Lansdown (b. Limehouse, London, 1857). In 1871, George Organ began to learn scale making at the long-established firm then headed by William Alfred Herbert at King's Cross. He was to remain with the firm for nearly thirty years, and became Herbert's highest paid scale maker. Meanwhile, in Swindon in 1877, architect Thomas Smith Lansdown leased land on Swindon quarries for the purpose of stone quarrying and lime burning.

In 1887, George Organ married Clara Lansdown at Shoreditch, and they lived at 25 Albion Street, Islington in a household of craft workers and artisans. Within four years, they had relocated to 174 Pentonville Road, London. The widowed Rachel Organ married Thomas Smith Lansdown in 1889. She was his second wife, and he was the brother of Edward Lansdown, whom her sister had married. Thomas died in 1895, leaving his lease at the Swindon quarries in the hands of his wife's son George. He gave up the scale-making trade and relocated from London to Swindon, where his family took up residence at 1 North View Cottages, Okus, and he became a 'quarry owner and lime burner'. His mother Rachel, now widowed for the second time, went to live with them.

When she died in 1899, she left her son £1,933. Within two years, he had built 1 Okus Road. By the time George died, his son with Clara, Henry James Organ (b. Islington, 1879; d. 1961), was a quarry owner in his own right at Swindon.

Parade, The The Parade was constructed, 1961-64, along the former site of the Wilts & Berks Canal where it ran through central Swindon. It was part of the redevelopment of the retail hub of the town, covering about 150 yards at right angles to either side of the main shopping street. On the western side, The Parade terminated at the west end of those buildings remaining that were at one time in the control of the New Swindon Gas Company (established 1863). It ended, to the east, where the Wilts & Berks Canal had formerly met with the North Wilts Canal. Throughout the development of this site, an old canal milestone advising 'Semington 26 miles' was retained, although it has been much moved about within the short stretch on the western side of Regent Street. In order to create The Parade, a number of properties and business premises were demolished. On the west side, to the south, were mainly the long back gardens of Cromwell Street, but to the north were the remains of the gas works. There was also a terrace known as Cambria Houses, and some properties still standing next to the site of the Golden Lion public house, which had been demolished in 1958. All of these were removed to facilitate The Parade. On the northern side of the canal site, to the east of Regent Street, had been Albion Cottages, a terrace that had faced the canal and had little front gardens. What remained of these was also taken down.

Initially, the site was built up on both sides only to the east; on the west side, only the north side was built up and shops put in. Here, a line of trees was planted, and a few seats were inserted facing the shops, from which they were effectively separated by the entire width of the former canal and towpath on the north bank. Thus, it remained until the development of the Brunel Centre and its environs in the 1970s. To the east of Regent Street, The Parade was 'enhanced' by regular bench seating and rectangular concrete containers for ornamental planting; it was also, for a decade from 1966, the site of the infamous and much disliked cube waterfall feature. The section to the west of Regent Street is now called Canal Walk; to the east, it is still The Parade.

Particular Baptist Chapel, South Street see Strict and Particular

Passmore, Richard Keylock (1845-1927) One of Swindon's earliest commercial photographers, Richard Passmore, was born at Bristol, the son of painter and glazier Hercules Passmore (b. Bristol, 1814) and his wife Mary née Keylock

(b. Latton, 1814). The couple married in 1837 and the family came to Swindon in the early 1850s, first to Albert Street and then to settle in Victoria Street. Photography, then in its infancy, appealed to Richard who, by the age of sixteen, was already styled 'artist in photography'. Initially, the enterprise was named H. & R. Passmore, probably to give some credibility in the face of Richard's comparative youth, but he was already a portrait painter and a supplier of artists' materials to the general public. However, when Hercules died in 1864, Richard relinquished his interest in photography in favour of his father's occupations, and became a painter and glazier. He lived at 1 Victoria Street, where his mother stayed on as housekeeper. In 1872, he married Jane Thorp (b. Swindon, 1852); they extended the premises to include 2 Victoria Street, and had two children. One was Hercules (b. 1884), who was killed in 1917, and the other was Arthur Dennis (b. 1887), who became an eminent archaeologist. Richard Passmore latterly became an antiques dealer. He lived and worked at 29 Wood Street, which was where he and his wife died in 1927, within two months of each other.

Paul, William Henry (1910-92) The son of a GWR clerk, Bill Paul was born in Swindon and became a draughtsman by profession. For six decades, his cartoons were featured in Swindon's *Evening Advertiser*, and his sporting comment on the town's football club's matches were printed in its weekly sister paper, *The Football Pink*. He was also involved in founding the Swindon Artists' Society.

Photographers, early practitioners in Swindon The earliest-known photograph of anywhere in Swindon came to light in 1974 when Denis Bird, himself an amateur photographer of considerable repute, obtained a picture taken c.1847 of Holy Rood church. This was the former parish church of Old Swindon, situated on the Goddard estate, most of which was demolished in 1852. The old photograph was taken by Nevil Story Maskelyne, a clergyman from Purton, who was a friend of Henry Fox Talbot of Lacock Abbey. Fox Talbot was the photography pioneer whose early experiments in the 1840s led to his invention of the calotype process, and who patented the negative-positive process for photography in 1842; Maskelyne was a clergyman with a penchant for photographing churches in the area. The picture of Holy Rood was not a commercial venture, and there is no evidence that any commercial photographers operated in Swindon before the 1860s. When they did, almost all of them had pursued other occupations to begin with, but had changed when it became evident that there was a growing and lucrative potential in photography. Also, most of those who started up in Swindon came from elsewhere. Swindon developed rapidly from the 1860s, so it was clear that there was the opportunity for the enterprising young man (and some of them were very young) to offer a new and exciting service in an expanding town.

The early photographers were inclined to list their areas of photographic expertise: 'cartes de visite portraits and vignettes, highly finished in colours', 'architectural views', or 'animals'. Several were embracing the potential of the developing art, but continuing to hedge their bets by incorporating it into their initial careers as artists and portrait painters. Few, to begin with, were prepared to take on photography as their sole occupation. (See Brooks, Henry Jamyn; Butler, Edward; Cannon, Charles; Dodson, Zephaniah; Grant, Edwin; Great Western Photographic Company; Guggenheim family; Hemmins, Henry; King, George; Passmore, Richard Keylock; Protheroe & Simons; Short, William.)

Pitt, Revd William Baker (1856-1936)

There is no corroborative proof of Pitt's claim in 1911 that he organised the football team that, within a few years, became Swindon Town F.C. He was certainly in at the birth of organised football in Swindon, and in 1879, Pitt allegedly formed and captained what was originally named Swindon Association Football Club (the name was soon changed to 'Spartans'). The matter is made more ambiguous in that there are three slightly different versions. The first is that in 1879 Revd Pitt met with some young Great Western Railway Works employees at King William School (which Revd Baily built in 1871) and formed a football club as a result. (Swindon Town F.C. currently claims 1879 as the year of its formation.) The second is that what became Swindon Town F.C. resulted from a suggestion by Pitt in 1881 for an amalgamation between the Old Swindon Cricket Club and the St Mark's Young Men's Friendly Society, who had just played a football match, with a view to becoming an amateur football club. The third, also suggesting 1881, is that it was Revd Pitt's Spartans who played St Mark's Young Men's Friendly Society, and it was these two sides that amalgamated. Pitt played for the Spartans from its formation in 1879 until 1881.

William Baker Pitt was born in Exeter, Devon. He was the son of a well-to-do grocer and provisions merchant, Thomas Baker (b.

Cadbury, Devon, 1818) and his wife Anna née Baker (b. Rewe, Devon, 1819). William's parents married in 1844, and the family lived in the high street at Exeter. William was ordained in 1879, and by the time he was twenty-three, he was a curate at Christ Church, Swindon, working under Revd Henry George Baily, largely through whose untiring efforts the church, built 1850-51, had been financed. William the curate was lodging at 38 Belle Vue Road, a stone's throw from Christ Church, in the household of Frederick Osman, a carrier and grocer.

In 1881, Revd Pitt became rector of All Saints', Liddington, where he went to live at Rectory House, ceasing his involvement with the football team in Swindon. The following year, he married Alice Mary Kinneir (b. Purton, 1859). She was the daughter of Henry Kinneir, the Swindon solicitor and attorney who, almost immediately after Alice's birth, moved into Redville House, High Street, Swindon. At Liddington, the Pitts always had at least two servants, and the number of staff increased with the size of their family. The 1911 census described William as 'a clerk in holy orders'. He resigned as rector of Liddington in 1935 and removed to Bournemouth for the sake of his deteriorating health, which was where he died. Alice Mary died in 1943.

Plaum's Pits This area of water is made out of former clay pits, once allied to brickworks, to the west of the point where Cheney Manor Road meets Vicarage Road, from which it is accessed. The area was known as Rodbourne Lake until it was taken over in the 1930s and turned into a leisure attraction by Frederick Hubert Plaum (1888-1954). Fred Plaum was born in Antwerp, Belgium, (as were his siblings George, b.

1882 and Robert, b. 1886), the son of an English mother and a Jewish German father. His mother, Clara Agnes (b. Malvern, 1857; d. Swindon, 1908), was a dressmaker, who was trading as such in Swindon by 1895 when the family lived at 18 Sanford Street. It is likely that she was already a widow by that time, which was possibly the reason for her return to England. By the end of the 1800s, they were at 21 Vilett Street, and they later relocated to 489 Ferndale Road.

Fred Plaum began his working life at fourteen in the GWR Works, becoming a wheelturner; George became a railway storekeeper, and Robert was classed as 'feeble-minded'. By 1911, Fred was a private in the Royal Army Medical Corps (he rose to sergeant), working as a male nurse. He married Martha Smallbone in Swindon in 1915, the year he joined the First World War, fought in Africa, and returned in 1918 on one of the vessels of the United Africa Steamship Company. During the 1920s, he was still in military service, and spent much time in Africa. By 1928, the family was at 36 Elmina Road.

By the end of the 1930s, Rodbourne Lake had become known locally as Plaum's Pits, and the area was administered by Fred Plaum. There was one way in, through a turnstile, where Fred charged 1d entrance fee, and 2d to those who wanted to swim in the muddy water. The lake was developed as a leisure area: little rowing boats were put on it; a two-stage, openwork wooden diving stage was installed; and a floating raft went into the middle of the water. A smaller pool was added in the late 1940s, using local volunteer labour, and a concrete-lined, sunken children's paddling pool was installed, with steps down to the water level. The site also had three old railway carriages:

two were used as male and female changing rooms, and the other was a shop, operated by a couple who sold mineral water, biscuits and confectionery.

Pliosaurus Brachyspondylus Excavations associated with the Swindon railway works' non-ferrous foundry in 1975 revealed the bones of a prehistoric creature. This was identified by Professor Appleby of Cardiff University and Professor Halstead of Reading University as the remains of a pliosaurus brachyspondylus, a crocodile-like animal that lived 130-150 million years ago. It was the most complete specimen of that creature discovered to date. Harry Roberts, the Works manager at the time, acceded to a request from BBC television's *Blue Peter* for the right to display the bones on television, and they were reset onto polystyrene so that a better likeness was obtained. The bones afterwards went on display at the Swindon Museum, and were later received into the British Museum collection.

Prospect Silver Band The Prospect Silver Band was formed in 1908 by Edward Paul Bullock, and continued until it disbanded in 1948. It became the Prospect Silver Prize Band after obtaining honours in competitions at Banbury and Market Lavington, after which it was successful in a number of competitions. At its height, it had around forty musicians. Edward Paul Bullock was the son of Dick William Bullock (b. Alderton, Wiltshire, 1856) and his wife Eliza née Holder (b. Swindon, 1857), who married in 1878. She was the daughter of a cordwainer who lived in Short Edge (part of what would become Devizes Road) in Old Town. The couple lived at first in Yeovil, Somerset, where two of their children,

Robert Joseph (b. 1886) and Edward Paul (b. 1888), were born. They came to Swindon in c.1889, where Dick William worked for the GWR as an engine driver, and his two sons entered the Swindon Works as engine fitters. Their daughter, Violett Eliza, was born in Swindon in 1891 and, when she left school, she became an assistant in the London Penny Bazaar in Regent Street. The family lived at 45 Curtis Street.

Dick, Robert and Edward all played brass instruments with the Salvation Army. When the sons had the idea of forming their own silver band, they named it after the Primitive Methodist Chapel at Prospect, where their Salvation Army parades regularly ended. In 1913, Edward Paul Bullock married Emily née Butler (b. Wroughton, 1882), the daughter and sister of GWR boilermakers. He taught musical instruments from their home in Curtis Street; his Prospect Silver Band played locally, always led the carnival parade in aid of funds for Swindon's Victoria Hospital, and was instrumental in fundraising for numerous good causes in the town. Edward died at Stratton hospital in 1946, and his funeral was held at the Prospect Chapel. His brother, Robert Joseph Bullock, led the Prospect Silver Prize Band for its remaining two years.

Protheroe, James Smith (1858-1929) and Simons, Thomas Henry (1875-1960) The only 19th-century Swindon photographer to claim royal patronage, J.S. Protheroe stated such an association with the Prince of Wales (later King Edward VII) in his advertisements and underlined the fact by also including the royal coat of arms. Protheroe was born in Swansea, Glamorgan, the son of a master tailor, and was himself in the trade until the 1880s. Then he came to Swindon with his nephew Thomas Henry Simons (b. Swansea, 1875) as his photographic assistant, and set up in business at 30 Regent Street, the late premises of Charles Cannon, photographer. Protheroe was a strict Baptist and, from the beginning in Swindon, he conducted the choir at the Baptist Tabernacle in Regent Circus. In 1894, he married Fanny Jane Redman (b. Swindon, 1858) and became involved in the Swindon Traders' Association. The photographic business continued at 30 Regent Street as J.S. Protheroe until 1901, when master and assistant went into partnership as Protheroe & Simons.

In 1905, Thomas Henry Simons married Esther Annie Brown (b. Swindon, 1882) and the couple moved into 15 Victoria Road, which became the business premises for the photographic partnership. By 1907, Protheroe was taking a back seat; he had become a collector of income tax in the town, with offices at 177 Victoria Road. Fanny Jane Protheroe died in 1925. Protheroe's own obituary notice in 1929 described how, among other appointments and interests, he had been a county Justice of the Peace, a prominent freemason in the town, long-term chairman of the Swindon & Highworth Board of Guardians, the first secretary of the Swindon Branch of the National Farmers' Union, a member of the Wiltshire County Council and of the County Education Committee, and chairman of the Wilts Joint Vagrancy Committee. After Protheroe's death, Simons continued as T.H. Simons, photographer, until 1939. He died at Westlecot Home for the Blind, Westlecot Road, Swindon. His widow Esther Annie died in 1964.

Pub landlords in 19th-century Swindon This is an alphabetic list of the named beerhouses and public houses listed in Swindon trade directories and other sources for the 19th century, together with their known keepers, listed in date order. The dates given are the earliest found at each venue for the person named. It should not be assumed that each keeper remained in charge until the next shown in the list, although that was true in most cases, and there are some examples of longevity. (The Wheelers, father then son, kept going what became the Wheatsheaf in Newport Street for over forty years; Richard Dunn was for forty years in charge at the Whale, Cetus Buildings; Stephen Cox had the Oddfellows Arms, Queen Street, for thirty-one years.) The list shows that some keepers moved from house to house in the trade, some houses remained in the same family, and wives frequently retained the business after the death of their husbands, and were sometimes followed by one of their sons. (Further information on most of the establishments listed below may be found under the separate entries for each in this book, or in its predecessor *The Swindon Book*. David W. Backhouse's book *Home Brewed* (revised edition, 1992) was the result of his painstaking research into the breweries, beerhouses, alehouses and pubs of the Swindon area, and is particularly rich in licensing details and information about individual houses, through sales to breweries, brewery mergers, etc.)

Artillery Arms, Regent Street
1855 James Edward Toe
1860 Charles Watts
1861 James Herbert
1869 Louisa Watts
1876 Thomas Latter

1893 Walter D. Cox

Baker's Arms, High Street (Emlyn Square)
1850 Richard Allnatt
1885 William James Keylock
1892 Alfred E. Morgan

Beehive, Prospect Hill
1871 Philip Cockbill
1893 T. Boulton
1894 Frederick Price

Bell, High Street
1830 Charles Rose
1839 Henry Pineger
1848 Edwin Frederick Franklin/ James
        Franklin
1850 John Woodroffe
1853 Henry Pineger
1858 Charlotte Pinnegar
1859 Napoleon King
1860 William Godwin
1875 Richard Tarrant
1877 Thomas Elliott
1885 John Mitchell
1888 Frederick Scott
1893 Walter Lawson Nicholson
1899 Frederick Levi Wilson

Bell and Shoulder of Mutton, Lower Town
1830 George Austin
1842 Martha Austin
1850 Jeremiah Smith
1855 Esther Austin
1858 William Hitchcock
1859 Edwin Pope
1875 Elizabeth Pope
1879 William Large
1893 Arthur A. Powell
1894 Joseph Powell

1899 George B. Pinneger

Belle Vue, Belle Vue Road
1864 Philip Cockbill
1873 William Cockbill
1884 George Bishop
1899 Susannah Hunt

Britannia/Fountain, Devizes Road
1849 Richard Stagg
1867 James Howe
1868 Caroline Watmore
1875 George Daniels
1891 Thomas Tranter
1899 Frederick Williams

Bull/Black Bull, Newport Street
1830 John Wyatt
1839 Joseph Browning
1848 Henry Hawes
1850 Sarah Hawkins
1852 John Palmer
1861 John C. Bingham
1875 Stephen Lawrence
1877 Edmund Brow
1879 John M. Marfell

Butcher's Arms/Gardener's Arms, Westcott Place
1875 John Bacon
1879 Eliza Bacon
1885 William Gilmor
1890 Ellen Stevens
1892 William Stevens

Castle Inn, Prospect
1863 Charles Barker
1875 Charles Benjamin Boniface
1878 Ann Pedder Boniface
1891 Robert Smith

Clifton Hotel, Clifton Street
1885 Henry Jefferies
1899 Frances Jefferies

County Ground Hotel, County Road
1897 Charles Williams

Cricketer's Arms, High Street (Emlyn Square)
1853 Edward Jeffcoate
1858 Samuel Dixon
1867 Martha Dixon
1869 Richard Skerten
1875 William Collard
1879 Thomas Phipps
1885 Thomas Wheeler
1899 Harry Wheeler

Cross Keys, Regent Street
1851 Ellen Horne
1856 James Edward Toe

Cross Keys, Wood Street
1873 Henry Lay
1885 Eliza Lay

Crown, Lower Town
1841 Charles Smith
1867 John H. Wheeler
1875 Henry Lailey
1885 Jacob Little
1885 Thomas Gale
1887 Jacob Little
1891 Mrs Little
1892 Joseph Moore

Dolphin, Rodbourne Road
1873 Robert Bishop
1879 Thomas Hayward
1900 Alfred Edward Morgan

Duke of Edinburgh, Gorse Hill
1875 Frederick Davis
1877 James Henry Vickery
1880 Frederick Davis
1885 Charles Kent
1890 William Marshall
1893 Arthur Bowker
1894 John C. Parsons
1895 Arthur Bowker

Duke of Wellington, Eastcott Hill
1876 James Henry Vickery
1886 ? Williams
1891 Christopher John Parsons

Duke of York, Westcott Place
1851 John Leighfield
1856 William Cox/Mary Cox

Eagle Inn, Regent Street
1867 William Thomas
1875 John William May
1876 Caleb Comley
1886 Mrs R. Thomas
1887 Henry W. Thomas

Engineer's Arms, Market House, High Street (Emlyn Square)
1869 Jane Edwards

Falcon, Westcott Place
1867 Robert Wattleworth
1885 Richard William Allnatt
1899 Edwin Richard Parfitt

Forester's Arms, Fleet Street
1858 John Forward
1876 George Shail
1890 Henry Penton
1892 John William Miles

Fox Inn, Regent Street

1864 John Forbes
1868 Robert Thompson
1876 William Harvey
1879 Joseph Warman
1885 Harry Batten
1887 Thomas Oakes
1890 William F. Draper
1893 Bertie C. Weight

George Inn, Eastcott Hill

1851 George Bishop
1854 Charles Hurt
1876 Henry Weeks
1879 Henry Sharps Lewis
1888 Eliza Lewis
1899 Alfred Webb

Globe, North Street

1871 Zillah Teale
1876 Edward Gould
1891 Thomas Strange

Glue Pot, High Street (Emlyn Square)

1851 William Warner
1865 William H. Thomas
1889 Arabella Thomas/Charles R. Thomas
1891 Thomas Charles Riddiford
1892 C.R. Thomas

Goddard Arms, High Street

1830 Joseph New
1848 Jane New
1855 William Westmacott
1875 Edward Sheppard
1877 W.D. Price
1879 Jane W. Price
1889 Miss H.M. Rosindell

Golden Lion, Bridge Street

1848 John Cross

1853 James Godwin
1859 John Gray
1867 Samuel Emery
1876 John Churchward Porter Stancombe
1885 Joseph Samuel Weight
1892 Ozias E. Weight
1893 Enoch Weight
1895 Charles Hall Barker

Grapes, Cambria Place

1863 Samuel Rowles
1867 James Kempster
1875 Ann Kempster
1880 Ann Kempster Saintbury
1885 John Blackford
1886 Frederick Bush
1890 Frederick William Dack

Great Western Hotel, Station Road

1876 Charles Barker
1879 Robert Bishop
1885 Colin McDonald
1890 James Mitchell

Greyhound, Faringdon Road

1847 John Young
1853 William Robinson
1875 Joseph Hunt
1879 Simeon Gibbs
1885 James Evans
1890 Frances Evans

Greyhound, Westcott Place

1853 John Dolman
1858 J. Haggard
1861 David Chapman
1867 Alfred Chapman
1877 Joseph Hunt

King of Prussia, High Street

1830 Mary Ellison

1848 William Webb
1858 William John
1860 William Jordan
1861 Henry Wicks
1863 G. Mann
1865 Edwin R. Fifield
1875 George Bishop
1876 Thomas Washbourn

King's Arms, Wood Street

1842 John Godwin (Snr)
1870 John Godwin (Jnr)
1892 Charles David Godwin

King's Head, Fleet Street

1865 George Hall
1879 James Perry
1887 W. Reynolds
1891 Thomas Richards
1894 Richard Miles

Lamb & Flag, Bridge Street

1851 George Bishop
1855 Amelia Barrett
1876 Edwin Bowker
1879 Frederick Cratchley
1885 George Thomas
1890 John Melling
1894 Thomas Gardiner

Locomotive, Fleetway (Fleet Street)

1853 Richard Pearce Smith
1858 Elizabeth Jeffcoate
1867 Robert Shelley
1869 George Smith
1882 Mary Ann Smith
1889 Thomas Greenwood
1890 George Greenwood
1893 J. Greenwood
1894 Walter James Greenwood

Lord Raglan, Cricklade Street

1847 Elijah Rushan
1857 George Prier
1868 George Trout
1871 Frederick Cratchley
1877 Joseph C. Ashton
1885 Henry William Bennett

Mason's Arms, High Street

1830 Richard Tarrant
1839 Richard Tarrant/William Hewers
1841 William Killard
1850 Caroline Killard
1853 Thomas Pearce Brown
1858 Henry Tarrant
1863 Henry Ellison
1863 John Washbourne
1869 Matthew Washbourn
1873 Thomas Wheeler
1889 Frederick Bush
1899 Charles Koeber Fenton

Mechanic's Arms, Cheltenham Street

1885 John Easter

New Inn, Cromwell Street

1876 Jacob Speck
1879 George Bishop
1885 George Smith
1888 Charles Preater

Oddfellows Arms/Plume of Feathers, Cricklade Street

1848 John Compton
1865 Frederick Cratchley
1876 Simeon Gibbs
1878 A. Bizley
1879 Stephen Cox
1885 Albert Bizley
1890 Mary Ann Bizley

Oddfellows Arms, North Street

1861 John Dyer

Oddfellows Arms, Queen Street

1859 Stephen Cox
1890 William Wilson
1891 J. Thomas
1892 William R. Crook
1894 Alice C. Crook

Old Locomotive, Station Road

1877 J. H. Matthews
1885 Edward Raven

Park Hotel, William Street

1879 Edwin Harvey
1885 William Crombie
1885 Elizabeth Ann Harvey
1895 Ozias Edwin Harvey

Plough, Devizes Road

1855 Aaron Pickett
1876 Henry Bristow
1892 Jane Bristow

Prince of Wales, Union Street

1869 George S. Hunt
1886 George Hunt (Jnr)

Prospect, Prospect Place

1848 John Jones
1850 Susannah Jones
1853 John Jones
1860 Elizabeth Jones

Queen's Arms, Corporation Street

1848 John Kitching
1850 James Davis
1869 Mary Davis
1877 John Reynault
1880 Richard Rudman

Queen's Head, Fleet Street

1890 Thomas Richards

Queen's Hotel, New Swindon Railway Station

1848 Samuel Young Griffith
1850 John Rouse Phillips
1859 Joseph Benskin
1867 John Rouse Phillips
1876 George Moss
1885 Henry George Lake
1893 Henry Sicklen
1899 John Read

Queen's Tap, Station Road

(Est. c.1841; extant)
1850 John Rouse Phillips
1880 James Chater
1885 S. Homewood

Railway Hotel, Newport Street

1885 Emily Adams
1887 F.J. Ferris
1889 Arthur Charles Hillier
1892 Gabriel Morrell
1893 Edwin Herbert Croad

Red Cow Inn, Cow Lane

1840 James Ellison
1847 Ann Page
1864 Joseph Paget
1876 Robert Dibbs
1899 Sarah Jane Dibbs

Red Cow, Princes Street

1877 Robert Dibbs
1890 George Dibbs

Rhinoceros, Albert Street

1845 Lucy Rogers
1847 Joseph Paget
1859 Reuben Edwards

Rifleman's Arms, Regent Street

1860 Jane L. Cameron
1865 Sarah S. Wright
1875 Joseph Rich
1876 Samuel Weight
1885 Charles Fox
1899 John Albert Horsell

Rising Sun/Roaring Donkey, Albert Street

1848 William Walker
1862 John Williams
1877 William Hammond
1878 Joseph Gosling
1887 O. Denneman
1891 John Wilkins

Rolleston Hotel, Commercial Road

1890 John Horsell

Rolling Mills, Bridge Street

1876 Heber Spencer
1879 Walter Guise
1885 John Tebbs
1886 S. Harris
1890 John William Jarman

Royal Oak Inn, Devizes Road

1876 Edmund Brown
1879 William Spackman
1885 Thomas Offer
1893 Lydia Offer

Running Horse/Horse and Jockey, Wootton Bassett Road

1848 George Firmin
1850 William Brooks
1859 John Jacobs
1885 Mark Beasant
1899 George Frederick Missen

Ship, Westcott Place

1850 James William Bannister
1853 Charles Stephens
1858 C.H. Townsend
1860 George Smith
1875 John Churchward Porter Stancombe
1876 John Looms
1877 Robert Looms
1880 George Looms
1888 Alfred Webb
1899 Walter John Groves

Sir Daniel, Fleet Street

1867 Charles Lea
1869 Robert Kempster
1876 William Jones
1885 Eliza Jones
1886 Rebecca Jones

Sun, Coate

1891 Ann Choules

Sun, Newport Street

1830 Thomas Lamb

Sun Inn, Bridge Street

1869 Thomas Claughan
1877 William Hammond
1879 Thomas Claughan
1885 Daniel Claughan
1893 Mary Claughan

Union Railway Inn, Sheppard Street

1848 John Crook
1855 Walter Bertram
1858 Judith Warmby
1859 Thomas Morris
1860 John Ford
1869 Thomas Washbourn
1875 Richard Bullen
1877 J.W. Long

1880 Frederick Cratchley
1888 George Thomas
1899 Daniel Jones

Victoria Inn, Victoria Street

1845 Emma Sparrow Pike
1851 James Herbert
1863 Richard Green
1869 Joseph Thorp
1875 Annie Thorp
1876 Charles Kent
1889 Martha Kent
1891 Charles G. Kent
1899 James A. Wight

Volunteer, Bridge Street

1867 Henry Smith
1880 Thomas Hofield
1885 George Thomas
1891 Horace Haydon Whitehead

Whale Inn, Cetus Buildings

1842 Jonas Head
1845 Richard Dunn
1885 Thomas Garland

Wheatsheaf, Newport Street

1832 Isaac Wheeler
1858 Thomas Wheeler
1875 William Kent
1879 George Day
1892 Emily Day

White Hart, Newport Street

1841 William Farmer
1858 Elizabeth Cocks
1868 ? Hammett
1869 Ann Bush
1875 Samuel Bond
1887 Sarah Bond

Wild Deer, Westcott Place

1853 Thomas Prowse
1858 John Wilcox
1860 Saunders
1861 Thomas Palmer
1876 Thomas Skinner
1890 William E. Reed

Pulse Wholefood Cooperative

In the 1970s, Dick Kitto, organic grower, author and educationalist, was the first warden in charge of Lower Shaw Farm, an educational, environmental and cultural resource in Old Shaw Lane, West Swindon. In 1976, he asked one of the farm's residents, Stephanie Futcher, to help him establish what became Swindon Pulse, the town's first health food outlet. That summer, they began fetching stock from the Community Wholesale Warehouse in London, using the farm's old Bedford van. They weighed out products like beans, rice and raisins, and then sold them in one-pound bags (21p for a pound of raisins) from a stall in Swindon's covered market hall in Cromwell Street, just before the place was closed down. Swindon Pulse's last initiative there was an 'Ideas for Swindon' exhibition, where residents and community groups made displays featuring what they would like to see in Swindon. This was the catalyst for a vegetarian catering business and a natural health initiative. The market hall was demolished in 1977.

That year, Swindon Pulse set up as a temporary measure in one room of empty shop premises on the south side of Regent Circus. By September, it had relocated to 107 Curtis Street, which also provided kitchen, lavatory and a Calor gas heater. Stock was kept upstairs, and the shop soon became the place where alternative-minded people from Swindon went to buy produce, and to talk about their ideas and dreams. Swindon Pulse formed strong links with Friends of the Earth, Campaign for Nuclear Disarmament (CND), and Swindon Quakers. A noticeboard was set up to publicise activities at Lower Shaw Farm and projects by other community groups, and Swindon Pulse published a newsletter.

Keen that the structures and way of working should be as alternative and progressive as the type of products Pulse sold, Stephanie Futcher reorganised the business into a worker's co-operative. Everyone had equal status, and decisions were made by consensus. Some of the first members lived at Lower Shaw Farm, others were customers. Two of these were Liz Williams and Helen Boyce, who wanted to open a vegetarian café, and who set up a wholefood vegetarian catering business called Take Two Cooks. The treasurer was Jenny Lancaster. Other people from Lower Shaw Farm who were involved from the beginning included Frances Dorman, Kay Fisher, Tony Fletcher, Ruth Garland, Sheila Pregnall, Ann Stringer and Pat Zeilinska. In the early years, the shop was open on four days each week: Tuesday, Thursday, Friday and Saturday. At first, people worked there for nothing, but later took a wage of £1 per day. By 1980, membership had increased to thirteen.

In 1985, no. 107 Curtis Street was scheduled for demolition, and the future of the business hung in the balance, although loyal customers and hard-core members urged survival. In May 1986, Swindon Pulse reopened at 27 Curtis Street, from where it continues to operate. Everyone involved is a director, manager, and worker, and all are fully committed to the cause and employed part-time for the national minimum wage.

Quarries, The: Trout's Folly Today, Trout's Folly is a single dwelling, made out of at least two former stone-built cottages. These were erected when the immediate vicinity was developed in the late 1860s. In 1867, George Trout, who was also keeper (1863-1870) of the infamous Lord Raglan beerhouse and lodging house in Cricklade Street, leased from Ambrose Lethbridge Goddard 'land on or near the Quarries', on which to build. This site was where Trout's Folly is today. Historians have suggested that Trout's intention was to build a slaughterhouse there. In this, he might have been influenced by the unpleasantness he experienced daily from the slaughterhouses in and adjacent to Cricklade Street, which in consequence frequently ran with blood. He might also have anticipated a business opportunity in opening a similar establishment away from residential Old Town. It is possible that Trout came from Street, Somerset, where he was a stonecutter. If so, he probably had enough experience to work the stone from his patch of the quarries and build the slaughterhouse himself. Whether or not he was responsible for all of the buildings that made up Trout's Folly, or whether others were added later, is unknown. The slaughterhouse theory is credible because a large-scale map of 1885 shows (and names) Trout's Folly comprising eleven buildings and what appears to be ten small pens and four larger ones, all arranged tightly around three sides of a rectangle. By 1899, all the pens had gone, as had the buildings on the north side, leaving just eight properties. Apart from the dwelling still known today as Trout's Folly, all the other buildings were subsequently demolished. George Trout left the Lord Raglan in 1870 and was declared bankrupt the following year. Historians have suggested that the slaughterhouse project caused this difficulty and was the reason why the site, from probably as early as the 1870s, was called Trout's Folly. (See also Lord Raglan.)

Queenstown This rather amorphous area is today bounded to the north by Station Road, Corporation Street to the east, Fleming Way to the south, and Cheltenham Street to the west. It is a part of Swindon that has been much destroyed by programmes of rebuilding and townscape remodelling that have taken place over the last few decades (bus station, office blocks, etc.), and by work that has started in the 21st century to regenerate that part of the central area of the town. Before the Great Western Railway set up in Swindon, this area was divided into fields, separated by farm tracks. Only its southern boundary, the line of the Wilts & Berks Canal, and the farm track that ran past Lower Eastcott Farm to the east, provided fixed points. The majority of Queenstown was built on fields known as Great Culvery and Great Breach.

The widely held belief that this area of Swindon was so called after Queen's Road, which was built in the late 1880s between Station Road East to the north and Haydon Street to the south, is incorrect. In fact, it was unofficially being referred to as 'Queen's Town' a decade and a half previously. Queen's Road was itself named after a number of royal references that were already in and around the railway station. These were the Queen's Tap of 1840, opposite the station; the Queen's Arms of 1841 a little to the east; and the Queen's Royal Hotel of 1842, within the station complex. There were hardly three hundred yards between them, and, as a final flourish, the Swindon

Permanent Building Society laid down Queen's Road, which had a terrace of ten properties to the east and one of seven to the west. All of the references were to Queen Victoria, so it was hardly surprising that this overload (she was also the inspiration for Queen Street, off Regent Street, and Victoria Street in Old Town), was slightly lessened when, in 1908, Queen's Road was renamed Alexandra Road. Victoria's successor in this regard was Queen Alexandra, the Danish wife of Victoria's son Edward VII.

Queenstown came about because the GWR, which had bought up land around the site of its Swindon Works, was not in a position to build sufficient houses on it for the increasing workforce. However, from 1868, the railway company had a considerable presence in the Swindon Permanent Benefit Building and Investment Society, whose president was Sir Daniel Gooch, the recently retired GWR locomotive superintendent. Other senior officers of the railway company were directors. There was clearly a networking initiative that enabled the building society to acquire GWR land and build speculatively on it.

Queenstown School This school was designed by Brightwen Binyon of Ipswich. It was built by Thomas Barrett of 11 Newport Street, Old Swindon for the Swindon School Board in 1880-81, on a site between the Wilts & Berks Canal and the southern ends of Merton Street and Oriel Street. This was the board's first project in central Swindon. In the school's intended catchment area were the residential terraces to the east of Wellington Street that ran between the railway station and the canal. When Queenstown School was erected, this area had been built up only as far as the old roadway that facilitated

Eastcott Farm. (This was to become Corporation Street.) Beyond that, in 1881, there were only the canal company's Cetus Buildings, the Whale Bridge and pub, and Medgbury Road. Within five years, there would be a push to terrace the land between Corporation Street and the County Ground. Queenstown School was built with this residential expansion in mind; it cost £1,890 to build on land that had cost £400 to buy. Initially, it accommodated 279 infants, but was extended in 1885, at a cost of £2,300, to include 285 girls. The infants were relocated to College Street Infant School in 1938, where they remained until 1946, and Queenstown School became wholly an infants' school until its closure in 1977. The following year, part of the building was remodelled as a magistrates' court. This closed in 1990, and the buildings were demolished in 1993.

Radio Rentals The Swindon branch was at 14 Victoria Road, and such was its saturation of rented television sets in the area in the 1950s and 1960s that many people thought it was a local firm; in reality the company ultimately had 500 stores nationwide. By the time it came to Swindon, Radio Rentals was an amalgamation of two firms that had been founded to rent out radio sets, then television sets after the end of the Second World War, and latterly video recorders. These firms were Radio Rentals, founded in Brighton in 1932 by Percy Perring-Thomas, and Joseph W.C. Robinson's Rentaset, which began in 1930. They merged in 1964, when Robinson became the chairman of Radio Relay.

The importance of Radio Rentals to Swindon was its registration of Viewpoint as a company name in 1958. Then, the intention was to run local television into

homes (once the Government would allow it, funded by local advertising) in the town via the cable network that Radio Rentals was operating for BBC and ITV channels. This system gave a better picture reception to that being provided to date through garden and rooftop television aerials. The distance of Swindon from the nearest transmitter meant that television reception in the town at the time was very poor. The community television scheme became viable when the Government of 1972 licensed five local television experiments. At the beginning, the rationale behind the project was that it should transmit local news, sports information and cultural events through the town's radio and television cable network, and enable people to use its equipment to make their own programmes. David Yates, famously the director of several Harry Potter motion pictures, used these facilities early in his career to make short films. Local programming was axed in the 1990s, due to problems with funding.

However, by that time, Radio Rentals had sold its hitherto Viewpoint initiative to Thorn Electrical Industries in 1968, and that organisation ran it as a separate entity, with its original name, within its Thorn Television Rentals Division. This became part of the Thorn-EMI merger in 1980, when it was called Radio Rentals Cable Television, and the name was eventually lost after the Radio Rentals operation merged with Granada Rentals in 2000. (See also Swindon Viewpoint.)

Radnor Street, West Swindon Club The Sheppard estate at Kingshill was sectioned off and made available for residential development throughout the 1870s. Late in that decade, Redcross Street was laid out. Its name was changed almost immediately to Radnor Street, after William Pleydell-Bouverie, 5th Earl of Radnor (1841-1900), one-time Member of Parliament for South Wiltshire. By 1885, the street had a terrace of thirty-three properties on the north side, and on the south side was a run of twenty, plus the lodge at the entrance to Radnor Street Cemetery (laid out 1880-81). The neat but utilitarian houses were each of two storeys and two bays, and were built in red brick, with depressed arch lintels and keystones in stone above windows and doors, and neat, bracketed sills beneath the windows. Over the next fifteen years, Radnor Street was extended towards the south-west; Clifton Street was inserted between Radnor Street and William Street, where the original part of the former met the later build, and by 1900, the northern side of Radnor Street had fifty-five properties.

One of these, built c.1885 and occupied by the West Swindon Club, was one of the oddest in the town. Of two storeys with basement, and effectively three bays, its central section, visually enclosed by flat pilasters, had three square-headed windows at street level and three round-headed windows to the upper storey. This whole section was given prominence by a significantly raised, triangular shoulder pediment picked out by string courses that ran across the front and tied in with the flat caps of the flanking pilasters. On either side of the central section were two-storey, single-bay wings. Blind parapets with flat string courses tied the wings into the pilasters that ran through the levels of the central section. The windows in the wings were square-headed. The entrance to the building, in the right-hand wing, was also square-headed, and had decorative, wavy jambs. Above this

was a square, recessed panel featuring scroll brackets; above that, between two horizontal bands of string courses right across the front elevation, was a blind panel with scroll decoration. The string course immediately beneath the upper storey was ostentatiously corbelled out with fluted corbels beneath and ball finials on plinths immediately above them. That immediately above the ground floor windows had plain, square brackets.

The club came to the attention of the law when, in 1887, William Smith and Caroline Smith, who was his wife and the stewardess, were brought to court with several others by the Excise authorities on charges of illegally selling beer, wine, whisky and tobacco to non-members, for which they were fined. On 4 October 1923, the West Swindon Club building and the accommodation for the steward and stewardess, Mr & Mrs E.H. Hemmins, were gutted by fire. The alarm was raised at 1.15 a.m. and an unsuccessful attempt was made to access the telephone in the nearby cemetery lodge (where a notice said 'For fire telephone from here'), in order to call out the fire brigade. Capt. W.H. Baker and his men eventually received the call at 2 a.m. The fire station was in nearby Cromwell Street, but soon after they arrived, the roof of the West Swindon Club collapsed. It took seven hours to put out the blaze, by which time all the fixtures and fittings had been destroyed, as had most of the stock, including upwards of forty barrels of beer, and there remained just the skeleton of a building. The cause of the fire was thought to have been a cigarette end or lighted match, dropped on to sawdust on the floor, where it smouldered before bursting into flames.

Regent Circus development In 2006, developers Ashfield Land acquired the freehold of the five-acre site adjacent to Regent Circus on which stood the abandoned Swindon College, with a view to demolishing the buildings (but not the Victorian former Technical College, fronting Victoria Road, that was on part of the site). The firm obtained outline planning permission to redevelop the area in 2007, but the financial recession put any progress on hold. Detailed consent was granted in 2011 for a major retail and leisure development there. Wring Demolition cleared the site in 2012, and the following year, construction contractor ISG was awarded a £16.5m contract to build the retail-led scheme. Building by ISG began in October 2013. The complex included space for a food superstore, eight restaurants, a six-screen, all-digital cinema, and a car park with 450 spaces. At the same time, the road approach into Regent Circus from the east was reconfigured and became a shared-use facility without traffic controls. Ashfield Land sold the whole Regent Circus scheme for £40.5m in 2014 to UK Commercial Property Trust. The first business to open on this site was Morrison's, which opened on 13 October 2014.

Regent Place Built 1879-80, immediately north of York Place (which became the north side of Regent Circus), and at right angles to it, the eastern side of Regent Place was the first to be built up. The site had previously been orchards to the north-west of Upper Eastcott Farm, which stood close to where Regent Circus is now. Regent Place initially comprised a single terrace of nineteen properties. At that time, its northern end terminated in a T-junction that led eastwards towards Cow Lane, and in particular to the old Red Cow public house, which had its origins in the middle of the 18th century. Other properties around this junction brought the total residential tally to twenty-nine by the time of the 1881 census. During the 1880s, the T-junction end of Regent Place was also terraced, and a small terrace was built on the western side, nearest York Place. This, by 1891, brought the total number of properties in Regent Place to fifty.

Most of the first occupiers of Regent Place were GWR workers (and their families) and many of them were then in their late twenties. The roll-call of the workers and their occupations in the first twenty-nine properties when they were newly built was:

1. Henry Walman, carpenter
2. Eli Rowland, blacksmith
3. Matthew Carbon, GWR stoker
4. Reuben Weaver, GWR labourer
5. James Bassett, GWR tin plate worker
6. Joseph Nutt, GWR coach body maker
7. George Deacon, GWR machine belt maker
8. Henry Kinneir, corn agent and brewer's traveller
9. Joseph Porter, GWR railway coach painter
10. Sarah Baker, widow
11. Alfred Luckett, foreman baker
12. Joseph R. Stevens, GWR ironworks foreman
13. Mary Ann Baker, shirtmaker
14. James Newman, GWR plate layer
15. Alfred Charles Baker, general labourer
16. David Porter, general labourer
17. John Randall, crane driver
18. William Easley, boot worker
19. Thomas Haines, general labourer
20. Isaac Comley, GWR Works watchman
21. William Collins, general labourer
22. Eliza Ford, widow, dressmaker
23. William Jones, GWR engine fitter

24. John Mudge, general labourer
25. John Price, painter's labourer
26. James Sprules, general labourer
27. Samuel Greenwood, GWR office porter
28. John Couling, GWR fireman
29. James Joseph Locke, GWR engine
     fireman

It would be reasonable to suppose that all but three of the working occupiers of Regent Place when it was first built were either railway employees or the widows of railway employees. At the time, the GWR Company had some 106 acres at New Swindon, of which the built-up area – the Locomotive Works, the Carriage and Wagon Works, and the Rail Mills – occupied twenty-eight acres. When Regent Place was built to accommodate the ever-increasing railway workforce, the company employed 5,000 men on its site; within ten years, that figure had doubled.

Because the several sections of Regent Place were built speculatively by different builders at different times, the terraces bore the hallmarks of individuality. Most were two-bay, two-storey properties, and the more attractive run was on the east side; they had sharply pointed arches to the doorways and windows, some with diamond-shaped keystones, all treated with a degree of polychromy. There were few buildings on the west side of Regent Place before 1899, when a breakaway group of the Christian Brethren, which had been in the town for almost two decades, built their Regent Hall, known as the Open Brethren Mission Room. It was designed by William Hooper, the Swindon photographer, who was a member of the Brethren, and who also project-managed the build. The Open Brethren thereafter expanded into other mission halls

in the town, notably in Florence Street and at Westcott Place.

There was never any direct access between Regent Place and Regent Circus. Initially, the shortest route between it and the main shopping street was across open land to the west, which had previously been part of the orchards. The way was then either through the back stable- and pump-yard of the Rifleman's Arms, or via a dogleg of a passage past Regent Villas, part of which still exists beside what became the Savoy cinema. Most of Regent Place was demolished 1962-63, and the Regent Hall was taken down in 1967.

Rehoboth Chapel, Prospect Early in the 1880s, a large number of the members of the Strict and Particular Baptist Chapel in Providence Road left, taking exception to the minister's 'ungodly expenditure' in having the interior repainted. In 1882, those Particular Baptists who broke away opened their little Rehoboth chapel, of red brick with stone quoins and window dressings, on Prospect Hill. It had seats for 100 people. When the nearby extension was being built to Swindon Technical College in the 1960s, the chapel suffered hairline cracks, which were repaired by Swindon Borough Council. During the Regent Circus development, on the site of the College extension, the chapel suffered structural damage, which forced it to close in February 2014.

Reilly, Noel (1946-2008) The Beehive public house on Prospect Hill remained a backstreet boozer of no particular interest until it was taken over by Noel Reilly, known as 'The Ginger Man' because of the colour of his hair and beard. Reilly was an Irishman who had briefly studied at university in

Galway, had been in the country's military, and had worked in several bars in America. He came to Swindon in 1982 and was in charge of the Beehive 1982-93, during which time he became bankrupt. He was a chain-smoking, hard-drinking eccentric who could be extremely rude to customers (he once took out an advertisement in the local press apologising for this), and might throw out someone just because he took a dislike to some element of their appearance.

Nonetheless, Reilly brought culture and philosophy to the Beehive, and took his customers to London art galleries and Shakespeare productions at Stratford-upon-Avon. He established the Beehive Arts Initiative, held exhibitions of art in the pub, had open music sessions there, and organised art lectures. He once famously packed in the Swindon Choral Society, which gave a two-hour recital of *Handel's Messiah*. In 1988, he established a philosopher-in-residence at the Beehive. This was Dr Julius Tomin (b. 1938), who had been persecuted, imprisoned, and forced into a mental institution in his own country (Czechoslovakia) for carrying out underground philosophy sessions in various flats in Prague. Reilly offered him £5,000 to deliver nine lectures at the Beehive (in the event only four took place), and even went so far as to be arrested in Wenceslas Square, Prague for defending Tomin and calling for his repatriation. After he became bankrupt at the Beehive, Noel Reilly went to study English Literature at Oxford University. However, this did not last, and he returned to the pub trade. He died at Oxford, following a fall.

Reliance Controls building, Drake's Way

This was a landmark building for Swindon as well as nationally, and one that influenced some of the subsequent, great 20th-century buildings in the world. Peter Parker commissioned Team 4 to design what was to be a single 3,200-square-metre composite research facility, factory and office space for a company that was manufacturing components for the electronics industry. It was the first major project (and the largest at that time) for Team 4, a partnership that was set up in 1965 and then consisting of Norman Foster (who later designed the iconic Renault building in West Swindon), Wendy Cheeseman (who became Foster's wife), Richard Rogers and his wife Su Rogers, Georgie Wolton and Tony Hunt. The Reliance Controls building was designed and erected 1966-67. It was fundamentally a large steel rectangle enclosing a flexible space wherein the accommodation could be readily altered by means of mostly glass partitions. It was called 'a flexible shed', influenced by Southern Californian design projects, and was built of cheap, lightweight, prefabricated components in sheet steel, with exposed joints and obvious external bracing. Externally, the corrugated steel cladding was plastic-coated and coloured grey; internally, the multi-layered steel sections were white. Crucially, it was the first building of its type to be designed in a way that facilitated new democratic standards in light industry by eliminating segregation between management and employees. Its single restaurant facility was an example of this, an innovation that bucked the previously normal trend for each level of employees in industrial concerns to have their own segregated restaurants. It was the first example in the UK of what became known as 'high-tech architecture'. The Reliance Controls building won the first *Financial Times* Industrial Architecture Award, and then the Architectural Design Project Award. Later, Foster Associates extended the original. Although there was a televised appeal for such an important building to be preserved, it was demolished in 1991.

Roaring Donkey, Albert Street

In the mid-1840s, this small backstreet beerhouse was built of local stone, as part of a terrace, and was originally called the Heart in Hand. It served the occupants of Albert Street, Union Row, and Little London. Its first keeper was William Walker (b. Blackthorne, Oxford, 1811), who stayed in charge until 1868, by which time the little premises were home to himself, his wife and their eight children. He combined this calling with that of a local carrier. However, the Heart in Hand survived as a name only until about 1862, when it was changed to the Rising Sun. Walker's successor was John Williams (b. Newbury, Berkshire, 1837). For some years prior to taking over the premises in 1868, Williams and his wife Hannah had lived just four doors away with their own growing family. They arrived in the pub with their eight children, and soon managed to squeeze in four lodgers as well. Williams made ends meet by combining the occupation of innkeeper with that of coachbuilder. He was gone by 1875, and was replaced by William Hammond, of whom nothing is known. Next, in 1878, came Joseph Gosling (b. Faringdon, 1827), whose simultaneous occupation was that of piano tuner. In 1885, James Taylor set up next door to the Rising Sun as an 'outdoor seller of beer', and three years later, an application to move the Rising Sun's licence onto these premises was refused. Alice Taylor was still

carrying on there as an 'outdoor beer retailer' in 1891, but shortly afterwards, her cottage was incorporated into the Rising Sun next door, which was then remodelled internally.

In 1891, Gosling passed the Rising Sun on to John Wilkins (b. Taunton, Somerset, 1847), who brought his wife, and his son William, who became a bootmaker in Swindon. Wilkins held the pub until well into the 20th century. It was known as the Roaring Donkey for many decades before it was officially so named. The most frequently offered explanation is that from 1857, when the *Swindon Advertiser* set up its premises across the road, the sound of the presses starting up was reminiscent of that made by a donkey. Another suggestion was that William Walker might have kept a donkey on the premises in order to facilitate his secondary occupation of carrier around the town. Whatever the true reason, the name of the Rising Sun was changed to that of Roaring Donkey in 1999.

Roberts, Harry Royston (1921-92)

When he was appointed Swindon's railway workshops manager in 1972, engineer Harry Roberts was a Yorkshireman with a purpose. It was not, however, the same purpose as that held by his bosses at British Rail Engineering Limited, which had been formed in 1970. BREL imagined that Harry would steer the Works through their last handful of years to closure, whilst he was set on trying to attract sufficient work to make a compelling case for keeping them open. When he took over in Swindon, years of underinvestment by the rail industry had taken their toll on machinery and workers. The demoralised workforce, reduced to around sixteen per cent of the 14,000 or so it had been at its height, were already anticipating redundancy and inevitable closure in the near future. Harry Roberts realised that the workers had skills, and discovered that they were behind him in trying to utilise all the abilities at their disposal. They were helped in this by the Transport Act, 1968, which enabled the Works to bid for manufacturing contracts that were outside the rail industry.

Harry Roberts's approach to diversification, coupled with his open style of management, quickly found favour with the workforce. It was a combination that enabled the reduced number of Swindon railway workshops to remain in production far beyond the initial expectations of BREL. Meanwhile, BREL, which was not at all happy with Harry's apparent success, allegedly put difficult and obscure jobs his way that no one else wanted to undertake. In some instances, they knew that Swindon had neither the tools nor the capacity to undertake them either, but the unions and the workforce always rose to the occasion under Harry's leadership. Thus, he continued with this policy, always a thorn in BREL's side and almost doubling the size of the workforce to around 3,800 by the time he retired in 1981. Harry Roberts threw a lifeline to the dwindling Swindon Works at a time in the early 1970s when closure seemed imminent and inevitable. He saved many jobs and created many others, and was always positive about a future for the business in Swindon if BREL was prepared to invest. It was not.

As soon as Harry retired, talks about closure began again in earnest. The Work's committee, realising that with their champion gone they had to take possible closure very seriously, began a programme of lobbying British Rail bosses; the workforce marched in protest, and unions and workers drew up plans to prevent work from being place elsewhere. In 1985, the Government announced that the Swindon Works would close after about a century and a half, and the following year they did.

Rodbourne Lake see Plaum's Pits

Rodbourne Lane crossing Rodbourne Lane was originally the name given to the whole of the street that progressed northwards from Fleet Street, immediately adjacent to the west side of the GWR park. This is now Park Lane until it reaches the Rodbourne railway bridge, and thereafter it is Rodbourne Road. For half a century after the railway line passed across the roadway at this point, the lines were unmanned, and although carriages were prevented from crossing by a gate that was closed when a train was due, pedestrians still had access. It seems to have been left to the signalman in the nearby signal box to close the crossing to carriages whenever a train was due, and warn pedestrians of any danger. A number of fatalities occurred when people attempted to cross and were hit by moving locomotives. Following two such accidents in 1888, when two hundred trains were passing through the station each day, and 2,000 people daily used the crossing, the GWR Company decided to act. The catalyst for this was the death on the line of George Nash, of 6 Jennings Street, just two days short of his 50th birthday. His case particularly caught public attention because he had married Sarah Emily Oakley in 1884, who came with her three children from a previous marriage, and she and George had two of their own, the last being born the year he was killed. Witnesses at his inquest, which was held in The Cricketer's public house, included George's son James Nash of 9 Oxford Street, who said that his father, when he called at James's house on the afternoon of the fatality, was 'the worse for beer'. He was disinclined to let the older man continue home by himself, but George exercised his 'determined temper'. A witness confirmed that George Nash was 'under the influence of drink' at the gates of the Rodbourne crossing and, despite her attempts to hold him back, he went on and was knocked down by a passenger train coming from the direction of Wootton Bassett. The coroner pointed out that as most of the people using the crossing were GWR employees, it was in the railway company's interests to make it safe.

In 1888, the GWR bought enough land to enable it to build 'a subway' beneath the Rodbourne Lane crossing. The undertaking necessitated lowering the road, building a bridge to take the main line, and constructing a walkway for pedestrians. Work began on the project in the middle of 1890, carried out by 'several hundred men, working in night and day shifts', and was completed early in 1891. When, in 1902, Rodbourne Road was chosen as one of the tramcar routes (the service began in 1904), the road beneath the bridge had to be lowered to accommodate them; it was further lowered to allow free passage for the buses that succeeded the trams in 1929.

Rockers Re-United Some of the Swindon bands who played in the rock n' roll era of the 1950s and 1960s were All Things Bright, Aquarius, Clive and the Cyclones, Power Four, Stryknees, The Offbeats, The Sapphires, The Satellites, The Strangers, Vince and the Vigilantes, and Whispers. A number of the musicians who had performed variously in these bands got together in 2012 (when their average age was seventy) and formed Rockers Re-United, with the objective of playing at public and private events to raise money for charities. The catalyst for their formation was the last 'Majestic Dance Night', established in 2000 by Bob Lewis, also as a charity fundraising event, in memory of the dances held in Swindon's Majestic Ballroom. This was the name given to the main Milton Road swimming bath when, during the winter months between 1948 and 1960, it was covered over and used as a public dance hall. Originally intended as a one-off occasion, the Majestic Dance Night became an annual event, always with a live band, and was organised by Bob Lewis until he retired in 2009. Thereafter, Debbie Lawrence co-ordinated the arrangements, and Rockers Re-United was formed to play the last of the series in 2012.

The personnel involved in Rockers Re-United were Geoff Exton, keyboards (formerly of The Sapphires, The Satellites, Vince and the Vigilantes, Us Limited); Keith Hart, lead guitar (Clive and the Cyclones, Power Four, the Strangers); Nigel Norman, bass guitar (All Things Bright, The Offbeats, Whispers); Neil Pike, rhythm guitar (The Sapphires); Dave King, vocals (All Things Bright, Stryknees); and Dave Prosser, drums (Aquarius, Ray River Jazz Band). Rockers Re-United rehearsed in Hook Village Hall, and quickly established a repertoire of fifty tunes. Their first gig, in aid of the Swindon Therapy Centre for Multiple Sclerosis (established in 1982), was held at Grange Drive Community Centre, Stratton St Margaret, in December 2012. The band was an instant success. Early in

2013, Rockers Re-United issued a twenty-two-track CD called *Rock'n'Roll Bonanza*, featuring their favourite tunes from the rock 'n' roll period. Such was their popularity that by the time they had completed their first four gigs, Rockers Re-United had raised £10,000 for charity. (See also Norman, Nigel; Swindon Music Scene.)

Rolleston Street This thoroughfare ran south from Regent Circus. It was begun in the 1870s, and the properties on its east side were demolished in the 1950s to make way for a car park and the six-storey extension to Swindon Technical College (which was itself demolished in 2011 to make way for a retail and leisure complex). The road was named after the Rolleston Estate, on part of which it stood, after the land passed from William Vilett to his nephew, Col. William Vilett Rolleston. Historically, until that time, the Vilett family had owned much of the land west of Regent Street, between Faringdon Street and Victoria Street, an area that was fundamental to the expansion of New Swindon towards Old Town on the hill. The development of the area had been planned, and speculative builders were poised to take advantage of this; Col. Rolleston was amenable to selling it off, but was prevented from doing so when he became bankrupt in 1874. Thereafter, the estate's trustees could only relinquish small plots at a time until the matter was settled, and much more of the estate became available between 1885 and 1887.

Rolleston was coined as a street name as early as 1873 because that was initially decided upon for the eastern side of Regent Circus (then still called York Place), and it was intended to continue this towards the Rolleston estate. However, the east side of Rolleston Street, a single terrace of twenty-six properties, was not built until the mid-1870s. There were two front-room shops in this run of houses, and when Rolleston Street was first occupied, almost every property had at least one person living there who worked in the GWR Works.

Initially, on its corner with Regent Circus, there were two businesses: an auction mart yard built by John G. Ham in 1873; and John Dowling, builder and beer seller. In 1874, Ham's premises were bought by auctioneer Fred Davis. He immediately opened them to Revd Frederick Rowland Young for use as a temporary Free Christian church. The upper part of this building, which had a plain parapet, set-off corner and round arched gable, was retained when shop fronts were put in at street level. In the twentieth century, this became the distinctive site of Barkham's 'the electrical homemakers' showroom and shop, flanked by Townsend & Clifford, and the Quick Service Boot Repairers, until it was all swept away in the 1960s. Barkham's also had another outlet, a little to the east, on the corner with Byron Street.

When houses were built on Rolleston Street, the position of the streets admitting onto the west side of it had already been planned, 1887-88, leaving gaps for what became Horsell Street (built by John Horsell of Commercial Road in 1891) and Edmund Street, which went up in 1894. The north-west end comprised the rear of the premises on the corner with Regent Circus and their outbuildings; there was a terrace of nine houses between the entrances to Horsell Street and Edmund Street, and another terrace of eight ascending a hill thereafter. Most the properties in these streets were also demolished in order for the college extension to be built. The Christian Science Society had a meeting hall in Rolleston Street between 1924 and 1958. The north-west corner of Rolleston Street and Regent Circus comprised the offices and depot of the Bristol Omnibus Company between the 1930s and 1967.

Rye, Arthur Joseph see Ironmongers in Wood Street

Saddlers and harness-makers Documents extant written between the seventeenth and the twentieth centuries suggest that the saddlery and harness-making trade was carried on almost continuously in Swindon, although by only one or two men at any given time. John Deacon of Newport Street was listed as the saddler in 1697 and 1705, and a saddlery still operated there in 1784. By 1830, it was in the hands of Robert Walker. His competitor at the time was Henry Coster of Wood Street, whose business was taken over in 1832 by William Westmacott. In 1857, Westmacott became landlord of the Goddard Arms, High Street, but kept on his Wood Street saddlery and harness-making business until 1863. Then, it was taken over by his son, John Valentine Westmacott, who died in 1867, after which his widow, Louisa Ethel, kept it going for another couple of years or so with the help of her father-in-law. William Westmacott retired from the Goddard Arms in 1870 and died three years later. Meanwhile, James Tarrant (b. Cricklade, 1838), who had pursued the occupation of saddler and harness-maker in Calne, opened up at 16 Newport Street, Swindon during the 1860s, and then relocated to 2 Wood Street, c.1872, and was operating in Cricklade Street by the 1890s.

From 1835, the Westmacotts also had a competitor in Daniel Smith, who that year set up as a saddler and harness-maker in High Street. He was born in Swindon in 1810, and married Elizabeth Keylock (b. Latton, 1807) in 1837. Smith usually had three apprentices, and his business flourished. When he died in 1884, it was immediately taken over by William Henry Norris (b. Marlborough, 1847), the son of master saddler George Norris (b. Great Bedwyn, 1804), who carried on his business in the High Street at Marlborough. W.H. Norris came to Swindon in 1884. He lived with his family at 4 North Street, then at 48 Prospect Place, and in Newport Street immediately prior to moving into Manchester House, High Street in 1897.

Manchester House was a rambling building, erected for a merchant early in the 18th century, and was demolished in 1964. Just before Norris opened for business there, Sidney Allen Burge set up as a saddler and harness-maker at 8 Wood Street. The two men went into partnership, and 'Burge and Norris' was painted on the signboard fixed to Manchester House. Norris died in 1915, and the Burge and Norris premises were taken over by Fred Cleverley, antiques dealer. Burge continued to trade at 8 Wood Street until he died in 1927.

Sanford Street This street was laid out c.1873, connecting College Street with Edgeware Road, and was named after the Sanford family of Nynehead Court, Somerset. This was an old land- and property-owning, politically motivated, county family, and its member who brought the name to Swindon was Charlotte Sanford (1825-1904). She was the daughter of Edward Ayshford Sanford (b. 1794), gentleman, magistrate, one-time Sheriff of Somerset, Member of Parliament, and his first wife, Henrietta (née Langhorn), who died in 1836. In 1847, at Wellington, Somerset, Charlotte married Ambrose Lethbridge Goddard (1820-98), who was then heir to the manor of Swindon, to which he succeeded his father, Ambrose Goddard, in 1852. The couple came to live at Swindon House, the name being changed in 1850 to The Lawn, on the Goddard estate.

Sanford Street was only 123 yards long. It had three short terraces that were built in brick, with freestone dressings, between 1873 and 1878. The two terraces at the southern end, at the junction with Edgeware Road, were the first to go in. These comprised a run of twelve properties on the east side, and ten properties on the west side. On the west side, the area immediately north of the ten houses was occupied by the Congregationalist's iron church, erected there in 1877 and, north of that, another terrace of three properties that ended in a grocer's shop (initially run by Francis Holloway) at the junction with College Street. One of the other properties on this side was a beerhouse. There was empty ground north of the terrace of ten properties on the west side of Sanford Street until 1880-81, when Sanford Street school for boys was built. All of the residential properties were demolished, with the exception of the former caretaker's house next to the school, and the street was redeveloped.

Sanford Street Congregational Church In 1876, the Old Swindon Congregationalists moved from their little 1,050 square-foot, brick-built chapel of 1804 in Newport Street to much larger, custom-built premises in Victoria Street. Almost at once, a chapel for part of this congregation was erected in Sanford Street. This was a corrugated iron building, the former Pembroke Chapel from Oakfield Road, Clifton, Bristol, which had been empty there since 1866 when the Bristol Congregationalists built alternative premises. It was opened in Swindon on 17 April 1877, and was described thus: 'It is an iron structure of decidedly ecclesiastical character, having its nave, side aisles, tower and spire. Between the corrugated iron and inside boarding there is a lining throughout of thick inodorous felt, which renders it impervious to summer heat and winter cold. The dimensions are 88 feet in length and 46 feet in breadth. There is a spacious gallery facing the pulpit, and a large vestry behind. The total accommodation provided is for 700'. Its first minister was Revd Joseph Lambert who, in the same year as his church opened, became a founding member of the Swindon School Board. A Sunday school building was added to the church, which opened next door on 24 September 1888.

The iron church remained until 1895 when it was superseded by a brick-built replacement, designed by Thomas B. Silcock of Bath. This was a neo-Gothic oddity with Jacobean-style embellishments, carved scrolls on the corners, and a stumpy porch tower. The façade featured top-heavy triangular pediments, and a large rose window with 14th-century-style tracery; the other windows were all square-headed, each with two lights and with different treatments in the spandrels. The short tower had an eccentrically designed, gabled parapet with an open turret above. It cost £6,080.

The schoolroom was badly damaged by fire on 18 October 1947. The replacement, with a large assembly hall and a stage, was designed by Thomas Burrington, built by H.J. Spackman & Sons of Swindon, and had lighting by the Strand Electrical & Engineering Company. It reopened on 2 November 1848. The new stage consolidated the church's reputation for theatrical productions, and it was also active in other areas of the arts, and in providing activities for children. Eventually, the Congregationalists joined with the Presbyterians and created the United Reformed Church. The Sanford Street Congregational Church was demolished in 1977.

Sanford Street Boys' School This school was built for the Swindon School Board, which commissioned the design from architect Brightwen Binyon of Ipswich. The site was offered by Ambrose Lethbridge Goddard, Lord of the Manor, and was on 'Wyatt's Ground at Eastcott', an area that had been mentioned as such in documents since the 17th century. The Great Western Railway Company had a first refusal on this site, but negotiations that involved closing their school in Bristol Street, and relocating its pupils under the authority of the then newly formed Swindon School Board, meant that a greater interest had shifted in favour of the latter. Sanford Street School was built by D.C. Jones & Co. of Gloucester, using red and grey bricks, and including moulded string courses and cornices. It was multi-gabled, with large windows with depressed arches, and above the front door was a decorated triangular pediment. The school was intended for 794 boys and it had eight classrooms, five of which were on the ground floor of the building and the remainder were on the floor above; there was a manager's room, headmaster's offices, cloakrooms and lavatories. There was a large playground outside at the rear, and play sheds. The school opened on 4 April 1881, mainly with boys relocated from the GWR's school in Bristol Street. The first headmaster was John Williams, who died in 1904 and was succeeded by George Pressey, who had previously been head at the Drill Hall. For two months in 1914, the school was relocated to the Wesleyan Sunday school building in Faringdon Road and the Primitive Methodist Sunday school building in Regent Street, whilst Sanford Street was requisitioned by the Ministry of War as a temporary hospital. Pressey retired in 1919. The original bell was rung daily by a boy at the school until, one day in the 1930s, Harold Glendower Ball tolled the bell and the clapper fell out, narrowly missing the head teacher. After that, a handbell was used. Sanford Street School was closed in 1966 when its pupils were amalgamated with those of Drove Road School. The school building became Sanford House, the Children's Services Department of Swindon Borough Council, which was relocated in December 2011.

Saracen's Head, Cricklade Street The males of the Horsell family who lived in Albert Street and Cricklade Street worked with their hands. One of them, Reuben Horsell (b. Wootton Bassett, 1792) was also well known for employing his as an extension of his violent temper. He was a plasterer and tiler by trade, and was also the owner of the Saracen's Head, a beerhouse adjacent to the Lord Raglan on the west side of Cricklade Street, immediately before the road dropped into Brock Hill. His son George Horsell (b. Swindon, 1839) became a plasterer in Old Town, and within a few years was employing several men. Another son, Charles Horsell (b. Swindon, 1831), set himself up as a slater, plasterer and turner. William Horsell (b. Swindon, 1824), was also a slater and plasterer. Reuben Horsell opened his lodging house and beerhouse before the 1840s, when it was run for him by the widow Rachael Heath, who was still there a decade later when she was in her mid-seventies. In 1852, he took over the running of the Saracen's Head, eventually styling himself beer retailer and wood turner. Both Horsell and his enterprise had bad reputations; the beer and lodging house was described as 'a low beerhouse', by Henry Haynes, the town's superintendent of police, adding that 'such places are nurseries for perjury and crime'. Being on the edge of Old Swindon's red-light area at the time, it accommodated prostitutes. At no time did Horsell live on the Cricklade Street premises, but was always domiciled at 17 Albert Street. His last appearance as a beer retailer was in 1860, after which he returned to the business of plasterer, and the Saracen's Head ceased to operate.

Scutts, Henry George (1873-1950) Harry Scutts was the self-styled 'Veteran Walking Champion of England'. He was the ninth of thirteen children born to Maurice Thompson Scutts (b. Ashton Keynes, 1840) and his wife Florence Eliza née Ody (b. Lydiard Millicent, 1840), who married at Cricklade in 1860. Harry was born at Bagendon, Gloucestershire, where the family had moved to in 1871. In the late 1870s, they relocated to Aldsworth and then went to Rodbourne Cheney, Swindon during the next decade. Maurice Scutts, who was an agricultural labourer, died in 1887. His widow Florence Eliza Scutts remarried in 1891; her new husband was Richard King

(b. Haydon Wick, 1836). He was a labourer in the railway carriage and wagon works, and they lived at 41 Edinburgh Street.

In 1898, Harry married Edith May Taylor (b. Swindon, 1876), the daughter of Frederick H. Taylor, a house painter living at 27 Providence Row. Edith had always been a servant, working in a succession of households, one of which was the Jefford family, the aerated water manufacturer of Wellington Street. Edith died in 1904, believed to be as a result of giving birth to twins, who also died soon afterwards, but were named Albert Scutts and Andrew John Scutts.

For a while, Harry was a private in the 3rd Wiltshire Regiment. In 1911, he was described as a farm labourer, and was living with his brother Francis (Frank) Norman Scutts and his family at 84 Beatrice Street, Swindon. Frank was then a drilling machinist at the GWR Works. In 1917, Harry married Ruth Beatrice Bryant at Eton, Buckinghamshire. There is a record of just one child, Harry Thomas Scutts (b. Swindon, 1918; d. Swindon, 2006).

After serving in the army, Harry Scutts carved out a career as a rag and bone man, and at the same time developed his interest in long-distance walking, often between the shafts of a closed cart in which were the provisions for his trip. When he walked to Manchester (326 miles in 84 hours and 41 minutes), his cart included a lucky horseshoe and the words 'Good Luck Harry! The Swindon Veteran. Walking from Swindon to Manchester & Back'. On another occasion, he walked between Salisbury and Edinburgh, covering 413 miles on foot in 98 hours and 36 minutes. Short distances (to Harry) included Cardiff to Swindon (just 89 miles in 18 hours), and Bristol to Swindon (8 hours and 27 minutes to cover the 45 miles). He died at 23 Laburnum Road, Swindon (where he had been the householder since 1932), on 27 June 1950.

Seaton, W.A. see Coronation Music Stores

Sheppard, John Henry Harding (1777-1868) and family John Henry Harding Sheppard was born in Swindon, the son of Samuel Sheppard and his wife Ann. He married Ann Holbrook of Pewsey in 1807. Two of their daughters married solicitors: Anna married Alfred Southby Crowdy, whose business was in Swindon, and Martha married John Matthews, solicitor of Cirencester.

Little is known of J.H.H. Sheppard's early life, except that he began as a farmer and seems to have bought up land from an early age. By 1818, he was established as a maltster in High Street, and for a while afterwards he was in the partnership of Sheppard & Tuck. At some point in the 1830s, his business became J. H. Sheppard & Co, hop merchants, brewers, and wholesalers of wine and spirits. By the 1840s, this was John Sheppard & Son, the latter being another John Harding Sheppard. His substantial three-storey, stone-built mansion, with bow windows to the ground floor and first floor, was opposite the market square in High Street, on the corner with Newport Street. It came to the attention of the authorities at the Court Leet in 1824, when its owner was indicted for putting a bow window on the front of the freehold property that encroached on the roadway. This misdemeanour cost him a quit rent (a tax), payable to the Lord of the Manor.

J.H.H. Sheppard operated his brewing business from premises between High Street and Devizes Road, although these were not in his ownership. After his death, these were sold to Richard Bowly, were built up by him in 1870, and became the North Wilts Brewery. At one time, J.H.H. Sheppard also owned the King of Prussia inn in High Street, and some land along what later became Marlborough Road. He also owned Kingshill Farm, the Kingshill estate, properties on Kingshill, cottages in Eastcott Lane, buildings in Bridge Street, the impressive Italianate Kingshill House on Bath Road (although he did not live in it), and Ladd's Mill and the Running Horse public house on the road to Wootton Bassett.

In fact, during his lifetime, John Henry Harding Sheppard amassed a considerable amount of land and property in Old Swindon and around Swindon hill. On a part of the latter, in the early 1840s, two short rows of cottages were built on either side of the North Wilts Canal, at the north end of a track that became Bridge Street, and these were called 'Sheppard's Cottages'. Here too, were two adjacent beerhouses, the Wholesome Barrel, which was owned by the Canal Company, next door to the Old Locomotive. The GWR House, later named the Union Railway Inn, was built in 1841 opposite Sheppard's Cottages, and was owned by Sheppard from then until 1868; from 1844 until his death, he also owned the White Hart beerhouse in Newport Street.

A little to the south of the railway line, near Fleet Street, a short roadway was put up on his land, which was at first named Chapel Street, but later renamed John Street, after him. By the time the Great Western Railway Company's line had gone past Swindon, and work had begun on the Works, J.H.H. Sheppard owned a considerable amount of land immediately to the east and west of Col. Thomas Vilett's holding where the GWR village was being built, and on part of which St Mark's church was erected. In order to extend its village eastwards, the railway company bought two of Sheppard's fields adjacent to Vilett's, and between 1845 and 1847 building contractors Joseph D. and Charles Rigby constructed London Street, Oxford Street and Reading Street on them.

John Henry Harding Sheppard died in 1868, and his property passed to his two sons, John Harding Sheppard (b. Swindon, 1815), and William Sheppard (b. Swindon, 1822). John Harding Sheppard, who did not marry, was, at the time of his father's death, an attorney at law and the chief bailiff at Stoke on Trent; William was a married general medical practitioner and an apothecary living in Ashford, Kent. J.H. Sheppard came back to Swindon to live at 32 High Street, and to organise a number of sales of his father's former holdings, carried out by William Dore. One of these was the sale of his father's old house in High Street, which was bought by solicitor Henry Kinneir, and another was the disposal of Kingshill House, which eventually went to Richard Bowly. In 1870, John released land next to the railway village on what had been known as 'Sheppard's Field' and 'Road Ground', into which, in 1873, were extended London Street, Oxford Street and Reading Street. However, John Harding Sheppard asked that these extensions should instead be called Sheppard Street, Harding Street and John Street. However, because Swindon already had a John Street, named after J.H.H. Sheppard, the new John Street was always known as Henry Street, to which the name was later officially changed.

John Henry Harding Sheppard's Kingshill estate went up for sale variously between 1870 and 1875. On this were built Albion Street, Clifton Street, Exmouth Street, Radnor Street (originally called Redcross Street), and William Street in the late 1870s. Radnor Street cemetery was laid out in 1881. Between 1886 and 1894, Ashford Road, Hythe Road, Folkestone Road, Maidstone Road and Kent Road were developed. When he retired, John Harding Sheppard relocated to Kent.

Short, William (1836-1879)

Born the son of a general labourer and sometime gardener at Coxstalls, Wootton Bassett, William Short eventually became one of Swindon's earliest commercial photographers. By the time he was in his early twenties, he had set up as a naturalist in London, living at 50 Praed Street, a stone's throw from Paddington Station. In 1859, he married, at St John's church Paddington, Charlotte Sophia Farmer (b. Hampstead Norreys, Berkshire, 1835). She was a baker's daughter, and was also at the time living in Praed Street, where their first two children were born. The family relocated to Swindon c.1865, living first in a cottage on the corner of Newport Street and Short Hedge (part of Devizes Road). Short advertised himself as a naturalist, and his wife as a milliner. Effectively, he was part-taxidermist, part-dealer in products made from fur and feather. He soon added photographer to his portfolio, and was advertising himself as such from 1867. The following year, the family removed to 7 Newport Street, where he renamed the business as London Photographic Establishment. Although cartes-de-visite were his bread and butter work, his agricultural upbringing enabled him to advertise his expertise in photographing landscapes, buildings and machinery. In

1874, he transferred the business to a better address at 15 Wood Street, opposite the King's Arms Hotel, and slightly changed its name to London Photographic Studio. Charlotte worked from the same address as a milliner, a cleaner of feather and fur, and a cleaner and dyer of bonnets and hats. So continued the dual business until 1879, when William died and his activities were taken over by the Great Western Photographic Company.

Sikh Temple, Kembrey Street In 1972, the small Swindon community of Sikhs took over the former Salvation Army citadel in North Street, where the number of people using the premises grew to three hundred Sikh families. In the early 1990s, they began a decade of planning and fundraising in order to establish a custom-built Gurdwara (temple) in Swindon. Swindon Borough Council, in 1994, offered land in Kembrey Street, Gorse Hill that it had previously earmarked for community use. The fundraising became international, as £1.2 million would be needed. The architects for what would be the Shri Guru Nanak Gurdwara were Patrick Wilson Architects of Pewsey; the structural engineer was the Springfield Design Partnership of Old Town; and the place was built in forty-six weeks by R.J. Leighfield of Swindon. It was the first custom-built Sikh temple in Wiltshire.

The foundation stone was laid on 9 June 2001, preceded by a forty-eight-hour continuous reading of the Guru Granth Sahib, the Sikh Holy Book, at the soon-to-be vacated North Street temple. An important contributor to the fundraising was Mata Chanan Kaur Virk, who provided £21,000 of her own money, in recognition of which a plaque was created. Following the atrocities at the World Trade Centre, New York, on 11 September 2001, ten windows were smashed at the temple, then under construction. The 'topping-out' ceremony, when the large dome was put into place, was on 13 October 2001. The building was officially opened on 20 January 2002 during a ceremony that involved three days of special prayers and a procession from the North Street temple to the new one in Kembrey Street. One of the speakers at the opening was Michael Doe, Bishop of Swindon. The temple was given a Wiltshire Police Secured by Design Award, when it was the first building of its kind in the country to be so honoured. In October 2003, the Swindon Sikhs opened a new Punjabi community centre adjacent to the Gurdwara, costing £700,000 and also built by R.J. Leighfield.

Simons, Thomas Henry see Protheroe, James Smith

Sir Daniel Arms, Fleet Street In the late 1840s, George Selby (b. Swindon, 1816), a tea dealer, bought a plot of land with a dwelling house on it, immediately south-east of the GWR Company's model village in New Swindon. The site was almost opposite the Locomotive public house, in a part of Fleetway (otherwise known as Fleet Street) that was then called Bleat Lane. By 1851, Selby had opened a grocery business there, and very soon afterwards, a short run of houses was erected adjacent, and called Fleetway Terrace. Selby's property was later to be numbered 11 Fleetway Terrace. George Selby, who married Elizabeth Thomas at Bristol in 1841 and was widowed in 1850, lived above the shop with his two sons, George (b. Bristol, 1841) and Theophilus (b. Swindon, 1847), his daughter Rhoda (b.

Swindon, 1846) and his mother-in-law, Mary Thomas (b. Rudghill, 1786), who was the family's housekeeper. These premises would eventually become the Sir Daniel Arms.

Living just around the corner with his wife and daughter, at 6 High Street in the railway village, was William Warner (b. Eastington, Gloucestershire, 1817), a draper and outfitter. At the same time, Charles Lea (b. Fairford, Gloucestershire, 1817), draper and tailor, was living and working in Cirencester. By 1857, he was in Swindon, where he opened his West of England Cloth Hall at 3 & 4 Bath Terrace, offering 'sewing by machinery'. By 1858, Selby's property was in Warner's hands, and Lea had set up there under lease as a draper and tailor. The 1861 census records him as employing six men and two boys at 11 Fleetway Terrace. Then, Charles Lea relocated his business there from the terrace in Bath Road, advertising it as a 'steam machine clothing manufactury'; whilst in High Street, William Warner turned his attention to beer retailing. In 1865, with Charles Lea still operating the latest technology, his wife opened a temperance hotel and refreshment rooms, apparently at the same address. She later advertised the premises, which she had set up as a commercial and family boarding house, as the 'New Swindon Boarding and Eating House' where 'comfort and economy (were) ensured'. Charles Lea continued to be occupied as a tailor and hatter in workshops at the rear, specialising in 'mourning at the shortest notice'.

Mrs Lea's involvement was just a means of easing the premises towards a change of status. By 1867, Charles Lea was advertising it as The Sir Daniel Private and Commercial Boarding House and, soon afterwards, himself there as 'Charles Lea, Sir Daniel

Fleetway'. It had been named after Daniel Gooch (1816-89), the man who effectively built Swindon's railway workshops and who was the GWR's Locomotive Superintendent, 1837-64. Lea did not stay there long, though long enough to install a 'first-class billiard room' containing a brand new table. He handed the Fleetway Terrace business over to Robert Kempster, who rebranded it the 'Sir Daniel Refreshment Rooms'. By 1876, William Jones was in charge of what had by then become the 'Sir Daniel Arms Inn', and was probably responsible for making internal refurbishments. Eventually, it was sold out of private hands and later became the property of Ushers.

This was a narrow, three-storey, three-bay building with a plain parapet, and the central section on levels two and three was slightly forward of the rest of the elevation. There were two square-headed windows, one above the other on levels two and three in the central section, with wide, flat surrounds. The decorative value was all at street level, where four lions rampant, made out of wood and carrying flags, stood above a moulded and decoratively bracketed cornice with brattishing above. This was all set forward on two slender stanchions that were partly barley-twisted. On the same plane were two decorated end pilasters, and the front entrance was recessed behind these features. With the exception of the brattishing, which disappeared, the front elevation remained remarkably unchanged. The premises were remodelled internally in 1970, and renovated again in 1984.

The Sir Daniel Arms acquired a poor reputation and, after a period of closure, was reopened in 1993 as The Sportsman. It closed again, and when the pub and its Victorian warehouses at the rear were demolished in 2000, only the pub sign, two stanchions, some front panels and one of the lions were saved. The other survivor was the name; in 2007, J. D. Wetherspoon opened its new Sir Daniel Arms, just a few yards from the site of the original. The architects of this new building were Tuffin Ferraby Taylor of Guildford.

Smith, A.E. undertakers Henry Smith was born into a family of Wesleyan Methodists at Chiseldon in 1842. He became a carpenter and joiner, and married Emma Sextone (b. Blunsdon, 1840) in 1870. Almost immediately, Henry went to London in the hope of gaining employment, where he lodged with a watchcase maker in Islington, while Emma stayed with her father, bailiff James Sextone, at The Lodge, Chiseldon. She had joined Henry in Islington by 1872, when their son James Henry was born there, returning to Swindon the following year to set up home at 12 Sanford Street. There, seven more children were born to them: Joseph William (b. 1873), Elizabeth (b. 1876), Albert Edward (b. 1877), Alice (b. 1879), Caroline (b. 1880), Ethel (b. 1883) and Frederick (b. 1886). During the 1880s, Henry turned his skills as a carpenter and joiner to making coffins, and established a business as undertaker. The family moved to 22 Gordon Road in the 1890s, and Henry died in 1917. Henry's little brick-built house in Sanford Street survived the much later redevelopment of the area, when all the other properties around it were pulled down, and it became home to the caretaker of the adjacent Sanford Street Boys' School.

It was Henry and Emma's fourth child, Albert Edward Smith, whose name is perpetuated in that of the firm. Albert joined his father's business when he left school, and in 1903 married Alberta Annie Foss (b. Wanborough, 1879). Just prior to the marriage, Alberta Annie was clerk and cashier at the Wellington Hotel, Gloucester Street, Swindon, which was run by her father Samuel B. Foss. In the 1880s, he had been proprietor of the Kooloo Coffee House at 23 Wood Street, Old Town, and, in New Swindon, of the Three Cups Coffee Palace at 92 Regent Street.

After their wedding, Albert and Alberta Annie lived at 22 Gordon Road with his parents and his siblings until the rest of the family relocated to 1 Clifton Street. Albert and Alberta Annie's first child, Marjorie Foss, was born in 1904; thereafter, were Donald Henry Beart (b. 1905, died 1906), Lester Albert (b. 1907), and Donald Samuel (b. 1910). Another son, Colin Foss, was born to them in 1922. Alberta Annie Smith died in 1942; Albert Edward Smith died in 1952 at his home, The Furrows, 241 Marlborough Road, Swindon. Their son Donald Samuel continued the business from Gordon Road. In the 1960s, that part of Swindon was demolished, and A.E. Smith Funeral Directors removed to Queen's Drive. In 1976, it was taken over by Lodge Brothers, a similar family firm that had begun in the 18th century, but they continued to trade in Swindon as A.E. Smith.

Smith family of butchers and farmers Eastcott House is a small, modern office development on the site of a sixteenth-century building in High Street. That building was previously a hostelry called the King's Head, and then the King of Prussia Inn. It closed in 1880, and soon afterwards became a butcher's shop. In 1981, ignoring a public outcry and a petition, Swindon Corporation permitted a property developer to carry out an act of total vandalism: the complete demolition of this ancient building. The office development that took its place was designed to have an external appearance that, to a degree, resembled what had been destroyed. In an effort to ameliorate public anger further, it was called Eastcott House. This took its name from that of Eastcott Smith, whose family had traded as butchers from this building for a century, since it ceased to be the King of Prussia Inn.

Eastcott Smith, more correctly Edward Eastcott Smith (b. Swindon, 1922), was named after Lower Eastcott Farm. Interestingly, in the eighteenth century, Lower Eastcott Farm was named to distinguish it from Eastcott farm, which was much closer to Swindon Hill; then Eastcott Farm changed its name to Upper Eastcott Farm to make things even clearer. Upper Eastcott Farm was demolished in the 1860s, whereupon Lower Eastcott Farm became just Eastcott Farm.

The 108-acre Lower Eastcott Farm was owned by Thomas Vilett when the Smith family took over as tenant farmers in 1850. They continued to work the farm until it was bought by Swindon Corporation in 1903, when the local authority immediately built its electricity works on the site. The Eastcott of the farm's title related to the name of the hamlet of Eastcott (north of the road between Old Town and Wootton Bassett, and west of the road between Old Town and Cricklade) in which it was situated. The first of the family to work it was Edward Smith.

Edward Smith was born in Cricklade in 1823. He married Jane Sexton (b. Coleshill, 1822) at Faringdon in 1848, and, two years later, the couple came to Lower Eastcott Farm, where Jane was to give birth to

ten children over the next fourteen years. Of this issue, William Eastcott Smith (b. 1857) and John King Smith (b. 1861) both became butchers. Meanwhile, Edward, who slaughtered and butchered his own beasts, was styled 'farmer and butcher'. In 1865, he established a butcher's shop in Wood Street (later to be numbered No. 33), and also began to sell meat from a stall in Market Square, High Street, New Swindon, (which name was changed to Emlyn Square in 1901). At Eastcott Farm, Edward employed 'two labourers and one boy'; by the 1870s, this had increased to 'four labourers and two women'.

It was Edward's son, William Eastcott Smith (b. Swindon, 1857) who moved the business into the former King Of Prussia Inn (which would become 4 High Street), c. 1880. Each of the two Old Town premises could be accessed from the rear of either. In 1882, he married Jesse Emily Morris (b. Swindon, 1858), whose father William Morris founded the *Evening Advertiser* in 1854. Edward Smith died in 1898, when he was also the owner of the 72-acre Greenmeadow Farm, Haydon Wick, said to be the residence of William Eastcott Smith. The executors of Edward Smith sold Greenmeadow Farm through the firm of Bishop & Pritchett at the Goddard Arms on 21 August 1900.

In 1907, Lord of the Manor, Fitzroy Pleydell Goddard assigned a five-year lease on Broome Farm to William Eastcott Smith. Two of his sons, William Edward Smith (b. Greenmeadow Farm, 1884) and Harry Morris Smith (b. Greenmeadow Farm, 1887), lived at Broome Farm. Initially, the former was the farmer and the latter was a butcher. In High Street, William Eastcott's wife Jesse Emily helped in the business, whilst their daughter Kathleen (b. Greenmeadow Farm,

1889) looked after the home. Following William Eastcott Smith's death in 1911, changes were made.

William Edward Smith of Broome Farm effectively took on responsibility for the business in High Street, as well as running the farm. He too, was then styled 'farmer and butcher', but he was more suited to farming, and it was not long before he retreated to Broome Farm. He married Gertrude Tanner in 1945, and died in 1959. Harry Morris Smith took over in High Street. He met Minnie Matthews (1898-1958), who worked in Lloyd's Bank opposite No. 4 High Street, and the couple married in 1921. They had three children, who were all born over the shop: Edward Eastcott Smith (b. 1922), Valerie Smith (b. 1924) and William Morris Smith (b. 1929).

When their father died in 1966, the boys took over the shop, and they were to become the last of the family to be involved with the former King of Prussia building. In 1951, Edward Eastcott married Elizabeth Harris (b. Cowbridge, 1923), whom he had met when supplying meat to the local authority food depot, where she worked in Broome Manor Lane. William Morris met his future wife Joan Gardner (b. Swindon, 1931) whilst they were both riding horses in Broome Manor Lane. She was the daughter of 'Lardy' Gardner, the famed Purton maker of lardy cake. They married in 1954. Broome Farm was bought by Swindon Borough Council in 1950. Harry Morris Smith took over the tenancy of Westlecot Farm in 1962; it continued with his son William Morris Smith until 2002.

Snell, Edward (1820-1880) Known today more for his valuable legacy of watercolours, painted in the 1840s, of the GWR Works and model village at Swindon, and of early locomotives in the Works, Snell nonetheless made a very significant contribution to the development of the site itself. Yet he was only in Swindon for six years. Edward Snell was born at Barnstable, Devon, where his father was a clock and watchmaker, jeweller and silversmith. He died in 1827; the business was sold, and the family continued to live partly on the proceeds. Edward's mother was Elizabeth Stothert, who, through family connections, was able to place her fourteen-year-old son with the well-established engineering firm of Stothert & Pitt in Bath. When his apprenticeship as an engineer and millwright was successfully completed in 1842, he relocated to the firm's works in Bristol, where he resigned within a year over pay and working conditions. An introduction to Daniel Gooch, then the GWR's Locomotive Superintendent and the man who effectively built the Swindon Works, secured Snell a job at Swindon. There, he became the head draughtsman by 1845, and in 1846 planned the extension to the Works. Latterly, he was the deputy manager under Archibald Sturrock, another of Gooch's protégés, with whom he did not get along. This prompted him to resign from the GWR in 1850 and sail for Australia, where he continued his engineering career, and his painting, before returning many years later to live in Cornwall.

Southern Exchange This was a professional repertory theatre company formed by Charles Savage in 1978 and based at the Wyvern Theatre, Swindon, where he was artistic director. Its original working title was The Southern Theatre Company. Savage's intention was to use a permanent company of fifteen actors and managerial support to mount top-quality productions in a bid to offset the increasing costs of buying-in touring plays with named principals. The cost of such plays was becoming generally prohibitive for many provincial theatres; the Hexagon Theatre, Reading, and Poole Centre for the Arts immediately came on board as part-sponsors of the project.

Southern Exchange was launched on 11 July 1978 with a press conference at the National Theatre on the South Bank in London. Its founding actors, all of whom came with a wealth of theatre, television, film and radio experience, were Brendan Barry, Ken Bones, Nigel Bradshaw, Tim Brierley, Adrienne Burgess, Hazel Douglas, John Fleming, Peter Forest, Meryl Hampton, Peter Mantle, Lloyd McGuire, Chris Mead, Michael Scholes, Mason Taylor and Sue Withers. Two of the group left soon afterwards, when they were offered television work and work in America. The backing management team comprised Vandra Edwards, company manager; Pat Dunne, wardrobe mistress; Anne Rafferty, wardrobe assistant; Janet Benge, costume designer; Alice Prier, design assistant; and Vicki Stirling, in charge of wigs. It also had its own press and publicity officer, Yorkshire-born and Ballet Rambert-trained Shelley Sutton. She had also done public relations for the Victoria & Albert Museum, been a BBC radio presenter, and a director and actor at Bristol Arts Centre. She joined Southern Exchange from a theatre in Harlech, North Wales.

Southern Exchange opened with *Lock Up Your Daughters*, by Bernard Miles, Laurie Johnson and Lionel Bart, and the rest of its opening season comprised *The Rivals*, by Richard Brinsley Sheridan; Alan Ayckbourn's *Time and Time Again*; Ronald

Gow and Walter Greenwood's *Love on the Dole*; and *The Ghost Train*, by Arnold Ridley. (See also Wyvern Theatre Company.)

Spiller's Furniture, Upholstery, & Cabinet Manufactory

Spiller's was one of Swindon's most enduring businesses. It began in New Swindon in 1843, and ended in Old Town in 2003. 'Where will be found every requisite for a complete furnish at the most reasonable charges', declared its Victorian publicity. The founder of the firm was John Spiller (1819-79), who was born the son of a farmer in Church Stanton, Somerset. John married his first wife, Hannah née Greedy, in 1843, which was when the couple settled in Swindon at 10 London Street, where he was described as a carpenter joiner. He married his second wife, Josephine Eliza née Downing, in 1857 and they immediately moved into 10 Bridge Street, which was where he established a business dealing in second-hand furniture, and making and selling new furniture. By then, he was describing himself as a cabinet maker. In c.1860, he set up in 1 and 2 Bath Buildings, on the corner of Bath Road and Devizes Road in Old Town, and the family lived on the two floors above.

The couple had several children: John Edward Albert Spiller (1858-1932), who was to take over the business from his father; twins Louiza Mary Ashley and James Wynn Clifton (b. 1860); Josephine Eliza (b. 1862); and Emily Sophia Augusta and Ada Hannah Downing (b. 1863). Their mother, Josephine Eliza, died in 1870, just as the Bath Buildings corner began to stock carpets and wallpaper, and to undertake framing for pictures and needlework.

When John the founder died, the business was taken over by J.E.A. Spiller. He had married Ruth Thorp (b. Swindon, 1855) in 1884, and they had three children: Mabel (b. 1884); Oscar Leopold (b. 1889), who was to become the third generation of Spiller to run the business; and Grace Marion (b. 1895). They lived nearby in Victoria Street, eventually moving into no. 132 early in the 1900s. Oscar Leopold Spiller married Barbara Yeo in 1916, took over Spiller's Furnishers in 1932, and retired in 1937, leaving the firm in the hands of Bernard Waldron, who had been his junior partner. Oscar Spiller died in 1941. In 1947, Waldron was joined by Kenneth Perkins; Waldron and Perkins operated Spiller's together until the latter died in 1970. The following year, Waldron opened a Spiller's bedding department at 76 Victoria Road. Two years later, the business was taken over by Trevor Whittle and his wife Elaine, who saw out its remaining years. Spiller's was still operating from 132 Victoria Road when it closed, although the warehouses at the rear had by then been converted to residential, as would be the shop.

Sports Ground opening, off County Road The sports ground was opened at the County Ground on 13 May 1893, at which time a celebratory 'athletic and cycling carnival' was held. It was organised by the committee of Swindon Amateur Athletic & Cycling Club, on whose secretary fell much of the preparatory work. This was Albert H. Noble, a railway clerk, who lived at 46 Rolleston Street. It was not a free occasion, however. Spectators who arrived in carriages had to pay 2/6d for their carriage and driver, and an extra 6d for each occupant; persons admitted to the pavilion and the enclosure that was immediately in front of it, each parted with 2/-; sixpence

was taken from individuals elsewhere in the grounds; and children under fourteen years of age were charged half the adult price for whichever part of the sports ground they were situated. Some 6,000 people turned up to watch Walter Long, MP, open the meeting; earlier in the proceedings, his wife, Lady Doreen Long, sat down to a luncheon in the company of one hundred guests in a large marquee on the site. A large number of on-site bets were openly called and taken on the outcomes of the various races, even though betting was strictly prohibited.

Races on the day, which were all handicapped and run on the flat, included one mile, 880 yards, 440 yards, 330 yards for local boys, and a 120 yards sprint. The bicycle races comprised a three-mile, open handicapped race, a one-mile scratch invitation race, a one-mile race for members of the Swindon Amateur Athletic & Cycling Club, a one-mile open handicapped race, and an 880 yards open handicapped race. A competitor in the one-mile race was James Kibblewhite of Purton, who, in 1889, set a world record for the three miles. Yet of the twenty starters who lined up for the mile at Swindon, only four completed the course, not including Kibblewhite, who had retired on the sixth lap. One of the competitors in the three-mile cycle race, G.P. Chandler of Reading, injured himself when he came off his cycle (which was a write-off as a result), crashing into a young spectator who was taken to hospital with head injuries.

Despite these disappointments, the day was such a success that the County Ground Company, which owned the site, considered laying a cinder running track and widening the cycle track. However, these improvements were not then made, but eventually a cycle track was installed to encircle the cricket area, with a surface of red ash.

Sprittles, Dorothy Ellen (1909-1989)

The Sprittles family came from Crewe, Cheshire, and was an example of generations of railway workers who moved with the industry. Dorothy's grandfather had been a boiler maker at Crewe, where her uncle had been an iron turner. Her own father, Albert John Sprittles (b. Crewe, 1882), was a steam engine fitter in the Crewe railway works, at age nineteen. In 1905, he married Isabella Buchan (b. Crewe, 1881) in Swindon, by which time he was employed as a boilermaker at the GWR Works. Their first child, Charles William, was born in Swindon in 1907, followed two years later by Dorothy. The family lived at 69 Redcliffe Street. At the beginning of the 1920s, Dorothy joined the West Swindon Youth Club, which was held at Jennings Street School, and she was active in its activities for the next half-century.

Dorothy never married. She was an unmistakable figure with short slicked-back hair, and a suit and tie, which gave her a rather manly appearance. She learnt to play the guitar, took a great interest in music, and was liked by children, who called her 'Auntie Dot'. People remember her for the music shop she ran opposite the park in Faringdon Road, between the 1930s and her retirement in the late 1960s, and the lessons she gave on a range of musical instruments in her flat above the retail premises. Pupils who went there came away smelling strongly of the Old Holborn roll-ups she smoked almost continuously, and the fug of smoke in which their lessons were held. Many had memories of her much-singed woolly sweaters. She ran a folk club in the 1960s, and put together a rock band of youngsters, which she called The Buccaneers, after her mother's maiden name. She was also a lifelong member of the Salvation Army in Swindon, and was buried in the cemetery at Whitworth Road.

St Tropez Massage Parlour

In the 1960s, Swindon reference library maintained a card index of local societies and other Swindon-related information. One of these cards was headed 'Brothels', and contained the addresses of those establishments that were then in Tenzing Gardens and Gordon Gardens (later demolished to make way for the Islington Road multi-storey car park) and Medgbury Road. The addresses had been provided by the prostitutes associated with them, who also did business around the town hall, wherein was the reference library. On cold nights, or when trade was slow, the girls often went in for a warm or a chat. The last entry on this card read 'Venereal Disease Clinic', followed by its daily opening times at the hospital. Brothels have long been set up in Swindon, raided, and put out of business, but none achieved the longevity of the St Tropez Massage Parlour, latterly known as the St Tropez Health Studio, at 137 Victoria Road.

It originated in the mid-1980s, behind blanked-out windows, and an ever-open doorway illuminated by a diffusion of reddish light. The brothel was referred to in various newspaper reports over the years, and in 2008, five women were sentenced for renting rooms there to prostitutes. Then, Diana Jones, a one-time Bridgend pub landlady, pleaded guilty and was sentenced at Merthyr Crown Court – although at the time absent whilst living in Cyprus – for running four brothels, of which the St Tropez in Swindon was one. The St Tropez remained in business, although occasionally interrupted by police raids, and in March 2013, a woman was arrested when the police raided the premises and found three suspected prostitutes on site. The brothel reopened within a week, and another arrest was made. The St Tropez finally closed in June 2013 in the wake of police activity following complaints from nearby residents. The premises were immediately put up for sale. The building, of 1,056 square feet, had a large yard at the rear, and had lately been fitted up with a kitchen and two reception rooms downstairs, and four separate bedrooms upstairs for the use of prostitutes and their clients.

Steam Railway Co. public house, Newport Street The impressive double-gabled front elevation, with its central-linking, former carriageway entrance, was put up on the south side of Newport Street in 1876, when the place was rebuilt and the interior remodelled. There had been a much smaller beerhouse or public house called the White Hart on this site since the 1700s, which was renamed the Bull in 1782. Thus, it remained until 1881, when it was renamed Railway Hotel. In 1976, it became the Old Town Tavern, and has been the Steam Railway Co. since 1992. (See also Bull public house, High Street; Bull public house, Newport Street.)

Stiles, Walter Robert John (1914-86) Born at Marlborough, Johnnie Stiles was much later to find fame as the eponymous leader of one of the best dance bands of the 1940s and '50s. He came from a line of rural bricklayers who worked in the Marlborough area. His grandfather, Tom Stiles (b. West Lavington, 1851), carried on the trade and was, at the same time, keeper

of the coffee tavern in Pewsey High Street. That was where Johnnie Stiles's father, Walter Tom Stiles (1877-1937), was born. He was also a bricklayer, and, in 1902, he married Marlborough-born Mary Ellen Taylor (1880-1924). Walter Robert John (Johnnie) was their third child.

After leaving school, Johnnie Stiles went into the carpentry trade for a living, and learnt to play the trumpet as a hobby, turning out for the Marlborough brass band. He came to Swindon early in the 1930s, and in 1935 joined the Harry Smith band, which had a residency at the Bradford Hall (where Smith was the manager, and which is now the Arts Centre) in Old Town. When Smith left to join the fire service at the start of the Second World War, Stiles took over the band and also became a volunteer fireman. It was during this period that he was severely burnt on the leg whilst fighting a blaze at Plymouth, an injury that troubled him for the rest of his life. By 1940, he had formed the Johnnie Stiles Band, taking with him Smith's young saxophone player Roger Summerfield, and often making a space for Harry Smith, also on saxophone. He gave Summerfield a special job: to keep a record of all the musicians who would henceforth play in his band. Also in 1940, Stiles's original twelve-piece line-up made their first radio recording, in the 'Music While You Work' half-hour at the BBC studios in Bristol. The original line-up included the violin player Charlie Comley, who was later to front his own band, and who took over the baton of the Empire Theatre in 1952, where he was the venue's last pit orchestra conductor. It also included clarinet and saxophone player John 'Jock' Walker, who played with most Swindon bands of the 1930s and '40s, and was a full-term fixture with the Stiles outfit, and Gordon Talbot, pianist and arranger for the same length of time.

Johnnie Stiles married Dorothy Joan Bingham (b. Swindon. 1921) at Battersea, London, in 1948. The band continued until 1958, playing at all of the dance venues in Swindon, but was particularly associated with the Majestic Ballroom, where it had a residency during the winter months. The Majestic was the name given to the boarded-over main bath used for dancing (1948-60) at the public baths in Milton Road. At its largest, the Johnnie Stiles Band had fifteen musicians; over the eighteen years it existed, more than fifty musicians played in its ranks. Its leader had the reputation of being a strict disciplinarian, which he had to be to keep a big dance band in order and encourage them to attain the standards he required.

Although the band had built up a substantial local following, it only began to achieve national success when it won a competition at Reading, and then entered the *Melody Maker* 'All Britain' Dance Band Championships, held at the King's Hall, Belle Vue, Manchester. It was placed third in 1945, second in 1946, dropped to seventh in 1947, and then bounced back to take the Championship title in 1948 with a programme of three scintillating numbers, during which Johnnie played very forcefully. One of the judges on that occasion was the black American trumpet player Rex Stewart, who had played with the Fletcher Henderson and Duke Ellington bands. When Johnnie collected the Championship trophy, Stewart leant across and said: 'Man, you sure can play that horn', which Johnnie always thereafter considered to have been the greatest compliment of his music career. Afterwards, the band went into the BBC studios in Manchester and recorded a fifteen-minute radio programme. It consolidated its lead position in the dance band world when, in 1949, it once again won the *Melody Maker* 'All Britain' Championships, and then the *Musical Express* Dance Band Championships at the Winter Garden, Blackpool. The Johnnie Stiles band was defeated in the *Melody Maker* Championships in 1950, which was the catalyst for its leader's decision to withdraw from further competitions.

Trophies won by the band from 1946, including the 'All Britain' successes, were displayed on a shelf behind the bar at the King's Head, Fleet Street, Swindon, which was known as 'the musician's pub'. During the 1950s, the band played during the summer months at the Regal Ballroom in the Mechanics' Institute building, Emlyn Square, returning to the Majestic in the winter.

After its founder's retirement in 1958, the Stiles band was taken over by Gordon Talbot; it was immediately renamed the Gordon Talbot Band and continued to play at the Majestic until 1960, when the venue decided it would no longer facilitate dancing. Johnnie Stiles became landlord of the White Hart public house at Stratton St Margaret, 1958-80. He then retired, which did not suit him, so he bought the Queensfield Stores in 1982. The life of a provisions retailer proved to be no more exciting than retirement, so he sold the business and took on the Freke Arms near Hannington. That was where he died, survived by Dorothy until 1988.

Stoddart, David Leonard (b. 1926), Lord Stoddart of Swindon

This independent Labour politician was Member of Parliament for Swindon, 1970-1983. Swindon had voted solidly for Labour between 1945 and 1969, when Francis E. Noel Baker, who had held Swindon since 1955, resigned. He had acquired a reputation as an absentee MP who took innumerable holidays in Greece, which earned him the title 'the Member for Athens West', and ultimately made him unpopular with the electorate. Such was the backlash against Noel Baker, that David Stoddart, who was put up as the Labour candidate at the by-election following Noel Baker's resignation, lost by 478 votes to Christopher John Ferguson Ward, the Conservative candidate. But Swindon was still Labour in its heart, and nine months later, at the 1970 general election, David Stoddart took Swindon back for Labour.

During his period as Swindon's MP, Stoddart was Parliamentary Private Secretary to the Minister of Housing & Construction, 1974-75; Assistant Government Whip, 1975; Lord Commissioner of the Treasury, 1976-77; and Junior Opposition Spokesman on Industry, 1982-83. His period as Swindon's MP was not a good one for the town. In 1975, unemployment in Swindon reached a post-war record high, well above the national average. Large manufacturing companies in the town either closed down or made many people redundant. In 1982, at a moment when a little success might have helped to lift Swindon spirits, Swindon Town Football Club dropped for the first time into the 4th Division of the Football League.

Stoddart's tenure as Swindon's MP coincided with the lead-up to the closure of the town's railway works, so he was much occupied in talks with British Rail Engineering Limited and the railway unions. In 1983, he prophesied to Parliament that the Swindon railway works had 'no future beyond 1986', adding that the workforce felt aggrieved at what they considered to be 'treachery by the Government and British Rail over a long period'. At the 1983 election, Stoddart was defeated by the Conservative Simon Christopher Coombs, who represented the town for three consecutive terms. Also in 1983, Stoddart was given his Life Peerage. His memorial in Swindon is David Stoddart Gardens, a sheltered housing development of seventy-eight flats in Omdurman Street, Gorse Hill.

Strict and Particular Baptist Chapel, South Street In 1845, a permanent building was erected in Provident Row, the eastern extension of South Street, Prospect, by disgruntled breakaway members of the Congregational Chapel in Newport Street and their supporters. Built of stone, the Provident Row chapel was set back some forty-two feet from the line of the road, and had a frontage of sixty-five feet, with a slight forward projection of what were effectively wings either side of a central core. A small burial ground was established between the chapel and the roadway, wherein the last burial took place in 1909. Inside, were seats for 220 people, but the place seems to have been without a regular minister until c.1875. Then, the office was taken on by corn merchant Robert Pigott of 15 North Street, Swindon, who was born into a Quaker family at Faringdon in 1830. He stayed there until 1902, after which the chapel was described only as being licensed for the solemnisation of marriages and confirmed that 'ministers supplied'. In 1979, Mike Welsh bought the chapel from the Baptist Union, for conversion to a family home. The graveyard was excavated and the remains found in thirty-six graves were reinterred in

Purton cemetery. (One headstone referred to a resident of Purton.) The removal was undertaken by Maslin's, with the services of a Wiltshire self-employed gravedigger called 'Lardy' Bristow, who regularly ate his sandwiches sitting on the graves. In 1981, the property was divided into two, and the following year, the larger of the two was sold to Revd Andrew Hake, who had led the Community Development Team in Swindon Borough Council. The smaller property was also sold; it contained a baptismal chamber with stone steps down, all secreted in the wooden floor. It has since been remodelled, and renamed Providence House.

Swindon 105.5 radio This is a non-commercial community radio station for Swindon, founded by Shirley Ludford, who became the station manager when it was launched on 16 March 2008. The date was chosen to coincide to the day with the thirty-ninth anniversary of Swindon Town Football Club's defeat of Arsenal, 3-1, to take the Football League Cup at Wembley in 1969. This also connected with the station's first venue, the studio at Swindon Town's County Ground. The station was licensed by Ofcom as a not-for-profit venture, which meant that it could not take commercial advertising. It had to be funded by grants, donations, corporate support, and by organising fundraising events. The initial licence was for five years, and this was extended by another five years in 2013. In 2011, Swindon Borough Council made it possible for *Swindon 105.5* to move into Eastcott Community Centre, and the following year, the radio station was looking to place a transmitter on the top of Swindon's tallest building, the David Murray John Tower in the centre of town. Instead, it moved to the Bentley Centre in Stratton Road, where it continues to operate with the help of up to 150 volunteers.

Swindon Athletic Club In 1920, a group of local business and professional men met with a view to forming an athletic club in Swindon. A provisional committee organised the preliminaries, and the first meeting, at which the committee of permanent officers was decided, was held in an upstairs room at the County Ground Hotel on 28 February 1921. Eighty members attended. The club's first president was solicitor Thomas Kimber, who had been part of the firm of Butterworth, Rose, Kimber and Bradford that had been dissolved in 1907, and who was, at the time of the SAC's formation, chairman of Swindon Town Football Club.

The SAC's vice-presidents included Sir Frederick William Young, MP for Swindon 1918-22; George Jackson Churchward, Chief Mechanical Engineer of the GWR; William Arthur Stanier, then GWR Works manager; Robert Hilton, solicitor and Swindon's Town Clerk; William Ewart Morse, department store owner and twice mayor of Swindon (1914-15 and 1915-16); Fitzroy Pleydell Goddard, Lord of the Manor of Swindon; Ernest Clement Skurray, flour mill owner; Albert John Gilbert, cabinet maker and furniture retailer; and Samuel A. Morley, proprietor of the Electra Palace cinema in Gorse Hill. The rest of the twenty-one-strong group of vice-presidents were military men, doctors, and owners of small local businesses. A twelve-man committee was elected, plus treasurer and trainer, and ninety-seven members were accepted. Within five months, this would rise to some three hundred. The colours for the club's vests were settled as yellow and blue hoops.

Its first official badge depicted a locomotive and tender, and the initials 'S.A.C', and the firm Fattorini of Birmingham made dies that featured a similar design for the club's medals.

The SAC's first organised event was a three-mile handicapped road race, held on 19 March 1921, which began and ended at the County Ground Hotel. There were twenty-five competitors. To coincide with the first athletics and cycling festival, the club organised an attempt to beat a world record set by Herbert Minton in 1906 for the 440-yard Swindon bicycle sprint from a standing start. It failed, but 300 spectators were at the finishing tape. The record was eventually beaten on the Cricket Ground in 1926. The town clerk resisted the club's request to use the County Ground and changing rooms for training, but offered the use of one of the huts remaining from the First World War on the cricket ground site, at a rent of £40 per annum. The SAC considered this to be excessive and applied to the Council to be included in the lease for the Cricket Club sports ground. This was rejected by the Cricket Club, and by the Town Clerk, who instead reduced the rent by half. The hut was also popular with local amateur football teams who had nowhere else to change. In a shrewd move, the SAC agreed to this, on the condition that those football club members who wished to use this facility also joined the Swindon Athletic Club.

The second event promoted by the SAC was a 120-yard flat handicap race held on 20 April 1921. On 2 July 1921, the club held its first annual sports day on the cricket ground. In the same year, ten women applied for membership. The committee vacillated for a while, but eventually agreed, and obtained permission for them to play netball

on Saturday afternoons at College Street School. At the end of its first season, SAC was described as 'the pride of the town'.

From the beginning, the club organised boxing matches, the first of which was held at the Milton Road swimming baths on 15 March 1922, in aid of the Victoria Hospital fund. This, and national charities, benefited regularly from other SAC sporting and social events, such as balls and whist drives. A boxing instructor was employed, and a sixteen-foot-square boxing ring was installed in the SAC's hut, as were vapour lamps. The ceiling was painted white and the hut was opened on several evenings of the week for boxing and general training. Also in 1922, two hundred and fifty wooden forms were bought by the club's committee at a munitions stores sale and, with the permission of Swindon Town FC's secretary Sam Allen, were stored beneath the stand at the County Ground. The club took over an old rifle range beside the canal in the centre of the town, which it used for boxing and exercise training, and became affiliated to the Amateur Boxing Association. The club settled into a routine of holding two open athletics meetings each year and two evening meetings for members only. Boxing tournaments were organised for the winter months. The SAC became affiliated to the Amateur Athletic Association and the National Cycle Union.

Organisations, firms and businessmen began to provide trophies to be won at SAC events. The GWR Mechanics' Institute gave a shield for a boys' 4 x 100-yards relay race, and a splendid shield was contributed by the entertainments committee of the Kinema Proprietors of Swindon, to be awarded for the girls' relay. Cinema owner Samuel A. Morley gave a cup, known as the Morley

Cup, which was thereafter awarded to the member who gained the most points during the year. The GWR Foreman's Association gave a silver cup for the 880-yards scratch championship. The 'Tradesmen of Swindon' came up with a silver cup and challenge bowl; the first was to be awarded to the winner of the five-mile cycle scratch race, and the other for an open mile medley relay.

The club's president (1925-31) was W.A. Stanier, then manager of the GWR Locomotive Department, and later to become its Chief Mechanical Engineer. He was knighted in 1943. In 1930, the GWR Social and Educational Union acquired a sports ground in Shrivenham Road, and Stanier used his influence in trying to affiliate the SAC with that body so that both might use it. Two years later, Swindon Cricket Club offered its facilities for training purposes.

In 1940, the military authorities took over the club's training hut, and other buildings on the site. The SAC suspended its activities for the duration of the Second World War. The headquarters of the club were relocated to 23 Albert Street, the home of the secretary, where all of the trophies were also placed for safekeeping. Other equipment was stored at the football ground. The full SAC committee did not reconvene until 1945. Its organised races began again in 1947, and the following year, two SAC members carried the 1948 Olympic torch between Salisbury and Torquay.

In 1950, the club made its headquarters in two long huts and a bridging hut, which it restored, behind the County Ground Hotel. It used the sports fields at Churchfield School and Kingsdown School for training, and carried out track training on a marked-out surface at the County Ground extension. By now, there was little public support for the big festivals that had been held since 1921, and which latterly took place on the sports ground at Ferndale School. After 1959, these were commuted to annual evening events, and the last one took place in 1963.

Through the perseverance of William Arthur Townsend, then President of the Swindon Athletic Club, and his son Robert Keith Townsend, who was to succeed him, and the good offices of Denys Hodson, Swindon's Director of Arts & Recreation, the SAC got its first official track in 1984 at the County Ground. The ceremonial first sod was cut by Emily Townsend, whose husband and son had been stalwarts of the club since its very first race. This was to be an 'all-weather' track with a polyurethane-based synthetic surface, and six lanes around each bend and eight lanes along each straight. It cost £480,000, and was opened on 24 August 1985. In 1996, Swindon Athletic Club joined with Swindon Road Runners (founded in the 1980s) to become Swindon Harriers. This organisation embraces the activities of both earlier organisations and is involved in track and field events, cross-country, and road running. (See also Townsend, W.A.; Townsend, R.K.)

Swindon FM radio station Swindon FM was a short-lived radio station that began in 2001 and 2002 as Swindon 107FM with test programmes from temporary premises in the Brunel Plaza. Its principals were businessman Rikki Hunt, one-time chairman of Swindon Town Football Club, and jazz musician Ray Butt, who had identified a niche market for music broadcasting in the town. In 2003, Swindon FM launched as the UK's first DAB-only radio station, from rooms in Old Town Court, Old Swindon. The station ceased broadcasting on 12 May 2006. (See also BBC Wiltshire Sound; Brunel FM; GWR Radio; Radio 105.5; Wiltshire Radio.)

Swindon Festival of Poetry This companion to the Swindon Festival of Literature was first held in October 2012, when it opened on National Poetry Day. It was inaugurated by Matt Holland, director of the literary festival, in response to a growing interest in poetry in the town as exemplified by the number of poetry groups operating in Swindon. A magazine, *Domestic Cherry*, was published in association with this undertaking, and Bluegate Poets, based at Lower Shaw Farm, West Swindon, and Poetry Swindon were involved in the project. The six days featured a touring poetry bus, and readings at various venues, including the Central Library in Regent Circus, the Artsite Gallery in Theatre Square, the Platform in Faringdon Road, and Lower Shaw Farm. The poetry festival was financed by the Arts Council, Swindon Borough Council, and the Swindon Festival of Literature. The star guest in 2012 was Pam Ayres; in 2013, it was Roger McGough.

Swindon Music Scene website This extensive and comprehensive website was created in 2009 by Nigel Norman, and subsequently developed by him, with the objective of gathering together details of all bands of every musical genre that were involved in the town's music scene from the 1930s to the present day. The site is a single point of reference for all the bands and the musicians who performed in them. By 2014, it featured comprehensive information on more than two hundred bands, details of the individual musicians who played in their various line-ups, sections on some of the professional bands that came to the town, and a gig guide for the period 1960 to 1969. It also published articles on venues in the town that hosted gigs, the bands that played them, and individual musicians. (See also Norman, Nigel; Rockers Re-United.)

Swindon Permanent Benefit Building & Investment Society Founded in 1868, this was largely a GWR initiative, albeit in the commercial sector, resulting from the railway company's need to significantly increase its workforce whilst being unable to itself finance the residential accommodation those workers and their families would need. It was the town's first building society, and it held its meetings at the Corn Exchange, Old Town, before relocating to the Council Room in the Mechanics' Institute. By 1870, some £20,000 had been taken up in shares, and the society was eager to attract the public: 'To Borrowers the advantages of the Society are apparent from the fact that there are no law charges, or charges in respect of amounts borrowed, to that if a person, a borrower, applies for £100, he gates that sum without abatement'. Its publicity, in *Dore's Swindon Almanack* of 1870, continued: 'In the Rules of the Society there is a tabular statement showing the amount at which the mortgaged premises can be redeemed at any time during the term for which the money was borrowed. This is well worth the attention of intending Borrowers, as they can at all times see the amount of their liability. We have compared the Subscription Terms with those of other Societies and find them much lower, at the same time the Prospectus of the Society shows the rates to have been carefully prepared, and to be certified by Arthur Scratchley Esq., MA, the eminent Actuary, as fairly and sufficiently remunerative to the Society'. By the 1880s, the society had been renamed the Swindon Permanent Building Society. Halfway through that decade, the take-up had not been good. Only forty-seven of its houses had been sold, forty-two of which had been re-mortgaged to the society for £6,925. The society still had ninety-three houses for disposal, and in an effort to attract custom, its advertisements pointed out that borrowers were not charged legal expenses. In 1888, the society was able to report that its stock was 'all let and in good repair'.

During this period, its officers remained remarkably stable, and were mainly representative of the GWR and the society's bankers (the County of Gloucestershire Bank). Sir Daniel Gooch (b. Bedlington, Northumberland, 1816), the GWR's Superintendent of Locomotive Engines, was the society's first president. Its directors included:

Henry Hill (b. Worcester, 1843), who lived in Park Lane, and was the GWR accountant;

Henry J. Birch (b. Kensington, 1827), who lived in Belle Vue Road, and was the GWR locomotive accountant;

William Dean (b. London, 1840), who lived at Marlow House, and later Newburn House, at the railway station, and was the GWR Chief Locomotive Engineer;

John Armstrong (b. Chester, 1852), who lived in the GWR Manager's House in the railway village, and was the company's Superintendent of the Locomotive & Carriage Department;

William Ellis (b. Merthyr Tydfil, Wales, 1825), who lived in Church Place, and was manager of the GWR rail mills;

James F. Carlyle (b. Badgworth, Gloucestershire, 1848), who lived in Fairview House, Bath Road, and was a civil engineer;

John Chandler (b. Pewsey, Wiltshire, 1819), who lived in Wood Street, and was a draper;

William Brewer Wearing (b. Trowbridge, 1818), who lived in Bath Road and was, until he retired in 1881, manager of the County of Gloucestershire Bank;

Lyttleton Etty (b. Wanborough, Wiltshire, 1843), who lived in Wood Street, was employed by the County of Gloucestershire Bank, where he took over W.B. Wearing's position in 1881.

By 1900, the Swindon Permanent Building Society's office was at 1 Commercial Road, where it was to remain. It merged with the Stroud Building Society in 1986 to form the Stroud & Swindon Building Society, but, soon after the Stroud & Swindon merged with the Coventry Building Society in 2010, all reference to the original name was lost.

Swindon Photographic Society

Begun in 1896, and given official status two years later when it was called North Wilts Field and Camera Club, the group held its meetings at the Technical College in Victoria Road. Its first president was Mervyn Herbert Nevil Story-Maskelyne of Bassett Down House, Lydiard Tregoze, a county magistrate and one-time keeper of the Mineral Department at the British Museum. Its secretary was William McLeod, a clerk in the Great Western Railway Company's analytical laboratory at the Swindon Works. Thomas Cuthbert Davison, who was a GWR assistant scientific analyst in Swindon, was the club's membership secretary. Laurence William Mathieson, a Swindon chemistry teacher, took on the job of curator and librarian, and solicitor and law accountant Abraham Coleman became the club's first auditor. Railway clerk Henry A. Stanier was the local secretary of the Selborne Society, which was formed in 1885 to commemorate the life and work of Hampshire naturalist Gilbert White. The Camera Club became associated with it after the society took on the management of a nature reserve in 1902, which facilitated the outdoor forays its members made during the summer. Throughout the winter months, the club held indoor meetings, and had a portfolio of pictures available for criticism. Initially, there was a seven-man committee, which increased to nine. The club became associated with the Royal Photographic Society in 1919. It was renamed Swindon Camera Club in 1958, and latterly Swindon Photographic Society.

Swindon 'Ranger' (Rugby) Football Club Swindon Rugby Club was formed in 1895, although rugby football in the town originated with the formation of the Swindon 'Ranger' Football Club. The origins of the club, c.1870, are obscure, but it was probably begun among employees at the GWR Works. Joseph Armstrong, the company's Locomotive Carriage & Wagon Works Superintendent, was for a while its president, and his son, John Armstrong, was an early captain in the rugby team. At the beginning, the rugby football team, which played in an all-white strip with a blue star, seems also to have been allied to the older Swindon 'Ranger' Cricket Club, with both organisations having C. Askew as captain, and John Armstrong as a player. Other GWR employees soon joined; A. Barns was deputy captain, and R.S. Edmonds was appointed treasurer, positions they both also held with the 'Ranger' Cricket Club. The first secretary of the rugby football club was William Sewell. After playing for a while on a field in Gorse Hill, the team was offered, c.1878, a site at The Croft, the Old Town home and estate belonging to solicitor John Copleston Townsend. By 1881, the Ranger's president was William Dean, Joseph Armstrong's protégé at the Works who would succeed him there. (This was also where Swindon Town Football Club played their home matches between 1884 and 1896.) In 1892, the 'Ranger' rugby team relocated to The Sands, where it remained until disbanding in 1895. The same year, the Swindon Rugby Club was formed, taking over the Ranger's site on The Sands.

Swindon School Board Until the late 1870s, children's education in New Swindon was in the hands of the Great Western Railway Company. In 1845, it built a school in Bristol Street for infants, boys and girls whose fathers were employed in the Swindon Works, and followed this up in 1873 with schools for infants and girls, in College Street. The company also held programmes of educational evening classes for young people aged fourteen years and upwards, at the Mechanics' Institute. This continued until 1877 when, on 10 November, the Swindon School Board was formed under the Education Act, 1870. The new board held its first meeting on 29 November 1877. The board comprised:

Philip Hawe Mason, grocer of High Street, Old Town, who was to be its first chairman;

James Holden, an engineer and the manager of the GWR carriage works;

Richard Lewis White, chief accountant at the GWR Works;

William Morris, founder and proprietor of the *Swindon Advertiser*;

Joseph Lambert, Congregationalist minister;

William Brewer Wearing, manager of the County of Gloucester Bank in Old Swindon;

Revd Henry George Baily, vicar of Christ Church in Old Swindon;

Henry Kinneir, solicitor, who was appointed clerk to the Swindon School Board, at an annual salary of £40.

Kinneir was also on the board of the King William Street School for boys, girls and infants, which had been built in Old Town in 1871 following a campaign led by Revd Baily.

Swindon School Board, which met every two weeks from 11 January 1878, immediately took a census of both parts of the town. This revealed that of a total population of 4,279 in Old Town, 1,505 were children, and in New Town there were 4,696 children in a total population of 12,334. Of these children, 4,344 fell into the three- to fourteen-years' age group. The board calculated that, after making deductions allowed by the Elementary Education Act, 1870, 3,160 children needed school places. At that time, the GWR schools could accommodate 1,294, and 690 places could be found at other parochial schools. The most pressing, immediate need was in the Gorse Hill area, and the board employed William Henry Read of Morovia House, Bath Road, and William Drew of North Street, architects and surveyors, to jointly submit a plan. Their school, for a total of 450 boys, girls and infants, and the adjacent teacher's house, was built in Avening Street by George Wiltshire of Clyde Villas, Bath Road, at a cost of £4,150.

The Mundella Act, 1880 made it compulsory for children aged between five years and ten years to attend school, although there was no free state education until 1891. This put pressure on the Swindon School Board to build more schools. The board followed Gorse Hill with Queenstown Infants' in 1880 for 275 pupils, Gilbert's Hill

or Eastcott Infants' in 1880 for 280 pupils, and Westcott Infants', Birch Street, in 1881 for 286 pupils. Sanford Street Boys' School was also opened in 1881 for 794 pupils, and in April of the same year, the board acquired the GWR's College Street Schools on a twenty-one-year lease. In order to finance its work thus far, Swindon School Board borrowed £12,185 from the Public Works Loan Commissioners, on variable rates repayable over fifty years.

Thereafter, the board built Clifton Street for boys, girls and infants (1895); Queenstown Girls' School (1885); Gilbert's Hill Girls' School 1890; Lethbridge Road for girls and boys (1891); Even Swindon for girls, boys and infants (1891); Westcott Place for boys and girls (1892); Swindon & North Wilts Technical School (the College in Victoria Road, 1895); and Clarence Street for boys and girls (1897). Some existing schools were also enlarged: Even Swindon (1894), College Street (1896) and Westcott Place Infants' (1896). Swindon School Board was abolished, as were all school boards, under the Balfour Act, 1902, after which matters of education devolved on local authority Education Committees.

Swindon Town Football Club Managers

The club was formed in 1881, following a game of football played between the Old Swindon Cricket Club and a team put together by the St Mark's Young Men's Friendly Society from New Town. The team began to engage professional players in 1884, when M.D. Robinson was the secretary. Caretaker managers are marked *

1881-1902 No management; the team was selected by the board of directors

1902-1933 Samuel Henry ('Sam') Allen (1868-1946)

1933-1939 Edward ('Ted') Vizard (1889-1973)

1939-1940 Neil Harris (1894-1941)

1940-1945 Football was suspended for the duration of the war

1945-1953 Louis Antonio Page (1899-1959)

1953-1955 Maurice Lindley (1915-1994)

1955-1956 No manager; the team was selected by a four-man committee

1956-1965 Bertram James ('Bert') Head (1916-2002)

1965-1969 Danny Williams (b. 1924)

1969-1971 Frederick George Luther ('Fred') Ford (1916-1981)

1971-1972 David Craig ('Dave') Mackay (b. 1934)

1972-1974 Leslie William ('Les') Allen (b. 1937)

1974-1978 Danny Williams (b. 1924)

1978-1980 Robert William ('Bobby') Smith (b. 1944)

1980-1983 Norman John ('John') Trollope (b. 1943)

1983-1984 Kenneth George ('Ken') Beamish (b. 1947)

1984-1989 Luigi ('Lou') Macari (b. 1949)

1989-1991 Osvaldo César ('Ossie') Ardiles (b. 1952)

1991-1993 Glenn Hoddle (b. 1957)

1993-1994 John Gorman (b. 1949)

1994-1994 Andrew Arthur ('Andy') Rowland (b. 1954)

1994-1998 Stephen Joseph ('Steve') McMahon (b. 1961)

1998-2000 James Martin ('Jimmy') Quinn (b. 1959)

2000-2000 Colin Todd (b. 1948)

2000-2001 Andrew Edward ('Andy') King (b. 1956)

2001-2001 Roy Quentin Echin Evans (b. 1948)

2001-2005 Andrew Edward ('Andy') King (b. 1956)

2005-2006 Ifem ('Iffy') Onuora (b. 1967)

2006-2006 Dennis Frank Wise (b. 1966)

2006-2006 David Philip ('Dave') Tuttle (b. 1972)*

2006-2006 Adrian ('Ady') Williams (b. 1971)

2006-2007 Paul Whitehead Sturrock (b. 1956)

2007-2008 David Stuart Byrne (b. 1961) *

2008-2008 Maurice Daniel Robert Malpass (b. 1962)

2008-2008 David Stuart Byrne (b. 1961) *

2008-2011 Daniel Joseph ('Danny Wilson') (b. 1960)

2011-2011 Paul Hart (b. 1953)

2011-2011 Paul John Bodin (b. 1964)*

2011-2013 Paolo Di Canio (b. 1968)

2013-2013 Fabrizio Piccareta (b. 1965)*

2013-2013 Thomas William ('Tommy') Miller (b. 1979)*

2013-2013 Darren Ward (b. 1978)*

2013-2013 Kevin Duncan MacDonald (b. 1960)

2013 - Mark Nicholas Cooper (b. 1968)

Swindon Town Railway Station, off Newport Street

Station Approach is a short stub of a road curving off Newport Street to the south-east. It ends at the Signal Way industrial estate. These railway names allude to the site of the former Old Swindon railway station on which part of the industrial estate now stands. The station (then called Swindon Town Station to avoid confusion with the Great Western Railway Company's Swindon Junction Station in New Town) was opened 27 July 1881. There was also an approach to the station off Marlborough Road. The Swindon town band was waiting at the station, and struck up as the first train drew in carrying officials of the railway company. It then processed around Old Town, ending at the

Corn Exchange where a reception was held.

The line through Swindon Town Station was built by the Swindon, Marlborough & Andover Railway which, on 24 June 1884, amalgamated with the Swindon & Cheltenham Railway Company (whose extension line from Swindon Town Station had opened on 18 December 1883) to become the Midland & South-west Junction Railway. Swindon Town Station was built where it could also take advantage of the movement of livestock by train in and out of William Dore's large and extremely successful, adjacent cattle sale yard, which had opened in 1873. To this end, a siding was put in at the station complex, with a cattle dock to the south-west, at a sufficient distance from the station to ensure it did not inconvenience passengers. A goods shed was built south of the cattle dock, and there were two signal boxes.

This was no backwater halt; it was intended to be the flagship station building for the M&SWJR, and was considered its finest. The station was constructed in red bricks by John Dover of Walton Street, Oxford. With its canopy, the main building was 144 feet wide and 42 feet deep, with a central covered entrance on the north side. Within it, were toilets, the station office, and a well-equipped refreshment room, which was first licensed in 1894 and survived the actual demise of the station. On the south side, there was a canopied building some 62 feet long and 16 feet deep. Both buildings were of brick, and the canopies were fretted – the one on the north side (the down line) being raised on a series of six slender stanchions with ornamental brackets. Initially, foot passengers crossed the lines on boards at rail level. In 1885, this was superseded by a raised walkway of wooden planks supported by a steel frame, which was subsequently given steel sides. The two nearest bridges over the line were built in local stone. The tracks were remodelled, 1904-5, and both platforms were widened and extended. New tracks were laid on the south side of the up platform, upon which new waiting rooms were built. Over the years, Swindon Town Station added several buildings to the complex, such as goods sheds, a locomotive shed, a small turntable, and a larger turntable.

The stationmaster's house, also of brick, stood between the station and the approach road from Newport Street. From the outset, the M&SWJR offices were in a large building a little closer to Newport Street, thereby imparting even greater importance to the Swindon Town Station.

Gradually, the station acquired a history and a persona of its own, independent of the railway line it served. It soon became renowned for its ornamental garden that railway staff developed alongside the down line, close to the open bridge across the lines. The garden included a manicured rectangle of grass enclosed by borders with bird baths, and it had an island feature. During the summer, staff were regularly required to release huge numbers of racing pigeons, sent down for the purpose from the north of England. Ernest Carpenter, the owner of Swindon's Empire Theatre from 1898, negotiated with the M&SWJR for cheap theatre tickets to be sold at Swindon Town Station, as well as on the trains themselves. One of the first things Alfred Manners did when he became manager of the Empire in 1904 was to arrange for special trains to run along the M&SWJR line to convey patrons to and from theatre shows. He also arranged for tram services to fetch patrons from Market Square in Old Town and return them afterwards to catch the waiting special trains. After a new boiler was installed at the station in 1908, passengers could obtain foot warmers.

It was from Swindon Town Station that the town's Territorial Army reservists departed on 6 August 1914. Thereafter, for the duration of the First World War, the station was often full of military personnel. This happened again during the Second World War, and at all times in between it was used by forces personnel visiting Swindon from the Tidworth area. Annually, a boat was delivered to Swindon Town Station on its way to the lake in Beatrice Street, in celebration of Lifeboat Day.

In 1923, the M&SWJR was taken over by the GWR, who had no real interest in making the line profitable. The last scheduled passenger train drew out of Swindon Town Station on 10 September 1961. The stationmasters at the Swindon Town Station were:

1881-82	J.W. Read
1882-83	Frederick J. Wilmott
1884-85	Henry Stevens
1886-92	Edwin Noble
1892-97	John Manning
1897-1902	Samuel Rumbold
1903-05	Alexander Bowd
1905-29	Henry Baker
1929-32	J. Jones
1932-35	H. F. Ludgate
1935-38	J. Jones
1938-53	John W. Philpin
1953-61	G.A. Webb

Goods traffic continued at Swindon Town Station until 1964. The station's refreshment rooms, latterly known as the 'Ghost Train', with their original Victorian and Edwardian fixtures and fittings, closed on 1 February 1965. The station buildings were demolished in 1968, and, over the following two or three years, most of the track and sidings were taken up, although there was, for a while, some use of the remaining track. It was all removed in 1978, and its site is now a linear nature walkway and cycle path.

Swindon Viewpoint In the early 1970s, the Government set up five experiments in community television and public access programme making. The only one to survive was Swindon Viewpoint, established in 1973 under the auspices of Thorn Electrical Industries, which five years before had acquired the Viewpoint initiative from Radio Rentals. Richard Dunn was appointed station manager; he left in 1976 and was eventually replaced by Rupert Kirkham, and the project was financed by EMI after its merger with Thorn in 1980. When private funding ceased, Swindon Viewpoint was sold into public ownership and became a not-for-profit organisation. In 1980, Martin Parry (b. Hereford, 1947) became involved with Swindon Viewpoint; he also ran film workshops teaching film and media to young people. In 1988, he founded Western Film Archive, which later worked in conjunction with Swindon Media Arts. Swindon Viewpoint ceased programming in the early 1990s, and Martin Parry began to digitise and make available online its huge archive of videotaped material. He also filmed new material for the archive and restored old films, and the valuable historic archive was made available online. When it achieved its fortieth anniversary in 2013, Arkell's brewery celebrated the occasion by creating a Swindon Viewpoint Anniversary Ale. In addition, a concert by current

Swindon bands and former artistes from the town was held at the Music Entertainment Cultural Arena (MECA) in Regent Circus. (See also Radio Rentals.)

Swindon Wildcats The ice hockey team was a Swindon Borough Council initiative, and played its first match on 14 June 1986. The following month, it was accepted into the Heineken-sponsored British Hockey League, then the major ice-hockey organisation in the UK. Its first match as Swindon Wildcats was played on 9 August 1986. Eventually, the local authority withdrew its financial support, and when the team reorganised in 1996, it emerged under new ownership as the Icelords, the change being necessitated by ownership issues surrounding the name. By 1997, it was set to be renamed Swindon Steamers, a name that had a more nautical feel to it rather than the nod to the town's railway heritage, which it was allegedly meant to signify. However, insufficient financial business backing meant that this initiative folded, and many of its potential players joined Oxford Chill. Problems with its Oxford ice rink resulted in Oxford Chill playing its opening match at Swindon Link Centre on 7 September 1997. Within the month, the move to Swindon had become permanent, and the name was changed to Swindon Chill. In 2000, another change of name resulted in Swindon Phoenix, which played for a single season when, in 2001, it won the English National Premier League title. That year, came Swindon Lynx, which remained until the club reverted to Swindon Wildcats in 2004.

Tarrant's *Recollections* (augmented) The *Recollections of Richard James Tarrant* were made orally when he was

in his eighties, and were written down. They relate to the Tarrant family and to the Noad family of his mother, and to people and places in High Street, Old Town, when he was a boy. There is a verbatim copy of the original in the Swindon Local Study Archive. Whilst this gives a snapshot of Swindon life in the 1840s and early 1850s, it is of little value today because its points of reference are no longer extant, and the names of people that so fleetingly appear are to a degree unfamiliar and require further explanation. In an attempt to make this more useful to a contemporary readership, Tarrant's *Recollections* are here remodelled and rewritten, in the third person, with much additional information, a number of factual corrections, and the removal of material that is not relevant to Swindon.

Tarrant Family

Richard James Tarrant peppered his *Recollections* with notes about members of his family, generations of which were all natives of Swindon. RJT was born in Lower Town (today, the northern end of Marlborough Road where it enters Old Town) in 1840. His father was James Richard Tarrant (b. 1810), a shoemaker with a shop and a number of employees in Newport Street. He was an ardent Wesleyan Methodist.

RJT began his schooling at 'a dame school in Dammas Lane kept by a Mrs Stubbs'. This was Elizabeth Stubbs (b. Upholland, Lancashire, 1785), whose husband Thomas was a painter and glazier. RJT then went to the boys' private day school in Lower Town run by James Steger (1814-89), who was born at Kelstone, Somerset. His wife, Emma Louisa née Green (b. London, 1812), whom he married in 1842, ran the companion ladies' school. Steger left the teaching profession and went to work as a clerk for the GWR. RJT was then taught by Taunton-born George Nourse (1801-75), who operated a private gentlemen's boarding and day school in Prospect Place. In 1826, Nourse married Catherine Turner (b. Middlesex, 1801), who in RJT's time ran the ladies' school in Prospect Place. Nourse is remembered for asking the boys what Swindon was noted for, before immediately supplying the answer himself: stone quarries and very bad boys. RJT left school at the age of twelve, and began to learn the boot-making business. 'I learnt the 'closing' process before machines were introduced.'

According to RJT, his father had an elder brother, Henry, who first inherited the shop. This had workshops at the rear, and stables, where a horse was kept. In the days before a police force was established, Henry Tarrant was a member of the Wiltshire Yeomanry, and was for many years Constable of Swindon, part of whose remit was to find accommodation for all the soldiers who came through the town. He was also in charge of the stocks in the market square, the dog pound on the Coate road, and all polling arrangements. RJT remembers him as a property buyer and speculator. When he retired from the business, Henry took over the Mason's Arms public house, which was run by Sam Tarrant after him.

RJT had another brother, John, who died when he was about thirty. James Richard's father was James Tarrant, a bootmaker who started the Newport Street shop, and James's brother, who died in 1812, was a retired overseer and freemason 'whose father was a quarry owner and property owner, one of the largest property owners and landowners outside the Goddards'.

James Richard Tarrant went to Canada 'in 1827 or 1828'. He 'went up the St Lawrence with a party of Red Indians, in one of their cork canoes, to the falls of Niagara' and 'got them to land on the British Territory of the Falls. There he sang the first verse of "God Save the King" to these Indians. Then he threw up his cap and gave three cheers for The King and Old England. He served in the Canadian Militia and wore the uniform of William IV. He used to practice firing from Halifax into the waters of Halifax, under the command of Colonel Bogg.' When he arrived home, James Richard Tarrant married Mary Noad (b. 1809), daughter of William Noad, bootmaker, 'who built a little factory in a house in Lower Town'. Richard James Tarrant was James and Mary's second child.

RJT said that his uncle, Henry Tarrant (b. 1807), a cordwainer employer, had three daughters. One of these was Louisa (b. 1835), who married Joseph New (b. Stepney, London, 1835), who was briefly in charge of the Goddard Arms Hotel. When RJT was born, another Joseph New (father of Louisa's husband) was landlord of the Goddard Arms. He died in the 1840s, and the inn was taken on by Jane, his widow. She later married William Westmacott, who had the place from 1857 to when he retired in 1870.

Henry's other two daughters were Emma (b. 1839), who married John H. Hanks (b. Malmesbury, 1829), postmaster, stationer, and organist at the abbey church; and Fanny (b. 1856). She remained an unmarried woman who, for a while, lived with her sister Louisa and Joseph New in North Street. After the Goddard Arms, he was variously an accountant and stationer. The News had one son who went to Somerset House, another who was apprenticed to the drapery trade in the north of England, where he set up business, and a third of whom nothing is known. Henry Tarrant also had a son, Charles (b. 1837), who died young, and Robert (b. 1851), who became a fitter in the GWR railway works. Eventually, he went to Scotland, where he was killed on the railway.

RJT's elder brother, Joseph Noad Tarrant (1838-1923) was later apprenticed to J. & H. Mason, grocers of Newbury and Swindon. When this was completed, he was employed by Messrs Felgate, grocers on the Isle of Wight, where he settled at Ryde. In his *Recollections*, RJT briefly describes Joseph's life on the Isle of Wight, and refers to his children, of whom none had any connection with Swindon.

Mary Tarrant, RJT's great-aunt, married John Theobald (b. 1766), wharfinger at Semington Lock. They had a son, also John Theobald (b. 1811), who became a farmer, coal dealer and corn merchant at Melksham wharf. James Richard Tarrant, RJT's father, lived with this family for two years. RJT recalled John the younger: 'Riding his charger through Swindon to the May Manoeuvres at Marlborough. That was in May 1853. A deep snow that day'.

Noad family

When RJT's father, James Richard Tarrant, came back from Canada, he married Mary Noad, daughter of William Noad, a bootmaker of Lower Town. Her mother was a former Miss Salt of Lambourn. The story that Wesleyan Methodism came to Swindon via William Noad originated with RJT's *Recollections.* He said that either at the end of the eighteenth century or very early in the nineteenth, the first Wesleyan Methodist sermon was preached to a large crowd one Sunday afternoon in the market square by George Pocock, travelling preacher and

a native of Kingswood, Bristol, who was 'well acquainted with the great work of John Wesley in that locality'. (RJT also mentioned that Pocock was the maternal grandfather of the cricketer W.G. Grace.) Afterwards, William Noad invited Pocock to his house in Lower Town, where the latter expressed a wish that 'the work he had commenced that day (in Swindon) should be perpetuated', and Noad offered his large kitchen for the purpose. Once he had secured a preaching licence, without which it was illegal to hold religious services in a private house, the town crier, James Hiscock, announced the services. These continued at Noad's house for several years, and the superintendent minister of the Hungerford Circuit paid a special visit to Swindon, preaching in William Noad's kitchen, where he issued quarterly membership tickets to those worshippers assembled there. Services there finished only when a dedicated Wesleyan Methodist chapel was built in 1813. RJT's mother, Mary, recalled seeing George Pocock at her father's house.

RJT thought the Noad family house in Lower Town had been in that family's hands for two hundred years, and he also suggested that a Noad had held the Bell Inn in 1600. Mary obtained the freehold of the Lower Town house, an entailed property which consequently caused difficulties, from an uncle, John Noad, who RJT said was a wholesale cheese factor. This John Noad emigrated to Canada in 1816, becoming, among other occupations, a merchant in Montreal who retained business interests in London. One of John's sons, Henry Noad, visited his cousin Mary in Swindon. RJT remembered walking with him along The Sands (the western part of present-day Bath Road), when Henry asked, 'Where's New

Swindon?'. When the direction was pointed out to him, Henry said, 'That's west, and in America we say all good things go west'.

High Street 1840-1855

In his *Recollections*, RJT attempted to list the occupants of adjacent properties in High Street. Here, his memory went awry, because whilst he recalled people who lived in the properties, they did not necessarily live concurrently in adjacent buildings; others he mentions as living next door to each other did not. RJT was recalling a time, mid-1840s to mid-1850s, when High Street was undergoing considerable change, in the style of houses and in the class of its occupants. With just a couple of long-term exceptions, he mentions no one who was there at the time of the 1841 census, and most of the people he recalls were not in High Street until the 1850s. The 1851 census (beginning at the southern end of High Street, on the corner with Newport Street, where the Co-op foodstore is now, then moving northwards) records the street's heads of household and occupations as:

1. **Samuel Shaw** (b. Islington, London, 1819), draper *Shaw was the son of Robert Elgie Shaw, 'a gentleman'. When Samuel came to Swindon, c.1848, he had just married Mary Packer (b. Oxfordshire, 1816). At first, he went into partnership with George Sewell (b. Scotland, 1819), a draper, tailor, haberdasher, hosier and outfitter of Wood Street. By 1851, he was working on his own account, and the family lived in High Street with a shopman, and their two children, Fanny (b. 1849) and Archibald (b. 1850). Mary died in the 1850s, and in 1857, Samuel married Mary Anne Thompson (b. Great Yarmouth, Norfolk, 1826). He was later to give up the drapery business, and became a commercial traveller. His early partner,*

George Sewell, also gave up the business and opened a grocer's shop at 27 High Street.

2. **William Butler** (b. Swindon, 1795), wine and spirits merchant *Butler was established as a maltster in Newport Street before 1830. In 1834, he married Elizabeth Campbell (b. Whitchurch, Middlesex, 1801), and his address is thereafter given variously as Newport Street and High Street, which suggests that his was a corner site. By 1863, his last listing in trade in Swindon, he was described as 'a licenced brewer, dealer in spirits, tea and coffee, and retailer of British wines'.*

3. **Edward Page** (b. Stroud, 1816), ironmonger *Page was there, c.1845-54, and RJT noted that this shop was afterwards kept by William Morris, and was where he printed his first copy of the Swindon Advertiser.*

4. **John Jefferies** (b. Rodbourne, 1785), baker *He is best remembered as the grandfather of the writer Richard Jefferies (1848-87), and father of the grocer James Luckett Jefferies (1816-96). Swindon people knew John for the lardy cakes that he made after 1840 when he took over the High Street business that his father James had acquired c.1800, at about the same time as he also bought what became Jefferies Farm at Coate, and the old mill on the Goddard estate. John Jefferies the baker died in 1868.*

5. **Thomas Strange** (b. Swindon, 1795), draper *RJT says that the draper was the son of Thomas Strange, banker. In about 1847, recalled RJT, the draper paid more than £5 in farthings to a man with whom he held a grudge. Although he took over his brother James's banking interests when the latter died in 1826, Thomas the banker was also a draper.*

6. **Edward Strange** (b. Swindon, 1823), draper *In 1847, Edward Strange*

married Sibbella Smith (b. Staines, Middlesex, 1826). Several of the High Street tradespeople lived in their houses with their growing families, servants and, in a number of instances, their apprentices or assistants. The draper was a case in point; his household in 1851 included his wife, two-year-old daughter, and twelve other drapers and tailors.

7. **Caroline Killard** (b. Nailsworth, 1820), The Mason's Arms *The Mason's Arms was run by Richard Tarrant until c.1840, when it was taken over by William Killard, who was the landlord until his death in 1849. His widow, Caroline, was then only twenty-nine years old and remained in charge until 1852, when it passed into the hands of Thomas Pearce Brown. The next landlord, in the mid-1850s, was Henry Tarrant.*

8. **William H. Heale** (b. Calne, 1837), nurseryman

9. **Sophia Jenner** (b. Walcot, Swindon, 1807) *RJT mentions that she was a bookseller in High Street. This must have been in the early 1840s. Formerly Sophia Baden, she married the very wealthy Robert Jenner (1796-1848) in 1834, and the family lived in Bath Road. How Robert made his money is unknown, but after she was widowed in 1847, she is described variously as a fund holder, and living on income from houses, lands and dividends. She lived in High Street with her daughter Alice Baden Jenner (b. Swindon, 1846) during the 1850s, then relocated to High Street, Highworth, where she lived with another daughter, Beatrice Baden Jenner (b. Highworth, 1840). She was the mother of Andrew John Baden Jenner (b. Highworth, 1836), a homeopathic physician who worked mostly in Australia. Sophia Jenner died in 1880.*

10. **Isaac Ann** (b. Alveston, Gloucestershire, 1805), stationer *Oddly, Isaac Ann is not mentioned in RJT's Reminiscences, although he was installed in High Street in the mid-1840s, probably taking over the bookselling part of Charles Anthony Wheeler's business. By 1848, Ann was a 'music seller, bookseller, stationer, printer, bookbinder, berlin wool repository, circulating library, dealer in patent medicines, registry office for servants, and depot to the Christian Knowledge Society'. He quickly added 'pianoforte seller and tuner', and became the Old Swindon Parish Clerk. In 1859, his eldest daughter, Mary Ann Ann (b. Alveston, Gloucestershire, 1837), had taken on the shop in High Street, soon adding a 'toy and fancy warehouse' to the premises. Isaac Ann concentrated on his work as parish clerk, and by 1861 had become a Professor of Music. About 1865, he removed to the old Manor House at the intersection of Wood Street and Bath Road, and styled himself 'music seller and Professor of Music'. Mary Ann also set up business in the Manor House, where her brother Thomas (b. Swindon, 1854) assisted her. Isaac Ann and his wife Charlotte both died in 1873, after which the business broke up. Mary Ann Ann became a schoolmistress, and went to live at 30 Vilett Street with her unmarried sister, Hannah Amelia Ann (b. Alveston, Gloucestershire, 1844), who was similarly employed.*

11. **Daniel Smith** (b. Swindon, 1811), saddler and harness maker *Smith's premises were on the east side of High Street, the last-but-one building before Market Place. 'He had only one child, a daughter, who died, and his wife died, and the house was empty for a long time. Then it was turned into a workmen's club.'*

12. **James Wise** (b. Devonport, 1821) journeyman

13. **Edward Acland Moore** (b. Plymouth, 1817), banker *Moore was a former insurance agent in Swindon. He became manager of the County of Gloucester Bank in High Street, which, in 1842, took over the Strange brothers' bank. He was also a member of the original 1852 committee of the Swindon Market Company.*

14. **Robert Fox** (b. Swindon, 1821) tinman

15. **Rachel Buckland** (b. Wroughton, 1779), pauper

16. **Sarah Strange** (b. Eye, Kent, 1768), independent means

17. **Henry Newton** (b. Berkshire, 1811), clerk

18. **James Bradford** (b. Swindon, 1795), solicitor and **James Edward Goddard Bradford** (b. Swindon, 1830), solicitor *RJT mentioned that the Bradfords were related to the Goddards, and were 'quite aristocrats, who kept a carriage and a pair of horses, coachmen, footmen, everything'.*

19. **Francis Broome Pinnegar** (b. West Kennet, 1822), chemist and druggist *Pinnegar worked in Charles Anthony Wheeler's chemist's shop, and then took it over. He was a member of the unsuccessful committee, formed in 1863 by Lord of the Manor, Ambrose Lethbridge Goddard, charged with finding a site on which to build a corn exchange.*

20. **Henry Reeves** (b. Westbury, 1826), draper

21. **Sarah Kemble** (b. Coleshill, 1765), retired *RJT said she was the sister of Preb. Kemble of Bath, who spent £80,000 of his own money in restoring the abbey there, and that she lived in High Street with two rich old maids.*

22. **John Henry Sheppard** (b. Swindon, 1815), brewer and maltster *RJT thought that the house John Henry Sheppard lived in was built by his father. He described it as being opposite the square. John Henry was a brewer who began what became the North Wilts Brewery, off High Street. RJT said that Sheppard charged the Wesleyans one guinea per inch for sufficient land for them to build their chapel. He lived to be ninety-one. Walter Kinneir, solicitor, had his offices 'for years' in this building.*

23. **John Woodroffe** (b. Ramsbury, 1823), Bell Inn *RJT remembers William Godwin as the landlord, but he did not take over until the 1860s. He also mentions Richard Tarrant, a later landlord. In 1870, William Godwin built the Belmont Steam Brewery close to, and in competition with, the Sheppard-built North Wilts Brewery.*

24. **Martha Owen** (b. Avebury, 1792), independent means

25. **Charles Anthony Wheeler** (b. Andover, 1805), house proprietor *RJT recalls him as a chemist, although Wheeler had so many different businesses that it is impossible to categorise him. He built The Hermitage, off High Street, and Rose Cottage, off Drove Road. This he sold against a deposit of £30 to Revd Frederick Rowland Young, Swindon's first Unitarian Minister, whom he met one day in the reading room that Revd Henry George Baily had created. F.B. Pinnegar took over his chemist's business in High Street. RJT knew Wheeler quite well, and said he was a considerable inventor who spent large sums of money on his patents, always tried to do good, but neglected himself. After Garibaldi visited Swindon in 1864, Wheeler copied the Italian's style of clothing. His wife Mary Jane had a private income of £400 per annum, but spent all of*

this as well as her husband's money. Their daughter Ellen Mary Wheeler (b. Swindon, 1837) eventually lived in Gloucester Terrace and kept apartments for bank clerks.

26. **William Webb** (b. Hungerford, 1811), King of Prussia Inn *This was 'Fat Billy' Webb, of such girth that it was said he could not fit through the door of his pub, and who kept a notoriously wayward house of ill repute. RJT recalled that it formerly had an inn sign depicting the king, believed that the stout landlord made a lot of money, but supposed that he killed himself with drink.*

RJT also mentions:

Elizabeth Petty (b. Minety, 1811), dressmaker and milliner *She was in High Street in the 1840s, and by 1850 was living and working in Victoria Street. Her husband, William Petty (b. Abingdon, 1812), was an accountant. In 1852, they relocated to Prospect Terrace, and by the middle of that decade, Elizabeth Petty was in partnership with William H. Sharpe (b. Shipton, Oxfordshire, 1832), working in Wood Street as Petty & Sharpe linen drapers. There, Sharpe remained, taking on his elder brother, Thomas Sharpe (b. Burford, Oxfordshire, 1828) as his linen draper's assistant. Elizabeth Petty left the business in the late 1850s when her husband became a Baptist Minister at the Stratton Chapel. When she was widowed, she continued to live on a pension at Prospect, with her sister and an aunt. Elizabeth Petty died in 1900.*

Coventry House

Standing next to the Bell Inn in RJT's memory was Coventry House, 'a beautiful house', owned by Thomas Coventry, whom RJT said was a London merchant. He described Coventry as being a small man, very rich, who kept a butler, a footman, and a carriage and pair. The butler was John Palmer (b. Purton, 1812), who became, when RJT was only a few years old, landlord of The Bull in Newport Street. Palmer also built 'two or three houses in Devizes Road'. He later returned to Purton where he was occupied as a greengrocer. His son, also John Palmer (b. Swindon, 1850), was employed as a solicitor's clerk in Henry Kinneir's Old Town offices. RJT also recalled when James and Thomas Pakeman 'transformed Coventry House into business premises, opened as drapers, and did a big business there'.

The first Pakemans, brothers James (b. Uxbridge, Middlesex, 1825) and Thomas (b. Uxbridge, Middlesex, 1827) came to Swindon in 1858, at first both living at 9 High Street, and both styled 'linen draper'. They were soon gone, however; Thomas went to Westbury-on-Trym, where he set up as a hosier, haberdasher and lacemaker, and James became a Swindon coal merchant, living in Byron Street. In Old Town, their place was taken, c.1863, by another brother, George Pakeman (b. Uxbridge, Middlesex, 1824), who had been living in Canterbury and had set up at 22 High Street. In his *Recollections*, RJT refers to him as 'Tailor Pakeman' who 'had a shop alongside the chemist's shop'. At the same time, James B. Daniel (b. South Petherton, Somerset, 1830) opened up what RJT called 'a splendid business' as a master draper in 20 High Street. 'But he took it into his head to give it up. All at once he turned round and sent out an advertisement that he would no longer give credit, and all his credit accounts would be closed. That ruined his business and he had to leave Swindon.' The premises were taken over by George Pakeman.

Limmex corner

This is the corner of High Street and Wood Street, known (even today) as Limmex Corner after the ironmongery business, and later also hardware store, that Samuel J. Limmex acquired in the early 1870s, and which continued to trade under his name until 1999. RJT refers to it: 'A very old place. Willis kept it when I was a little boy ... an ironmonger's shop. Then Mr Wise took it; then George Deacon bought it and took it. Then a man named Walters came to manage it and eventually it was bought by Walters who carried it on for some years and then sold it to Mr Sam Limmex's father, a retired Wesleyan missionary'. In fact, the ironmonger on the site when RJT was born was Lawrence Laurence. He was succeeded, c.1845, by Edward Page; John Ambrose Willis took over in 1847; and in 1852 came James Wise. George Deacon is first mentioned as the owner in 1862 and Joseph Walter in 1867.

Humphreys the hairdressers

Henry Pruce (b. Highworth, 1830) was the son of Highworth barber Edward Pruce. He took up the trade and remained in Highworth, whilst his contemporary, John Humphreys (b. Highworth, 1826), who had been apprenticed to Edward Pruce in Highworth, was operating as a hairdresser in Wood Street by the end of the 1840s. RJT recalls his business as being in High Street on a corner (where Lloyds Bank is now), immediately south of the Goddard Arms, to where he must have relocated during the 1850s. He married butcher's daughter Maria Blackford (b. Swindon, 1835), had eight children, and remained there, in what became 3 High Street. His sons William Henry Humphreys (b. Swindon,

1861) and Frank (b. Swindon 1871) also became hairdressers. RJT recalls that John Humphreys 'every night after he had shut his shop up, year in year out, would be seen leaving his house and going for a run right up to the top of The Sands and back again'. By 1900, the business had relocated to a property known as the old manor house in Wood Street, where John, by then widowed, continued as a hairdresser, and his daughter Blanche was occupied in the same building as a tobacconist's assistant. Frank, an assistant in his father's business, and who would take it over, lived next door with his family. John Humphreys died in 1905, and Frank in 1950.

East side of High Street 1840-1855

Next door to Humphreys on the east side of High Street and, according to RJT, long before the hairdressers moved in, were the Strange family. RJT described them as drapers, tallow chandlers, moneylenders, and bankers. They were non-Conformists who attended the old chapel in Newport Street. The bank they founded, which became Thomas and Richard Strange & Co., was eventually taken over by the North Wilts Bank. Next door, in High Street, was the County of Gloucestershire Bank. RJT recalled that when the old premises of the Stranges were being rebuilt by Thomas Barrett, part of the building collapsed one afternoon and killed five children who were on site collecting rotten wood to take home. RJT's parents 'were so alarmed at the news that they sent the servants to fetch us home'. He continued: 'I   remember seeing one of the children who were buried carried down the street with a face as black as soot. I saw five or six, black as soot. The dead bodies were carried away'. When the premises were rebuilt, the Strange family remodelled the interior to make business and living accommodation. Richard Bowly came from Cirencester, of a wealthy Quaker family. He 'took the drapery and carpet business from the Stranges, and then gave up. The building became Horder's the drapers, and was later demolished. Bowly bought Sheppard's North Wilts Brewery.

East of High Street, between the roadway and the Hermitage, is a large brick-built house. That, according to RJT, was where Henry Kinneir, solicitor, lived and worked, from the moment he came to Swindon. There his son Walter was born.

At the south-west end of High Street, just before Market Square, stood several small buildings. One of these had been the Bull public house. Another was a grocer's shop: John Howe – grocer and candle maker, according to RJT. This, in the mid-1840s, was taken over by Charles Elgar Owen, advertised as tea dealer and grocer, oil and Italian warehouseman, and dealer in British wines. He was, said RJT, 'a great man in the town in those days; a Goddard Arms man, and a great church man'. He was followed by a tea dealer named Stokes. Then these two properties, and another adjacent, were bought by three brothers from Newbury: Philip Hawe Mason, John Hawe Mason, and James Henry Mason. Mason's at Swindon was in the charge of the first named, who eventually 'retired and went to New Zealand for the benefit of his wife's health'.

RJT described the corner premises with Market Square thus: 'The corn stores where Toomers are now was rebuilt by Philip Pavey, of Wroughton, a great miller who lived at Elcombe Hall. His brother was a physician to Queen Victoria; a very noted family. Then came A.W. Deacon, who is a magistrate. He took the business and carried it on until John Toomer & Sons took over.'

Circus at Bell Close

There was a large field at the rear of the Bell Inn when RJT was a child, with a private thoroughfare to it from the pub. He tells how all the circuses that visited the town would there set up a big tent, drumming up support by marching around the town with a band and riders. 'Men and women and little piebald ponies went round and down to New Swindon, and returned to (Bell) Close to give their performance, just for a day; then they were off.' Three years after the Belmont Brewery was founded in 1870, it began a programme of expansion that gradually spread across Bell Close.

Cricket at The Butts

The Butts was a field south of present-day St Margaret's Road, then adjacent to the grounds of The Croft, and admitting onto Marlborough Road. It is mentioned in Goddard documents from the 1700s and was, as the name implies, an area set aside for archery practice in medieval times. The Midland & South West Junction Railway line, which opened to Swindon in 1881, passed through part of The Butts. Here, cricket was played by Swindon teams, which RJT remembered as being 'a very aristocratic affair', involving 'a good many professional men', and theoretically open only to those over the age of sixteen. These included John Gay, the surgeon; solicitors William Crowdy, and James Bradford and his son James Edward Goddard Bradford; and Charles Bradford, who was rector of Clyffe Pypard and 'a noted wicket keeper'. RJT says it was about 1847 when he saw Edward Hayward Budd and his son Thomas

Budd play cricket at The Butts. These were both gentlemen of easy means who lived at Elcombe Hall, Wroughton and, according to RJT, were both members of the All England Eleven. 'Old Budd played in a silk top hat, and I can see him now active as a panther or a leopard or a cat.'

The players allowed the local boys to field for them during practice evenings in the summer, and RJT was so taken with the game that he asked his mother whether he might join the club. She put the matter to Revd George Driver, superintendent of the Methodist Circuit in Swindon, who agreed. When RJT joined, it 'brought the membership of the Tarrants in the Club, all first cousins, up to nine'. Sam Tarrant of Newport Street, the eldest son of RJT's uncle Henry, was the team scorer, and so had a tent to himself. Sam, who never married, went into the boot business but failed at it, and went to work in the GWR as a clerk.

'At that time, Revd Henry George Baily [vicar of Holy Rood church, demolished 1852, and of its successor, Christ Church] had gentlemen pupils, aristocrats' sons, at the vicarage, and all of them were good cricketers. One belonged to the noted Jessop cricketing family; another, a nephew of Lord Nelson, was a magnificent cricketer and one of the most accomplished batsmen you ever witnessed. There was great rivalry between the Old Swindon Cricket Club and the club from New Swindon who played on The Plantation, the former name of what became the Faringdon Road Park.'

Chimney Sweeping
The Old Swindon chimney sweep of RJT's childhood was the inebriate Matthew Tuck (b. Purton, 1814), who lived in Newport Street from where he ran his business,

employing a number of small boys. 'He was a drunken sweep and one of the foulest men, and when drunk he used to race round the town in a frenzied state.' RJT described where Tuck lived: 'If you were to go down [High Street] and turn to the right, about halfway up [Newport Street] there was a little lot of wretched tenements behind and they lived in one of these, a squalid place'. Tuck sent his boys up inside the chimneys (RJT says his was 'eight feet thick'), and when they got to the top, they waved their brushes and shouted. However, they were badly treated by their master and some of the clients. One of the boys recounted how, when he went to sweep the chimneys at Burderop Park where they 'kept a tremendous dog at the entrance', the butler 'for a bit of a spree' might unchain the animal and let it fly at the sweep. It was alleged that the dog was even more savage on account of the sweep's black face, and the latter had to beat off the creature with his brush before he could get into the house.

Telephone Exchange On 9 July 1888, a meeting was held at the Goddard Arms with a view to establishing a telephone exchange at Swindon. The first one was opened in 1893, and the first number – Swindon 1 – was allocated to the Swindon Charabanc Company.

Temperance movement in Swindon The temperance movement in Swindon was always predominantly a class issue. It devolved on early initiatives by the often-intemperate upper class, the gentry, and middle-class tradespeople of the town to exert pressure on the labouring poor. Whilst degrees of wealth concealed what the former considered to be acceptable amounts of drunkenness and moral laxity in themselves, it was always the lowest levels of society that were thought to be at the greatest risk from drink. Nationally, the temperance movement began in the mid-1830s, and was led by individual social reformers, groups of social reformers, and non-conformist preachers.

Arguably, the earliest of the organised temperance activities in Swindon were the penny readings. These were established in the 1850s in Swindon, and their patron was the demonstrably intemperate Lord of the Manor. Their apparent purpose was to provide Swindon's urban poor with instruction and entertainment, but the underlying principle was to offer an alternative to the public house. Of course, it was a flawed concept. The readings took place once a week or every other week, firstly at the Goddard Arms Hotel, then the town hall in Old Swindon from 1853, and later, from 1855, at the Mechanics' Institute building in New Town. But the readings were not held sufficiently frequently to make a direct impact. However, they were deeply moralistic in tone, and the choice of pieces often reflected the benefits of abstinence or the dangers of inebriation. Penny readings often involved the weighty presence of church leaders, and were mostly attended by poor women whose menfolk were probably elsewhere getting drunk. The messages from penny readings were intended to seep by osmosis into the conscious of the female urban poor, and thence through to their errant menfolk. It would never have been enough to achieve the required result, but the social demographic in the early development of New Swindon at about the same time meant that much more would be called for in the future.

In the 1860s, the Church of England Young Men's Association came into being,

meeting in the Victoria Rooms, Victoria Street, a strictly non-alcoholic venue. It included a lending library supplied by the Limited Liability Library Company, offered daily, weekly, and local papers, had facilities for chess and draughts, and accommodated occasional lectures. In 1865, the Salvation Army was formed in the East End of London, and it would be nearly twenty years before it came to Swindon.

The temperance movement in Swindon went into full swing in the 1870s. Part of this, even if their purpose was not overtly so, were the coffee houses that sprung up, then and in the 1880s, advertising themselves as an alternative to alcoholic liquor. When the temperance organisations became established, they usually held their meetings in the town's coffee houses, which also provided wholesome meals and a range of reading material. During the 1880s and 1890s, coffee taverns proliferated in Swindon and, by the end of the century, they had more or less left behind their temperance associations and were being enjoyed in their own right. Whereas they had started out by advertising themselves as a non-alcoholic alternative for the working man, they were soon also providing rooms in which women might indulge in their blandishments.

Other organisations that were subtly working against the consumption of alcohol in Swindon were the designated reading rooms. These included the Victoria Street Reading Room, whose president was solicitor Henry Kinneir, which was open daily between 10 a.m. and 10 p.m., and wherein no alcohol was to be had, and the Workman's Hall, which opened in Belle Vue Road in 1877. It advertised itself as 'a free place of resort for men on every weekday evening'. By 1880, it had relocated to

Cricklade Street, where its president was the solicitor James Edward Goddard Bradford, and William Henry Read, the surveyor, was its secretary. It opened between 5 a.m. and 10 p.m., and advertised itself thus: 'At this useful resort of the working classes, refreshments disassociated from intoxicating drinks can be had, and breakfasts, dinners, tea and coffee, are supplied at a reasonable charge. Newspapers and periodical literature, with chess, draughts, bagatelle, and smoking, contribute to its popularity'.

In 1878, the Swindon Church of England Temperance Society was formed, which was to prove of some longevity. It met at first in King William Street School, and in St Mark's parish rooms from 1881. Its objectives were: (a) 'the moral, intellectual, and social improvement of its members, which include non-abstainers as well as total abstainers, upon a perfectly equal basis' and (b) 'the furtherance of all legislative enactments tending to promote healthy amusements for the people, and the establishment of clubs and places of public resort dissociated from intoxicating drinks'. People who joined had to sign a promise. Abstainers: 'I hereby agree to abstain from the use of alcoholic liquors, except for religious purposes or under medical orders'. Non-abstainers: 'I recognise my duty as a Christian, to exert myself for the suppression of intemperance; and having hereby become a member of this society, will do my utmost, both by example and effort, to promote its objects'. Its president was Revd Henry George Baily, and forty people joined at the first meeting. It was still going strong immediately before the First World War, when its mission was to 'carry on organised temperance work in the five parishes of the borough of Swindon unitedly, and police court mission work'.

By the 1880s, however, a good many temperance organisations had formed, most of which were associated with non-conformist churches. From early in that decade, their main ally in the fight against drink was the Salvation Army, which first set up in Old Town. The Swindon Branch of the Young Men's Christian Association, whose president was Joseph Armstrong of the GWR, met at the reading room in Station Road. The Bands of Hope associations proliferated there, with an aim to obtain temperance by encouraging children to sign the pledge. The 1870s and 1880s saw the rise of:

Baptist Band of Hope
British Women's Temperance Association, Swindon Branch
Church of England Temperance Society, St Mark's branch
Even Swindon Wesleyan Band of Hope
Gilbert's Hill Total Abstinence Society
GWR Temperance Union
Independent Order of Good Templars 'Anchor of Swindon' Lodge
Independent Order of Good Templars 'Star of Hope' Lodge
Independent Order of Good Templars 'True to the Core' Lodge
Independent Order of Rechabites
New Swindon Adult Temperance Society
New Swindon Primitive Methodist Band of Hope
New Swindon Wesleyan Band of Hope and Temperance Society
Old Swindon Band of Hope
Princes Street Wesleyan Band of Hope
Presbyterian Band of Hope
Prospect Primitive Methodist Band of Hope
Regent Street Primitive Methodist Band of Hope
Sanford Street Congregational Band of Hope

Sons of Temperance 'True Friendship'
Swindon Temperance Cavaliers
Swindon Wesleyan Band of Hope
Trinity Presbyterian Band of Hope
Victoria Street Band of Hope
Wroughton Wesleyan Band of Hope

Most of these were allied to the Swindon United Temperance Board, formed in 1884 and which met firstly at the Three Cups Coffee House in Regent Street (as did a number of independent temperance groups that did not have their own denominational schoolrooms), and afterwards at the auction mart in Regent Street. Other churches, some of which had no bands of hope, soon joined this umbrella temperance organisation, as did a few non-sectarian organisations. The Central Hall sent delegates to its meetings, as did the Highworth Total Abstinence Committee. Swindon area Church of England parishes also sent delegates. Towards the close of the century, another organisation, the Swindon & District United Temperance Council, met at Flock's Dining Rooms, Regent Street. In the GWR Works, senior management actively encouraged the aims of the temperance movement, and the Railway Mission in Wellington Street provided 'total abstinence' cards.

By this time, temperance hotels were advertising as such: the Wellington Temperance and Commercial House was in Gloucester Street, run by Samuel and Elizabeth Tarrant, who also had a coffee house there; George Eatwell was in charge of the Temperance Hotel, Station Road; and, in Old Town, Annie Thomas had the Temperance Hotel in Bath Road in the 1890s. Also by this time, there were probably more dedicated beer retailers in Swindon than there had ever been, and an ever-increasing

number of general store owners advertised that they too, were beer retailers. The public houses by no means had the monopoly, and the temperance movement found that it was fighting on two fronts.

In 1894, the Swindon Adult School was formed, which spawned several offspring, each with its ominous-sounding 'vigilance committee'. It met firstly at the Albion Coffee Tavern, Bridge Street, moving to the Friends' Meeting House on Eastcott Hill in the 1890s, and to Sanford Street Boys' School by 1904. At first, this organisation admitted only men. A women's branch was formed in 1901, but each met at a different time on Eastcott Hill. The following year, both sections of the Swindon Adult School relocated to 2 Bridge Street, and there established the Swindon Adult School Club. This was 'the outcome of an effort to provide some counter attraction to the public house', and the premises were described as 'a home of social intercourse for working men'. A men's branch was formed in Gorse Hill in 1904, and a women's section in 1906. Both met at Avening Street School, and between them they ran a coal club, early attendance prize scheme, male voice choir, old people's tea fund, outing club, savings bank and string band. Eastcott Hill Men's Adult School was formed in 1907, taking over the vacant slot in the Friends' Meeting House.

Another organisation was the Swindon branch of the radical British Women's Temperance Association, whose work devolved on a series of 'At Homes'. This was particularly strong in the town in the early years of the 20th century, when it organised lectures on temperance reform, held mothers' meetings, and undertook police court mission work. By this time, there were around 11,000 men in the GWR's

Swindon Works; this figure was to reach nearly 14,000 at its highest. The town's many public houses were open for business for much of each day, and many cases of drunkenness were brought before the Swindon magistrates every week. By the 1920s, the Adult Schools had become part of a Sub-Union, and the temperance societies that had survived the war years were few indeed. The Swindon branch of the Church of England Temperance Society, the GWR Temperance Union, and the International Order of Good Templars were still in existence. By the end of that decade, only the Church of England Temperance Society was still listed.

Thompson, John Bell Langhorn (1891-1961)

Born in Carlisle, Cumbria, the son of Robert Thompson, a company secretary for a firm of tinplate printers and photomakers, and his wife Jane Ann née Langhorn, who married in 1874, J.B. L. Thompson was destined to spend forty-one years in local government service. Whilst one of his brothers became a 'chromo artist', and another a solicitor, he was articled to the City Engineer at Carlisle in 1907, where he later became Chief Engineering Assistant. During the First World War, he served as an officer in the Royal Engineers, saw action in France, and was awarded the Military Cross. In 1922, he resumed his job in Carlisle, then almost immediately, but for only a brief period, relocated to Hastings, Sussex as Deputy Engineer and Water Engineer before coming to Swindon. As Swindon Borough Surveyor, 1924-48, Thompson was a crucial figure in formulating the town's plans for regeneration after the Second World War, in particular a scheme in 1943 for the town's redevelopment, and in their early implementation after hostilities ended. He built houses and roads in the town, and was responsible for the sewerage system. Thompson added the turret and clock to the bandstand in Swindon's town gardens in 1927; the nearby rose garden of c.1930 is to his design; and he designed the Art Deco bandstand, concert bowl and entrance, which were built in the town gardens in 1934. The concrete diving stage of 1935 at Coate Water is also one of his projects. In 1947, he was made president of the Institution of Municipal Engineers. He was succeeded at Swindon by J. Ackroyd, and retired to Hastings, which was where he died.

Timms, Peter Robert (b. 1953)

Born in Chiswick, London W4, the son of an inspector at Marine Mountings, later Lister's, in Wroughton. Peter Timms came to Swindon in 1957 when his family were four of the 14,000 people – the so-called 'London Overspill' – who came to live in the town during that decade, after Swindon had been designated under the Town Development Act, 1952. The family lived at Park South, and Peter was educated at Lawn, Park South, Churchfields and Park Senior schools. He was apprenticed to mechanical engineering at Vickers' South Marston works between 1970 and 1974, but gave that up because of an ever-present threat of redundancies. He trained to be an Operating Department Assistant and worked in hospitals in Swindon and Exeter. Always interested in steam railways, his interest in the GWR widened during his time at Princess Margaret and Great Western hospitals by talking to older patients. He learned, first-hand, about the railway works and the community around it during the steam era. At the same time, in the mid-1970s, he bought books and ephemera relating to the subject through his adverts in the local press. Early retirement taken in 2008 enabled him to research and write a detailed two-part history of the GWR Swindon Works through three decades. Peter is married and lives in Swindon. His publications are:

Working at Swindon Works 1930-1960 (History Press, 2007)
revised, enlarged and republished as
Swindon Works 1930-1960 (Amberley, 2014)
In and Around Swindon Works (Amberley, 2012)
Swindon Works Through Time (with Andy Binks) (Amberley, 2015)

Town Crier see Ferris, Frederick

Townsend, Robert Keith (b. 1941)
The son of William Arthur Townsend (see next entry), Bob followed in his father's footsteps as a notable cross-country runner and long-distance road racer. He was born at Kingshill maternity hospital, and he first became involved in athletics by selling programmes at the sports meeting held annually at the County Ground. He showed early prowess as a runner when he ran for Ferndale School in the Swindon Schools Championships. In 1956, he represented Pinehurst School in a 3-mile cross-country race against Bristol South Harriers. He went on to set a Wiltshire record for the 3,000-metres senior steeplechase at Marlborough College. For sixteen years, Bob was a fitter, turner and erector for British Rail at Swindon; he then maintained Royal Navy helicopters for the Ministry of Defence at Wroughton aerodrome for a similar period, and was latterly employed for the Science Museum on the same site. In 1966, he married Gillian Blood (a nurse), and the couple had two daughters.

In 1961, Bob Townsend was on the winning team in the South of the Thames Junior Championships; in 1962, he was part of the medal-winning team at the USIC championships in Leipzig, Germany, and again at Tinero, Switzerland in 1966, and Bergen, Norway in 1970. He was elected to the committee of Swindon Athletic Club in 1964, became its chairman in 1970, holding the office until 1978, and remained on the committee until 1985. In 1965, he was elected to the committee of the Wiltshire Amateur Athletics Association, on which he served as race secretary for the cross-country events and team manager of the cross-country championships from 1970 to 1997. In the latter position, he was responsible for selecting the athletes to represent Wiltshire in the National Inter-county Cross-country Championships. Also in 1997, the Wiltshire AAA made him Life Vice-president. In 2003, Bob Townsend received the South of England Athletic Association long-service award for his contribution to athletics in Wiltshire over forty years.

Townsend, William Arthur (1903-1982) The man who was to become firstly a keen competitor in amateur athletics in Swindon, and then a driving force in its development through his long association with the Swindon Athletic Club, was the son of a GWR labourer. A mild-mannered person, he was a committed Methodist, and a sidesman at Gorse Hill Methodist Church. William was apprenticed as a boilermaker at the GWR Works in Swindon, worked for a short period at Garrard's, then returned to the Works, where he was an assistant warehouseman when he retired in 1965.

In 1932, William married Emily Annie Walters. She was the niece of Samuel Edward

Walters who, during his year as mayor of Swindon, 1919-20, inaugurated the town's cenotaph. The couple had four children: John (b. 1940); Robert Keith (b. 1941); Malcolm (b. 1943); and Marilyn (b. 1950). John and Robert were both to become involved with the Swindon Athletic Club.

In 1921, William won the first timed, handicapped road race organised by the Swindon Athletic Club. He later won the mile in the International Railway Cross Country and Track Championships, and his position in the Inter-county Championships was sufficiently high for him to be chosen to compete for his country, although inexplicably he was never actually selected. In a twenty-five-year career, for which he was awarded a Southern Counties Amateur Athletic Association plaque, he was twice (1929 and 1931) winner of the South of the Thames Senior Cross Country event, and was for many years the acknowledged best cross-country runner in Wiltshire. He also ran cross-country for Westbury Harriers of Westbury on Trym, Bristol. During the Second World War, he served in the GWR Division of the Home Guard.

William retired from competitive running in 1948, and took on the role of Wiltshire County Team Manager, becoming a member of the Wiltshire AAA committee, then its president. He was the Swindon Athletic Club secretary between 1951 and 1977, and it was largely through his enthusiasm that the club kept going throughout the 1960s, when interested runners and public support were at a low ebb. He was president of the club between 1977 and 1982. Swindon Athletic Club celebrated its Diamond Jubilee in 1981, with a dinner at the Goddard Arms Hotel, High Street. Deteriorating health prevented William from attending, but his son Bob (see

entry above) gave an address on his behalf and was presented with the carriage clock that marked his father's long service.

Tramcar No.13 Swindon Corporation's tramways undertaking opened in 1904, with nine tramcars in cream and crimson lake livery. These were increased to thirteen in 1907, and all remained in service until tramcar No.1 made a ceremonial last journey in 1929, by which time the corporation had installed the motor buses that would take their place. Tramcar No.13, the last to be supplied, is also the only one of which parts are extant. An open-top tram, it was built by Dick Kerr & Company at Preston, Lancashire.

When it was retired after twenty-two years in service, Tramcar No.13 was bought by John Liddiard, the village undertaker at Chiseldon, who took it to Webb's Farm. He covered the upper deck, in order to store his timber there, and kept paint and wallpaper in the lower saloon. After his death in 1951, it was acquired by Arthur Payne, a builder of Wanborough (whose father had been that village's carpenter, builder and undertaker). Payne removed the upper deck, but had no further use for it. After a period of disuse, the Swindon & Blunsdon (later Swindon & Cricklade) Railway Society removed the lower deck to Blunsdon in the early 1980s. It sojourned at their depot, but was not restored, and was eventually taken over by Thamesdown Transport, who kept it in a barn. When the barn was destroyed by fire, the remains of the tramcar were relocated to Braydon Manor, Purton, before spending some time in 1999 in the former Swindon Railway Works. It was rescued from there by enthusiast Bill Parker and installed at his quarry site at Coleford in the Forest of Dean.

Trayhurn, Roger John (b. 1946)
Between 1971 and 2011, when he retired, Roger Trayhurn became the face of Swindon Reference Library and Information Service, the keeper of the town's local studies material, and one of the longest-serving librarians in the country. He also became a very talented amateur character actor. Born at Kingshill Nursing Home, Swindon, he was the son of Jack Trayhurn (b. Dursley, Gloucestershire, 1909) and his wife Constance née Powell (b. Dursley, Gloucestershire, 1908), who married in 1933. They had two other children, Mary Louise (1936-38) and Judith Ann (1941 -2008).

Roger was educated at Drove Road Infants' School, where he made his stage debut as Joseph in a nativity play, then at Clarence St Junior School, and Headlands Grammar School. Time spent in the reference library whilst studying for his A Levels convinced him that he would like to be a librarian, and he started his career in Swindon Central Library in July 1964, then worked alongside Mark Child in the reference library until starting a two-year course at Loughborough School of Librarianship from 1965, becoming a Chartered Librarian.

Back in Swindon, he returned to the reference library until 1969, had a two-year spell at Park Library, before settling in the reference library in 1971. This enabled him to develop his interest in Swindon's history, a field in which he continued to work for the rest of his career. His love of acting and the theatre was fostered in his late teens, and whilst at library school he was a member of the Loughborough College Drama Group. Since the 1960s, he has been an avid theatregoer to London and the provinces. He has been a member of the now defunct Adastrian Drama Group, the Phoenix Players since 1971, and the Western Players. When the Loughborough group of colleges (now Loughborough University) celebrated its centenary in 2010, it awarded Roger a retrospective honorary BA.

When it became clear that there was very little published material on Swindon's Empire Theatre (1898-1954), Roger set himself the task of listing all the performances that took place there, and undertook further extensive research into its history. This eventually resulted in the publication of the book *All for the Empire*, written with Mark Child, which was published in 2013 by Hobnob Press.

Triangle, The In October 2009, Swindon Borough Council granted permission for a small housing development of forty-two dwellings to be built on the site of a former caravan park and plant nursery behind Northern Road. Sixteen people submitted written objections to the proposed development, which comprised low-cost, low-energy properties made of sustainable materials and created in such a way that the development would promote sustainable lifestyles and engender a sense of community. The originator of the £4.2 million scheme was the architect and television presenter Kevin McCloud, who had formed Haboakus (Happiness Architecture Beauty) to carry out sustainable residential projects of this nature, and whose first development was The Triangle. The estate comprised sixteen two-bedroom houses, thirteen three-bedroom houses, seven four-bedroom houses, four one-bedroom apartments, and two two-bedroom apartments, arranged in a triangular shape around a small central green and play area.

Haboakus developed the scheme in conjunction with Green Square of

Chippenham. The design was by Max Fordham of Glen Howells, architects of Birmingham, in conjunction with the national engineering consultancy Curtins Consulting; landscaping was by Studio Engleback of Tunbridge Wells; and the builders were the national group, Willmott Dixon. Some 2.5 million pounds-worth of the cost came from the Home and Communities Agency's National Affordable Housing Programme, and the Department of Energy and Climate Change's Low Carbon Investment Fund contributed another £840,000 because the project used environmentally sustainable materials. Work began on site in May 2010, at a ceremony in the presence of luminaries of several of these organisations, and Grant Shapps, MP, the Minister of State for Housing and Local Government.

Visually, the properties were designed to give a contemporary interpretation of the cottages in the town's railway village, although what appeared to be chimneys were, in fact, roof ventilators. The walls of the buildings were made of tradical hemcrete, a hemp and lime thermal walling system that retained carbon in its structure. The development featured rainwater harvesting, air-sourced heat pumping, low-water-usage fixtures and a means of tracking individual energy usage. There were shared polytunnels, vegetable beds and edible hedgerows. Haboakus became involved with Go! Co-operative Limited, developing Swindon's first car club online bookings service for the residents of The Triangle who, instead of owning a car, could simply hire one whenever required.

The idea was that properties in The Triangle would be available to people registered with Swindon Borough Council for rent or for rent-to-buy. Seven hundred and twenty-seven people applied for the forty-two properties, and those who were successful were selected by interview. The first occupants of The Triangle, who took up residency in June 2011, were Tracey Hackett, then manager of the Bulldog public house, her partner Russ Wheeler, and her son Sam Hackett. In December 2011, the development was featured on Kevin McCloud's *Grand Designs* television programme for Channel 4. Among the awards The Triangle collected were the Landscape Institute Award for Communication and Presentation 2011, RIBA Award for Sustainability 2012, Civic Trust Award 2012, and the Sustainable Water Industry Group Award 2013.

Trout, George see Lord Raglan

Trout's Folly see Quarries, The

Tunley's Stores In 1870, the Cheltenham & Gloucester Building Society was laying out Cheltenham Street, parallel with the North Wilts Canal, and Wellington Street was being built on the same plane about 100 yards to the east. In 1874, the same building society erected Gloucester Street between the two. The new Swindon Local Board built New Bridge across the North Wilts Canal in 1878, and the line of Milford Street was then laid down, bisecting Cheltenham Street, Gloucester Street and Wellington Street, and thereby linking the new town to the west of the canal with the developing Swindon to the east of Wellington Street. Gloucester Street comprised terraces of houses with shop premises at either end; the large house on the eastern corner of Gloucester Street and Milford Street was, by 1895, the premises of A.E. Tunley, plumber and painter. It was a brick-built property; the doorway into the ground-floor shop was on the diagonal, and there were display windows facing both thoroughfares.

What became one of the most famous businesses in Swindon might instead have been named Price's. The story begins with the birth of John Tunley in Painswick, Gloucestershire, in 1820. He became a painter and decorator, and by 1841 was living at the Phoenix Inn, 22 Park Street, Cirencester. That year, he married Eliza Thirza Spring, and the couple relocated to Dollar Street; their daughter Alice was born at Cirencester in 1843, as was Sarah in 1848. Also living with them latterly was an unmarried laundress, Mary Price of Maisey Hampton, and her three Cirencester-born, illegitimate children: Alice Price (b. 1843), William Price (b. 1848), and Fanny Price (b. 1850).

In 1852, John Tunley married Mary Price, and they had four children of their own: Esther (b. 1852), Mary (b. 1854), Harriet (b. 1856) and John (b. 1860). John (the father) gave up painting and decorating, and became a plumber. He died in Cirencester in 1891, and his widow survived him for a decade. However, she was registered as a lunatic, and died in 1901 at the Gloucester County Lunatic Asylum, Wotton.

Meanwhile, her illegitimate son William Price had added Tunley to his name and, as William Price Tunley, married Priscilla Matilda Robins (b. Lechlade, 1848) at Cheltenham in 1867. Until the 1860s, he too, was a plumber; by 1871, he had included 'painter' in his advertised accomplishments. William and Priscilla had seven children, and all the boys became house painters. In the 1870s, the family were briefly in Swindon, before living for some time in

Highworth. Late in the 1880s, William Price Tunley brought his family to 17 Sanford Street, Swindon, from where he carried on the trade of plumber and painter, and where he was to remain for the rest of his life. Priscilla Matilda died in 1911, and William Price in 1918.

It was their second child, Albert Edward Tunley (b. Swindon, 1873), who, c.1895, put his name above the door on the corner of Gloucester Street and Milford Street, and there set up as a picture frame maker, later adding 'wallpaper and picture mould dealer', and house decorator. The site became known as 'Tunley's Corner'. On a gable was painted 'established 1880', which probably referred to when William Price Tunley started in business at Highworth. Early in the 20th century, the whole of the ground floor at street level was remodelled, with large wrap-around picture windows. The adjacent house in Milford Street was demolished in the 1920s, and Tunley's business premises were extended eastwards, with large picture windows running along the length of the upper floor of the extension.

Albert Edward Tunley married Eliza Snell in 1892. (Eliza lived just around the corner at 8 Wellington Street, and Albert Edward's sister, Ethel, married Eliza's brother, George.) The following year, they had a son, Albert Edward, who, when he left school, became a picture frame maker, and then a decorator, in the family business. Albert Edward senior and his wife Eliza both died in 1924, just over a month apart. They had latterly been living at 8 Wellington Street.

Union Tavern, Sheppard Street The Union Tavern or Union Hotel (sometimes called the GWR House, the Union Railway

Hotel, the Union Railway Inn, or just The Railway) was built by John Henry Harding Sheppard on his own land, and opened in 1841. It remained Sheppard's property until his death in 1868. The tavern was on one of the main routes taken by men employed at the GWR Works, for which reason it served hot drinks from six o'clock in the morning. It had a succession of early landlords: John Crook, 1840s; James K. Copeland, 1851; Judith Warmby, 1858; Thomas Morris, 1859; John Ford, 1860; Thomas Washbourne 1868; and Richard Bullen in 1873. By 1881, it was in the hands of Frederick Cratchley, and George Thomas, in charge by 1891, took it towards the twentieth century.

At the time of the 1851 census, James Copeland (b. Abingdon, Berkshire, 1821) styled himself 'butcher and innkeeper', whose retail outlet for meat was a stall in the octagonal market, beside the Mechanics' Institute building in High Street, New Town. The Tavern was at that time occupied only by his family. John Ford (b. Tickenham, Somerset, 1819) lived there with his wife, two sons, and a servant at the date of the 1861 census, as well as nine lodgers who were all employed at the nearby GWR Works. Ten years later, there was no room in the Union Tavern for many lodgers; Thomas Washbourne (b. Inkpen, Berkshire, 1832) and his wife had their five children and a servant there, and lodging with them were a gardener and a dressmaker. Frederick Cratchley, his wife and four children – one of whom was the barmaid – were, in 1881, hosting a hobbyhorse proprietor and his wife who were travelling in their wares. By 1891, George Thomas (b. Cannington, Somerset, 1855) lived at the Union Tavern with his wife and one servant. There were no lodgers.

The Union Tavern continued in business until it was acquired in the 1950s by Compton, Sons & Webb, who had built their clothing factory next door in 1876 and thereafter gradually extended it. The firm closed the Union Tavern in 1958, and it was demolished to facilitate further expansion of the clothing works.

Vicarage, Bath Road This is an example of Swindon's Victorian community coming together to raise funds for what it saw as being a worthy local project. Until the 1880s, by which time it had fallen into considerable decay, the vicarage and adjacent garden associated with Christ Church, Old Swindon, was situated on the Planks, where previously had been the Priory, part of which was incorporated in the vicar's house. In 1886, a committee of churchmen and leading Swindon businessmen was formed with the aim of facilitating a new vicarage; the incumbent at the time was Revd Newton Ebenezer Howe. They began by raising capital through the sale of the old vicarage and its garden, and then bought about three-quarters of an acre of land in Bath Road, from Ambrose Lethbridge Goddard, Lord of the Manor, almost opposite Eastcott Hill and next to the Old Town fire engine station. The committee retained architect William Henry Read of 10 Bath Road to design the new vicarage. The cost of the land, the building, and Read's fees came to just over £3,400; income from the sale and £200 worth of grants still left a shortfall of almost £1,000.

By 1889, it had become imperative that at least some of this be paid off. A three-day bazaar or 'Grand Fancy Fair and Ice Carnival' was held at the Corn Exchange, Old Town, 11-13 June 1889, with this in mind. There were ten stalls, each distinguished by the name of a cold country, entertainments, and afternoon and evening performances by The Orchestral Band of the 2nd Vol. Battalion the Duke of Edinburgh's (Wiltshire Regiment). Daytime admission cost 6d; 3d was the evening charge. The event was opened on the first day by Lady Doreen Blanche Long, wife of the Member of Parliament for Devizes Walter H. Long, who accompanied her. Charlotte, wife of A.L. Goddard, of The Lawn, High Street, opened day two. Proceedings were inaugurated on the third day by Thereza Mary, wife of the geologist and politician Nevil Story-Maskelyne, who lived at Bassett Down, Wroughton. The event reduced the debt by £282.14s.

A further attempt was made in 1892 to clear just under £453 that remained outstanding against the new vicarage by mounting a 'Military Bazaar and Mess Canteen' at the Corn Exchange, 9-11 November. Patriotism was the theme, and the event was opened by the Countess of Craven. There were exhibitions and display stalls by the Black Watch 42nd Highlanders, Dorsetshire Regiment, Grenadier Guards, Prince of Wales' Own Royal 19th Hussars, Royal Scots Greys, Royal Horseguards (The Blues), Royal Marines, Wiltshire Regiment 62nd Foot, Wiltshire Regiment 99th Foot, and the Wiltshire Yeomanry. There was a Volunteer Cyclists Encampment; a fancy stall, children's stall, sweet stall, curiosities, advertisement stall, flowers and an arts tent. The Swindon Town Orchestral Band performed; there were other musical and theatrical entertainments in the canteen, and a performance of *Cinderella*.

Victoria Bookshop, Wood Street

Victoria Bookshop was one of the best-loved independent traders of Old Town. Wood Street was numbered in the 1840s. No. 30 is an early Victorian building, put up as the left-hand of a pair of stone-built, semi-detached houses, ashlar-faced but thereafter rough-coursed. It was originally of two storeys and three bays with a tiled roof admitting two dormer windows. It retained its original stone frontage until the 1870s, when, together with the semi-detached house next door, both were extended upwards, and the whole elevation was remodelled in brick. Later, shop fronts were created of a piece at street level. The thin, vertical, ornamental glazing bars, and the ground-floor windows extant, are from the date of this refacing. From the late 1800s until the 1960s, the premises housed Morris's sweetshop.

In 1965, James Kenneth Austin (1919-85) leased 30 Wood Street as a showroom and retail outlet, and called the business Victoria Antiques. He was born in Birmingham, of a family that had long been associated with Calne, Wiltshire. Prior to the Second World War, during which he served in the army, he was a carpenter and joiner, a trade that he briefly returned to after hostilities ended. In 1941, he married Joan Reason in Birmingham; she became a domestic science teacher, and in 1950, their son Steven Kim Austin was born. The family moved to Guildford, Surrey in 1956, where James had a teaching job, and relocated to Swindon in 1961, where Joan secured a post at Swindon College.

By this time, James had become bored with teaching, and had taken up furniture restoration. He bought from local auctions, worked on the pieces in the large cellar of the family home at 74 Bath Road, and sold them on. Meanwhile Stephen, who had been educated at Dauntsey's School, West

Lavington, was also at Swindon College, and helped out at Victoria Antiques in his spare time. James often bought cheap boxes of books during his forays to local auctions for old furniture, and these too, were sold in the shop. Stephen had long held an ambition to become a bookseller, and underlined his intention by removing the bookcase from his bedroom into the shop, and there setting up the stock. Soon, books occupied two or three rooms. In 1968, the business was renamed Victoria Antiques & Books.

At the end of the 1960s, the antiques side of the business was relocated to 58 Devizes Road (later the site of the Talk of the Town hairdressers, beauty salon and solarium), and a small tearoom was operated for a couple of years upstairs in the Wood Street premises. Out of college, Stephen trained in retail bookselling; he began with W.H. Smith in their Fleet Street, Swindon shop and was latterly for three years with the same company in Bedford. By the time he returned to Swindon in 1973, and effectively took over the business, the Wood Street premises were entirely given over to a second-hand bookshop. Stephen introduced new books and new bargain paperbacks, which quickly became the more profitable side of the business. The business was renamed Victoria Bookshop. A concrete floor was laid over the flagstones in the cellar, where second-hand paperbacks, children's books and magazines were displayed. Non-fiction books, arranged by subject, occupied the whole of the three floors above, and also lined the staircases. James built a lean-to at the rear of the building, and this became the home of second-hand fiction. New books were shelved, and placed on tables behind the Victorian glass front, at street level.

In 1975, James retired, and relocated with Joan to Sidmouth, Devon, where he opened another Victoria Bookshop, which he ran for the next ten years. After 74 Bath Road was sold, Stephen turned the top two floors of 30 Wood Street into a flat, and lived over the business for the next ten years. Victoria Bookshop closed in 2004, a victim of supermarkets' ability to sell books to the customer at prices that were less than independent booksellers could buy them in. The premises were taken over and converted to offices by estate agents Dreweatt Neate, which at the time occupied next door.

Victoria Garage, Victoria Road In 1925, a firm named Bath Garages Limited opened the Victoria Garage in a purpose-built property on the corner of Victoria Road and Durham Street. When it closed down in 1977, the garage was under the control of Dutton Forshaw, and its managing director was Percy Gerrish. He began his career there as a mechanic, earning five shillings per week in 1949, and worked his way to the top via a spell as the firm's supreme salesman. For many years, this had been the town centre's premier garage, the distributor for Morris, Wolseley, MG and Riley cars. Anyone who bought a new car from the Victoria Garage between the wars was taught how to drive by garage staff. Two of the garage's employees became well known in the music field in the town. One was mechanic Thomas 'Tim' Coxon, who played piano and violin in the town's Empire Theatre orchestra from 1924 to 1939 when he joined the Victoria Garage. He was still employed there between 1949 and 1952 when he was also the conductor of the pit orchestra at the theatre. The other was John 'Jock' Walker, clarinet and saxophone player, who also played in the Empire's orchestra, as well as in virtually every other

Swindon band between the 1930s and 1950s, including the multi-award winning Johnny Stiles Band.

There were eventually three parts to the Victoria Garage. Initially, doors from Victoria Road admitted into the new car showroom, which had a polished wooden floor with a smaller area to the right that was ramped to a higher level to accommodate the gradient of the hill on which the premises were built. Offices were at the back of the showroom. A workshop was added on the end of Durham Street (immediately north of what is now the Durham Street entrance to Queen's Park). The rear of the Victoria Road showroom was remodelled as the workshop stores, and the part of that property which now forms a small car park was the garage's tyre store. In contrast to the warm, plush surroundings of the Victoria Road showroom, the Durham Street workshop was a cold, draughty place, long and narrow and built of breezeblocks. Just inside the entrance, immediately to the left, was a small office wherein toiled the workshop clerk, surrounded by cabinets of customer files. It was his job to make workshop appointments, make out job cards, book customers in and out, and keep all the records of their dealings with the Victoria Garage. Next to this office was the toilet block, which was usually awash with, and smelling of, green Swarfiga. The rest of the property was the workshop proper, with an inspection pit near its rear.

Latterly, when the business had been acquired by Dutton Forshaw, another outlet was added. This was the used car sales area, close to the Groundwell Road entrance to Queen's Park. Percy Gerrish achieved national fame when, four years after the Morris Minor (in production 1948-1970) had been discontinued, he accepted a commission to build one for a client from new spare parts. This involved obtaining parts from British Leyland, other garages in the Dutton Forshaw group, independent traders, and help from Bampton Brothers in Swindon. The new Morris Minor was built in the Victoria Road showroom window in full view of the public.

Vincent's Coffee Tavern For about thirty years, Frederick William Vincent ran a coffee house in Bridge Street. He was born at Garsdon, Wiltshire in 1861, the son of William Vincent, a local haulier. His early adult life was spent as a labourer and then as a servant to a farmer. This changed after he married Hannah Annie Woodman (b. Great Somerford, 1866) at Malmesbury in 1890, and the couple took up residence at 4 Fleet Street, Swindon. The occupant of this address, since c.1890, was Frederick Jesse Edwards, who ran a coffee refreshment house on the premises. (The place had previously been part of a working men's club, managed by George Dade, who lived on the premises, but had been converted to three residences in the 1890s.) Vincent took over Edwards's coffee house at no. 4 in 1893, when Edwards moved into 22a Bridge Street and became a baker; Vincent remained at no. 4 until 1899. Then, he relocated Vincent's Coffee Tavern to 72 Bridge Street; his widowed father also lived there; the Vincents' daughter Victoria had just been born (1900), and they accommodated two boarders and a servant. Their son Stanley was born there in 1902. When premises were built on the corner of Bridge Street and Sheppard Street, sometime after 1901, and numbered 78 Bridge Street, Vincent moved his coffee tavern there, into what was a prime location to attract trade from the hundreds of railway workers that passed by each day. This was a particularly pleasant little two-storey building, of brick with stone dressings; the windows to Sheppard Street on both levels were grouped in threes, round-headed, and nicely moulded with decorative scroll brackets on the jambs and beneath the sills. The entrance to the shop was on the diagonal, and that to the private quarters was in Bridge Street. Vincent continued to run his coffee tavern at no. 78 until he retired in 1926, and he and his wife went to live at 40 York Road. Hannah died in 1940, and Frederick William died in 1941. Subsequent remodelling of the former coffee tavern premises swept away the fine windows to Sheppard Street.

Volunteer, Bridge Street The site of the Volunteer public house was on the north-east corner of Bridge Street with Fleet Street. It began, c.1855, as a beerhouse called the Jolly Sailor, run by James Cook until, still named as such, it was taken over in 1860 by Henry Smith (b. Uley, Gloucestershire, 1824), who initially combined the trades of carpenter and publican. Smith lived there with his wife Ellen (b. Uley, 1819), and their daughter Rose, who was born in 1857 in America. The name of the house was changed to the Volunteer in 1862, and Henry Smith continued in charge until 1879. Early in this period, the building was remodelled, presenting a three-bay, two-storey façade to each street, large windows at ground level, a main entrance on the diagonal, and a private entrance from Fleet Street. Wrapped around the top of the building was a blank parapet, with the name of the establishment writ large within it on both elevations, and panels proclaiming the services of the house between each of the square-headed sash windows of the upper storey.

After Smith, the Volunteer was taken over by John Thomas Hofield (b. Northumberland, 1849), who had previously been a GWR railway clerk. George Thomas (b. Cannington, Somerset, 1855) replaced him in the early 1880s, and then went on to run the Union Hotel in Sheppard Street and later the Lamb & Flag in Bridge Street. The next landlord, who took over in 1886, was Frederick Cratchley (b. Randwick, Gloucestershire, 1831), who had lately been at the Union Hotel. At the Volunteer, he carried on a side trade as a 'mourning shillibier and hearse proprietor'. His career in the pub trade in Swindon saw him variously in charge of seven houses in Swindon, including the infamous Lord Raglan in Cricklade Street. By 1890, he had retired from the trade and was living in King William Street; he died in 1911. Cratchley was succeeded at the Volunteer in 1890 by Horace Haydon Whitehead. The former landlord's two daughters, Annie Louisa Cratchley (b. Swindon, 1870) and Winifred Cratchley (b. Swindon, 1872) both continued to live at the Volunteer, where they worked as barmaids. Whitehead took the pub into the 20th century, and John Tallyn (b. Barnstaple, Devon, 1869) was the landlord by 1903. Until recently, he had been a blacksmith in Old Town, and, after leaving Swindon, he continued as a publican in London. Tallyn was followed by Henry Nock when the premises were remodelled in 1911.

The alterations reduced the depth of the parapet and added a large pediment with scroll brackets above the diagonal, flatter pediments facing each street, moulded cornices, and string courses with heavy brackets running through them that visually tied together the whole property. The advertising panels were removed. The Volunteer was renamed the Oxford Hotel in 1912, and by 1915, it was being run by William Garlick. Albert Edward Griffiths followed him in the first half of the 1920s, and Lewis Marsh Gardner (b. Woodchester, Gloucestershire, 1874), who had run a fancy goods depository and tobacconist's shop in Fleet Street, afterwards took the Oxford Hotel towards its closure in 1929. This same year, another Oxford Hotel was opened in Drove Road. The property in Bridge Street was immediately demolished, and Montague Burton, the national firm of tailors, custom-built a conservatively art deco shop on the site.

Westcott Place Westcott was once a hamlet adjacent to the west of Eastcott. Before 1840, it comprised Westcott Farm, a water mill, and some isolated cottages. The name was applied to Westcott Place, which was built up from the mid-1840s, flanking the line of the old Fleetway track, running south-west of the planned railway village. The land had been bought, c.1843, by William Large, who then owned nearby Westcott Farm and was responsible for building a number of cottages and shop premises in what became Westcott Place. It was the comparatively slow start to the GWR's own model village development that gave the impetus to erect what was regarded from the beginning as a relatively contained satellite village. The early introduction of shops along Westcott Place shows that this was intended as a mixed usage high street, perhaps complementing the fewer traders in the focal square of the railway village, which was officially named High Street. In the hands of other speculative builders, Westcott Place expanded rapidly during the latter part of the 1840s and into the 1850s, as the GWR struggled to keep pace with

the amount of accommodation required for its workers and their families. It is 1848 before we have reference to some of the early traders in Westcott Place, namely:

John Blackford, butcher
John Carpenter, chandler
Elizabeth Cave, beer retailer
John Chandler, coal carter
Henry Cross, beer retailer
William Hassall, furniture broker
Harry Hinton, beer retailer
Tobias Hurcombe, beer retailer and tailor
John Martin, general dealer and baker
John Millard, boot and shoemaker
William Stone, boot and shoemaker
James Toe, boot and shoemaker

Although Westcott Place and the stubby Westcott Street that ran off to the north were both part of private development, the houses in them were internally cramped and intended for working-class tenants. The terraces that were built up in Westcott Place had none of the style of those planned throughout the railway village. There, irrespective of their internal arrangement, it was important that externally they should present the kind of visual character that suggested the GWR was providing superior accommodation for even its humblest workers. The builders of Westcott Place had nothing to prove with their unpretentious and functional properties. To this day, the street contains a house that has the narrowest kerbside frontage of any in Swindon. It is likely that these were also built with railway workers and their families in mind, and although many were occupied in this way, others became, from the outset, the homes of people who provided services to the fledgling New Swindon. At the time of the 1851 census, there were nineteen uninhabited houses in Westcott Place and Westcott Street, and a dozen shops. Here are the names and the occupations of the people living in the other properties:

Robert Alexander, innkeeper
Edward Allnatt, grocer
Frances Arnold, schoolmistress
Thomas Arnold, boilersmith
Thomas Bannister, publican
Charles Bealls, labourer
Emma Bealls, laundrywoman
Susan Beazley, laundress
George Broadhurst, butcher
Joseph Burridge, striker smith
William Burton, blacksmith
Thomas Camp, labourer
James Chandler, millwright
Alfred Chapman, blacksmith
David Chapman, labourer
Elizabeth Chapman, dressmaker
Stephen Checker, farm labourer
Frederick Collinson, railway guard
William Couling, boilersmith
Edward Davis, journeyman baker
William Davis, master baker
John Dolman, coal merchant
John Douling, engineer
Lewis Dubison, railway clerk
George Edwards, labourer
Albert Elson, retired farmer
William Estcott, labourer
William Evans, boilermaker
Samuel Farmer, engine fitter
George Fisher, shoe and boot maker
John Fuller, railway porter
Henry Garlick, farm labourer
George Gibbs, blacksmith
John Gregory, boilermaker
John Grey, engineer
John Hall, labourer
Ann Hampton, washerwoman
William Hardiman, labourer
William Harding, railway porter
George Harris, labourer
Ozias Head, contractor
Robert Henby, foreman
Thomas Hinder, labourer
Henry Hinton, labourer
Elizabeth Hounsell, pauper
Thomas Howden, fitter
Joseph Hunt, gardener
William Hunt, carpenter
William Jackson, mason
William King, labourer
James John Larkby, mechanic
George Leighfield, innkeeper
Andrew Long, boilersmith
William Martin, schoolmaster
John May, milkman
Joseph Miles, GWR porter
James Millard, GWR engineer
James Millard, GWR policeman
John Millard, master shoe and boot maker
Thomas Morris, practical engineer
Johnathon Nicholson, turner and fitter
William Nicholson, foreman and engine fitter
Robert Peer, cattle dealer
Susan Plummer, farmer
William Robinson, iron moulder
John Rogers, tailor
Charles Saunders, tailor
John Saunders, tailor
John Sellwood, labourer
Richard Sheward, metal plainer
Elizabeth Smith, dressmaker
William Stone, master shoemaker employing 5 men
John Stroud, labourer
Albert Sykes, engine maker
John Tarrant, labourer
Nevil Taylor, plasterer
Elizabeth Thatcher, lady annuitant
James Edward Toe, boot and shoemaker

Joseph Thompson, boilersmith
Thomas Thompson, spring maker
Thomas Turner, labourer
William Turner, smith
Richard Walford, driller
John Wise, journeyman shoemaker
Elizabeth Withers, pauper
James Woodman, carpenter
Cornelius Workman, machine worker

Very few of these people or their families were natives of Swindon, or even Wiltshire. Perhaps attracted by the low rents that were being asked for this sub-standard accommodation, the area appealed to Irish families, although there seems to have been no attempt to establish a permanent Irish community in Westcott Place. Westcott Place continued to be expanded; Falcon Terrace, for example, was still being extended at the end of the 1860s. (See also Westcott Place Infants' School.)

Westcott Place Infants' School, Westcott Street One of the first projects undertaken by the Swindon School Board was to take over part of the Drill Hall in New Swindon, which it opened on 25 March 1878 as a temporary school for infants. This remained in use until the board's Westcott Place Infants' School was opened on 4 April 1881, to accommodate 286 children. It was built by Forse & Ashley, a Bristol firm that comprised Benjamin Forse, of Broad Street, and Henry Ashley, of Temple Street, and cost £2,750. Its first headmistress was Jane Harrison, who lived at 7 Gloucester Terrace. The school was enlarged in 1896 at a cost of £1,132.

White Hart public house, Newport Street The origins of this business on the north side of Newport Street are obscure and much older than the name by which it was known. This was probably assumed around 1782 when a beerhouse previously called the White Hart, on the opposite side of the road, changed its name to the Bull. The brewer, property owner and landowner John Henry Harding Sheppard acquired the White Hart in 1844, and remodelled it into a beerhouse; it was always a small, squalid-looking place. Between 1850 and 1854, its keeper was Philip Cockbill, who built the Belle Vue tavern and brewery – between Victoria Road and Bell Vue Road – and the Beehive on Prospect Hill. After Cockbill, in 1855, came Eliza Cocks, who advertised her food. The White Hart remained Sheppard's property until his death in 1868, when it was bought for Bowly's North Wilts Brewery, which was hardly more than a stone's throw away. The last landlord, during the 1950s, was M.R. Matthews. The building was demolished in the early 1960s to facilitate the Newport Street road-widening scheme. (See also Bull public house, Newport Street.)

White Horse beerhouse No dates are known for this beerhouse, on the east side of Cricklade Street, but it had not traded as such for some time when the property was sold to William Vilett in 1728. Vilett was a merchant, landowner and property owner, and acquired the building as one of an adjacent pair of houses formerly in the ownership of Thomas Morse, a Wroughton tailor. Almost at once, he sold them on to the Harding family, who demolished them sometime before 1743 and erected on the site what became No.42 Cricklade Street, which Niklaus Pevsner described as 'the best house in Swindon by far', and which was 'one of the most distinguished town houses in Wiltshire' in the opinion of John Betjeman. The only 'evidence' remaining for the existence of the former White Horse beerhouse is the substantial tunnel-like cellars of a kind unlikely to have been built beneath a residential property at the time, and therefore assumed to pre-date the house and to be the storage areas for trade.

Whitehouse Bridge On 15 October 1996, a professional stuntman, John Carr, who had hitherto been best known for his daredevil work in *Cadbury's Milk Tray* television advertisements, took a one-hundred-yard run-up and drove a green double-decker bus at 25 mph into Whitehouse Bridge. The bus came from a scrapyard. As a result of the collision, most of its top deck was ripped off, but Mr Carr, who was insured for £2 million, was unhurt. The bridge was unscathed. The present Whitehouse Bridge, which gives a clearance of ten feet (3.1 metres) was built in 1910 to carry the main line from Paddington across the road at that point. It has long been officially the most battered railway bridge in Britain, with high-sided vans, articulated lorries, buses and horse boxes regularly coming to an unscheduled halt beneath it. In the 1990s, an average of one vehicle per month fell foul of Whitehouse Bridge. This is why Railtrack employed John Carr and the doomed bus to remind the public that more care needed to be taken at low bridges, and of the costs involved every time a vehicle became stuck beneath one of them. In March 1998, the bridge was painted bright yellow, but drivers have since continued to misjudge the clearance. Between 2008 and 2014, there were forty-three strikes of the bridge.

Wholesome Barrel, Sheppard's Cottages John Harding Sheppard built some cottages, c.1840-41, on land he owned beside the North Wilts Canal, adjacent to the north side of the canal bridge that was itself a little to the north of the new railway bridge that carried the GWR's tracks over the canal. The dwellings were known as 'Sheppard's Cottages'. Among those on the west side of the canal were two beerhouses, the Old Locomotive, nearest the canal bridge, and the Wholesome Barrel, which was the smaller of the two. Both premises were owned by the Wilts & Berks Canal Company, which had taken over the North Wilts Canal in 1822.

John Luckett Jefferies, artist and uncle of Swindon author Richard Jefferies, made a sketch of the site, which largely provides the information about the buildings. In the drawing, the Wholesome Barrel appears to be a single-storey building with a thatched roof. The first 'beer seller' there was Samuel Harris (b. Swindon, 1816). The business closed in 1849, and was empty at the time of the 1851 census.

The census records that at that time, Sheppard's Cottages housed, with their families, Charles Irestone (b. Grove, Berkshire, 1817), a railway haulier; the widowed James Taylor (b. Ireland, 1792); model and pattern maker George Taylor (b. Ceylon, 1824); butcher Reuben Ford (b. Hinton, Somerset, 1806; Francis Fox (b. Elton Stratford, Buckinghamshire, 1823), who was a store labourer; journeyman butcher Charles Lewington (b. Chilton, Buckinghamshire 1825); Samuel Gray (b. Bath, 1803), carpenter; iron planer William Musto (b. Fairford, 1823); and Samuel Lay (b. Bradwell, Buckinghamshire, 1803), keeper of the Old Locomotive Inn, two of whose daughters were at the time dressmakers. The Wholesome Barrel did not re-open after 1849, and was probably let as a dwelling for a short period before being demolished.

Wight, Clifford Seymour (1891-1961) Another of Swindon's hitherto 'lost' sons. Clifford Wight has been forgotten by Swindon because, around the mid-1920s, about fifteen years after he left England and was living in the Americas, he changed his surname from the family name of Weight to Wight. A small change perhaps, but one that meant that the 'two' people were not thereafter reconciled as the same person.

The Weight family had a history of working for the GWR, principally as fitters and turners. Enoch Weight (b. Stroud, 1798) was an engineer. The family lived in Stroud, then Kingswood, Bristol, where one son, Henry, was to find employment as a machinist. Two more, John Weight (b. Stroud, 1831) and Samuel J. Weight (b. Kingswood, 1839) came to Swindon. John arrived at some time between 1852 and 1855, and took up employment with the GWR as a fitter and turner; Samuel, similarly employed, soon took up residence with the family at 17 Reading Street. John's firstborn was Albert John Griffiths Weight (b. Kingswood, 1852), who, by 1871, was living with his recently married uncle Samuel, a GWR Works fitter, at 5 Cromwell Street. Also living in the same household was Mary Weight, Samuel's mother, and relict of the late Enoch. In 1878, A.J.G. Weight married Emma Ford; they set up home at 25 William Street, and he was at first a GWR machine man and later a fitter and millwright. The family was living at 17 William Street when Clifford Seymour Weight was born to them in 1891. A.J.G. Weight was a sawmill machinery fitter by 1901, and his children, with the exception of Clifford, either went into the GWR or trained to be teachers. By 1911, the family lived at 32 The Mall, and Clifford was an agricultural student.

Clifford Weight went to Canada in 1913 where, within two years, he had joined the Royal Canadian Mounted Police, and he was part of the Canadian Overseas Expeditionary Force at the time of the First World War. By the mid-1920s, he was in California, where he qualified as an architect and became a sculptor. Then he met the left-wing, politically inspired muralist Diego Rivera, changed his own name, and was depicted on one of Rivera's frescos in Mexico City. In 1931, Rivera painted Weight in five different poses for San Francisco's Art Institute. Over the next few years, the pair worked together on many frescos, notably for the Detroit Institute of Arts and the New York Museum of Modern Art, before Weight, now as Wight, created his own series of frescos for the Coit Tower in San Francisco.

He returned to England in 1936, together with his wife Jean née Abbott, and took up residence in London, where he was a bomb-disposal officer during the Blitz. Thereafter, he taught sculpture at Camberwell School of Art, became separated from his wife, and lived with a former student. After a couple of years touring Europe, the couple settled near Cheltenham. Clifford Seymour Wight died in Barcelona, following a fall from a tram.

Wiltshire, George (1821-1897) By the time George Wiltshire reached his sixties, he was a master builder in Swindon, where he employed 140 men. Along the way, he built the Aylesbury Dairy building, Station Road; Cattle Market, Marlborough Road; County of Gloucester Bank, Fleet Street;

Gilbert's Hill School, Dixon Street; the Primitive Methodist Church, Regent Street; and the Vale of the White Horse Repository, High Street.

Born at Studley, near Calne, George Wiltshire began his working life as an agricultural labourer. During the 1840s, he set up as a stonemason on the Swindon quarries in Old Town. In 1845, he married Louisa Haddrell (b. Charlcutt, 1824) at Calne, and the couple lived in Swindon at 8 Prospect Place. There, they had their children: Simeon (1848) and Louisa (1850); in 1860, their third child, Mary, was born. His wife Louisa died early in the year, and, a few months later, Wiltshire married Caroline Belsher (b. 1827) in her native town of Westbury. The family moved into 22 Bath Road, where George and Caroline lived for the rest of their lives together. This was the only property to be built at right angles to the thoroughfare, and is close to the junction with Eastcott Hill. When they married, George was in charge of seven masons, four labourers, and four boys. He continued to expand his building business, and also his work as a lime burner at the quarries. When he died, he left £3,829. Caroline soon afterwards sold 22 Bath Road, and went to live at 15 Stanley Street with another widow. Her former home was bought in 1898 by Alfred Bartlett, a monumental mason from Cricklade. (See also Bartlett Brothers.)

Wiltshire Radio *Wiltshire Radio*, the first radio station dedicated to Swindon and its surrounding area, was launched on 12 October 1982. It broadcast from Lime Kiln Studios, Wootton Bassett, which were custom-designed by the then newly founded London office of the Nicholas Grimshaw practice of architects. The complex of six studios was adjacent to a seventeenth-century country house, and the radio station opened with a staff of thirty, seven of whom were presenters. Its tag line was 'More to Say', and it adopted a black and red livery on its vehicles and its T-shirts as part of its publicity campaign. It also commissioned the Royal Philharmonic Orchestra to record its theme tune, and this was backed by Scott Joplin's 'The Entertainer' and was issued as a single record, which cost £1. *Wiltshire Radio* was a very successful station, which, in 1985, acquired *Radio West* of Bristol. At that point, *Wiltshire Radio* rebranded itself, and relaunched as *GWR Radio*. (See also BBC Wiltshire Sound; Brunel FM; GWR Radio; Radio 105.5; Swindon FM.)

Wood Street, No. 27 see Cross Keys

Wyvern Club On 3 November 1971, the Wyvern Club was formed as a private members' club, allied to the Wyvern Theatre. Its premises were a large room on the second floor of the theatre building, for which it initially paid an annual rent of £5. Its first chairman, elected by a twelve-member committee, was Keith Hardy, a reference librarian who was the founder of Swindon Opera. Brien Chitty, the artistic director of the Wyvern Theatre, was appointed secretary; Garth Michelmore, the assistant manager of the Midland Bank in Regent Circus, was named as the club's treasurer; and David Maggs, manager of the same bank, became the assistant treasurer. Stanley Jones became the first public relations officer. The committee authorised the club to borrow up to £500, as required. Its clubroom had a licensed bar, a small kitchen, a dining area for light meals, a small dance floor, and a lounge area overlooking Theatre

Square. The first opening of its bar was in the presence of entertainer Sandy Powell and his wife Kay, and veteran comedy actor and songwriter Leslie Sarony.

Entry was at all times restricted to members and their guests. The club invited members of the cast to have lunch in the club's restaurant area; many visiting stars took advantage of this, and also relaxed there after the shows, well into the night. Many an enjoyable evening saw club members in one-to-one conversation with cast members and sometimes dancing with them, some of whom were considerable stars. Very early on, an arts sub-committee was formed to attract exhibitions of different types of paintings, photography, sculpture, pottery and ceramics, all by local, professional artists and craft workers. In this, they were successful, and some fine exhibitions were mounted in the clubroom.

At its height of popularity, the club had 1,000 members, but it also had a chequered history. At one point, its public relations officer, Stanley Jones, complained that: 'There are twelve Wyvern Club committee members and seven or eight of them are "dead". Some of those elected have never been seen again, and about four of us run the club on our own'. Its attempts to be an all-day members' drop-in clubroom were thwarted, and there were numerous complaints about the standard of the food. Club subscriptions (which had to be raised as a result) were used to provide an extractor unit in the club's kitchen on the second floor, and its bar area was often unbearably hot because the building was not air conditioned throughout.

The club was charged with elitism; that it operated as a clique; and it was alleged that the reputation of the theatre suffered as a result of late night and under-age drinking. In 1989, with the membership at around 600, each paying a fee of £6 per annum, the Wyvern Arts Trust decided that the space it took up in the building could be better used as a restaurant for the general public, and refused to renew its lease. In the September, the Wyvern Club took the Wyvern Trust to court, but lost. The club moved out of the premises in January 1990, and thereafter existed in name only until May 1990, when it was officially wound up. The former clubroom in the Wyvern Theatre was refurbished at a cost to the Swindon taxpayer of about £100,000, and became the Harlequin Restaurant.

Wyvern Theatre Company The Swindon theatre's first professional repertory company was formed in January 1975 by Tony Clayton, who had the year before taken over from Brien Chitty, the Wyvern's first artistic director. The Wyvern Theatre Company's home was the newly remodelled, 120-seat, Harold Jolliffe Studio Theatre on the third floor of the building. The initial company included Bruce Bennett, David Creedon, Warwick Evans, Ann Hamilton (who was married to Tony Clayton and who, even with many other theatrical commitments, remained a stalwart of the Wyvern Theatre Company), Sidney Kean, Alan Leith, Isabelle Lucas, Peter Mantle, Gwyneth Powell and Shirin Tayler (an extremely versatile actress who also remained in the company to the end). Their first performance was held on 22 January 1975, and the first season consisted of seven plays. Each play presented by the company was rehearsed for two weeks and then performed for two weeks. They were:
Prisoners by James Dawson
Rattle of a Simple Man by Charles Dyer

The Caretaker by Harold Pinter
Who's Afraid of Virginia Woolf by Edward Albee
Staircase by Charles Dyer
The Promise by Aleksei Arbuzov
Alpha Beta by E.A. Whitehead
The Owl and the Pussycat by Bill Manhoff
Ghosts by Henrik Ibsen
The Maids by Jean Genet
The Night I Chased the Women with an Eel by William Payne
The Glass Menagerie by Tennessee Williams
Gaslight by Patrick Hamilton
Miss Julie by August Strindberg
Two for the Seesaw by William Gibson
The Unexpected Guest by Agatha Christie (in main theatre)
Entertaining Mr Sloane by Joe Orton
Enemy by Robin Maugham
The Price by Arthur Miller
Four Seasons by Arnold Wesker
The First Night of Pygmalion by Richard Huggett
The Wizard of Oz by Alfred Bradley (in main theatre)
The Late Edwina Black by William Dinner & William Morum
The Maids (second run) by Jean Genet
Statements After an Arrest Under the

Immorality Act by Athol Fugard
The Knack by Anne Jellicoe
Look Back in Anger by John Osborne
Spoiled by Simon Gray
Kennedy's Children by Robert Patrick
Wise Child by Simon Gray
Happy Family by Giles Cooper
Treats by Christopher Hampton
To Dorothy, a Son by Roger MacDougall
A Day in the Death of Joe Egg by Peter Nichols
Butterflies Are Free by Leonard Gershe
The Advertisement by Natalia Ginzburg
The Taming of the Shrew by William Shakespeare

The Shakespeare, performed in June 1977, was the last production by the Wyvern Theatre Company in the Harold Jolliffe Studio Theatre, and the penultimate performance of their existence. In April 1978, Clayton's successor as artistic director, Charles Savage, directed them on the main stage at the Wyvern in a performance of *French Without Tears* by Terence Rattigan, in an attempt to gauge whether Swindon's theatregoers would support professional repertory theatre in the main auditorium. (See also Southern Exchange.)

About the author

MARK CHILD was born at Stratton St Margaret, Wiltshire, in 1943. He was educated at King Alfred's School, Wantage, and thereafter has lived all his adult life in Swindon. His first published material included individual architectural guides to parish churches, and articles on church architecture written for county magazines. Concurrent with this, and having joined Swindon Library Service in 1960, he edited the magazine of the south-west branch of the Association of Assistant Librarians, and was appointed reference librarian with special responsibilities for building the local history collection. His involvement with Volume 9 (the Swindon volume) of the *Victoria History of Wiltshire* led to years of original research on aspects of Swindon's history, from which a number of printed monographs were written. A full list of his published work on Swindon, the monographs, and his other titles, can be found at the front of this book. In 1986, he began a long association with *Cotswold Life* magazine, writing on architecture, history, and the towns and villages of the area. He continued to write a monthly column for the magazine on aspects of Cotswold history, until 2015. He lives with his second wife, and has four adult children.

Lightning Source UK Ltd.
Milton Keynes UK
UKOW02f1520170116

266476UK00002B/59/P